SQL Clearly Explained

SQL Clearly
Explained
Third Edition

Jan L. Harrington

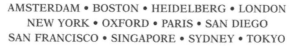

AMSTERDAM • BOSTON • HEIDELBERG • LONDON
NEW YORK • OXFORD • PARIS • SAN DIEGO
SAN FRANCISCO • SINGAPORE • SYDNEY • TOKYO

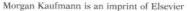

Morgan Kaufmann is an imprint of Elsevier

Morgan Kaufmann Publishers is an imprint of Elsevier.
30 Corporate Drive, Suite 400, Burlington, MA 01803, USA

This book is printed on acid-free paper.

Library of Congress Cataloging-in-Publication Data
Harrington, Jan L.
 SQL clearly explained / Jan L. Harrington. -- 3rd ed.
    p. cm.
 Includes indexes.
 ISBN 978-0-12-375697-8
 1. SQL (Computer program language) I. Title.
 QA76.73.S67H37 2010
 005.13'3--dc22   2010009181

British Library Cataloguing-in-Publication Data
A catalogue record for this book is available from the British Library.

For information on all Morgan Kaufmann publications,
visit our Web site at www.mkp.com or www.elsevierdirect.com

Printed and bound by CPI Group (UK) Ltd, Croydon, CR0 4YY

Transferred to digital print 2012

Working together to grow
libraries in developing countries

www.elsevier.com | www.bookaid.org | www.sabre.org

ELSEVIER   BOOK AID
             International   Sabre Foundation

Contents

Part I: Introduction

Part VI: Appendices

Preface to the Third Edition

If you have had any contact with a relational database, then it is very likely that you have seen the letters "SQL." SQL (Structured Query Language) is a computer language designed to manipulate relational databases. You can use it to define a database's structure, to modify data, and to retrieve data.

This book has been written to give you an in-depth introduction to using SQL, providing a gentle but complete approach to learning the language. You will learn not only SQL syntax, but also how SQL works. Understanding the "how" as well as the "what" will help you create SQL statements that execute as quickly as possible.

The elements of the SQL language covered in the first four parts of this book are based on those parts of the SQL standard that are for use with pure relational databases. Part V covers two non-relational extensions (XML and object-relational capabilities) that have been part of SQL since 2003. Virtually all database management systems that support SQL will provide the bulk of what you will find in Parts I–IV; implementations of the features in Part V are less common and tend to vary from the standard.

There have been some substantial enhancements to the SQL standard since the second edition of this book, both in the relational core features and the non-relational features. These features have been integrated throughout this third edition.

Organization of This Book

The five parts of this book take you from theory to practice:

◊ Part I: The theoretical material underlying relational databases and SQL has been moved into two chapters at the beginning of the book. In previous editions, the material in Chapter 2 (relational algebra) was scattered throughout the book. This organization should make it easier to find. The third chapter in Part I provides an overview of SQL environments.

◊ Part II: Part II covers interactive SQL retrieval. At first, this might seem backwards. Why discuss retrieving data before creating a database and getting data into that database? There is actually a very good reason for this.

SQL presents someone trying to learn the language with a bit of a catch-22. You need to know how to retrieve data before you can modify it, because modifying data means finding the data you want to change. On the other hand, you need to be able to create a database and enter some data before you have some data on which you can perform retrievals. Like Yossarian trying to meet with Major Major, it doesn't seem that you can win!

The best alternative is to have someone who knows how to do it create a sample database and load it with data for you. Then you can learn to query that database and carry those techniques over to modifying data. At that point, you'll have an understanding of SQL basics and will be ready to learn to create databases.

◊ Part III: Part III discusses creating and managing database structure. It also covers non-data elements in the database environment, such as managing users/ user accounts and transaction control.

◊ Part IV: When SQL-based database environments are being developed, programmers and database administrators do a lot of work using a command-line interface. There are, however, at least two reasons why SQL programming is very common:

    o The typical end-user should not (or cannot) work directly from the SQL command line. We therefore create application programs to isolate them from direct interaction with the SQL command processor by writing application programs for them to use.

    o In many cases, there are actions the database should perform in specific circumstances. We don't want to require users to remember to do these actions, so we write blocks of program code that are stored within the database to be executed automatically at the appropriate time.

Part IV introduces several techniques for SQL programming: embedded SQL (using a high-level host language), dynamic SQL, and triggers/stored procedures. These chapters teach you syntax of SQL programming constructs, but do not teach programming.

◊ Part V: Part V discusses the non-relational extensions that have been added to the SQL standard: XML and object-relational capabilities. Just as Chapter 1 presents a brief introduction to the relational data model, Chapter 18 covers object-oriented concepts, including the differences between pure object-oriented databases and object-relational databases. Chapter 19 then looks at SQL's object-relational features.

Database Software

Much of today's commercial database software is very expensive and requires expensive hardware on which to run. If you are looking for a database management system for your own use, you needn't purchase anything should you choose not to. There are at least two open-source products that will run on reasonable hardware configurations: mySQL (http://www. mysql.com) and PostgreSQL (http://www.postgresql.org). Both are certainly used in commercial settings, but can also function well as learning environments. Distributions are available for Windows, Linux, and Mac OS X.

The SQL commands to create the sample database used in the first four parts of this book and the SQL commands to insert data into those tables can be downloaded from the Morgan Kaufmann Web site.

Teaching Materials

If you are using this book as a college text (perhaps jointly with its companion volume, *Relational Database Design and Implementation Clearly Explained*), you can find teaching support materials on the Morgan Kaufmann Web site. These include a sample syllabus, assignments (and where appropriate, solutions), a project description, and exams.

Acknowledgements

Although an author spends a lot of time alone in front of the computer, no book can come into being without the cooperation and hard work of many people. It may be my name on the cover, but without the people at Morgan Kaufmann, you wouldn't be holding this book right now.

First I'd like to thank the editorial staff, Rick Adams (Senior Acquisitions Editor) and Heather Scherer (Assistant Editor). You're a joy to work with (as always). Second, I am forever grateful for the production staff, who have done everything they can to make my life easier and to produce a great volume: Anne McGee (Project Manager), Joanne Blank (Designer), and Carol Lewis (Copyeditor).

I also can't forget my support staff: my mother, my son, and the four fur kids. (Now, if the kittens could just distinguish between my leg and a scratching post, my world would be at peace.)

Part I

Introduction

The Relational Data Model

You don't need to be a database designer to use SQL successfully. However, you do need to know a bit about how relational databases are structured and how to manipulate those structures. This chapter therefore will acquaint you with the basic elements of the relational data model and its terminology. We'll finish by looking at the design of the sample database used throughout this book.[1]

Schemas and Entities

A database is a place where we store data, but there is more to it than that: We also store information about the relationships between pieces of data. The organization of a database is a logical concept rather than a physical one. Yes, there are files that store the data in a database, but the physical structure of those files usually isn't a concern for those who use the data.

The software that organizes, stores, retrieves, and analyzes database data is known as a *database management system* (DBMS). It isolates the user from the physical data storage mechanisms and structures and lets the user work with data in terms of the logical structure of the data.

---

[1] If you have been reading this book's companion volume, *Relational Database Design and Implementation Clearly Explained*, then you will be familiar with the concepts presented in this chapter. You can therefore skip to the last section of this chapter to review the design of the sample database.

Relational Data Model Origins

The theory of the relational data model was developed by Edgar (E. F.) Codd and introduced to the world in a paper published in 1970.[1] Codd continued to refine the model throughout his life, in 1985 publishing 12 rules to which relational DBMSs should adhere.[2] At that time, no DBMS met the rules and some commercially successful products met none of them. Eventually, Codd wrote a book that contained 330 rules.[3] He felt that DBMSs had met most of the original 12 rules and he wanted to give developers something to strive for.

---

[1]   Codd, E.F. (1970). "A Relational MOdel for Large Shared Data Banks", *Communications of the ACM*, 13 (6): pp. 377–387.

[2]   Codd, E.F. (1985). "Is Your DBMS Really Relational?", *ComputerWorld*, 14 October, and "Does Your DBMS Run By the Rules?" *ComputerWorld*, 21 October.

[3]   Codd, E.F. (1990). *The Relational Model for Database Management, 2nd ed.* Addison Wesley.

The overall logical plan of a database is known as a *schema*. A schema has two types of elements:

◊ Entities: An *entity* is something about which we store data, such as a customer or a product or an order for a product. Entities are described by pieces of data known as *attributes*. When we have a collection of data for all the attributes of an entity, we say we have an *occurrence* of the entity. Databases actually store occurrences of entities. Schemas show us what entities will be in the database and what attributes are used to represent those entities.

◊ Relationships: Relationships define how entities interact. For example, a customer entity is typically related to many order entities. There are three types of relationships, all of which we will discuss shortly.

The most important thing to keep in mind is that a schema shows the logical plan for a database, what entities and relationships could possibly be stored. However, inside the real-world database, we have many occurrences of many entities, each represented by descriptive data. We may not have occurrences of every entity in the schema or we may have thousands (even hundreds of thousands) of occurrences of entities.

Relations and Tables

A relational database takes its name from the structure used to represent an entity: a two-dimensional table with special characteristics taken from mathematical set theory, where such a structure is known as a *relation*.[2] To begin, let's look at the simple relation in Figure 1-1. At first glance, the relation looks like any table, but unlike other tables you may have encountered (for example, rectangular areas of spreadsheets), it has some very specific characteristics.

Cust. #	First name	Last name	Phone
0001	Jane	Doe	(555) 555-1111
0002	John	Doe	(555) 555-2222
0003	Jane	Smith	(555) 555-3333
0004	John	Smith	(555) 555-4444

Figure 1-1: A simple customer relation

Columns and Rows

A relation is a two-dimensional table with *no repeating groups*. That means that if you look at the intersection of a column and a row, there will be only one value. What you see in Figure

---

[2]   Don't let anyone try to convince you that a relational database is called so because there are "relationships between files." That is just plain wrong.

Cust. #	First name	Last name	Phone	Children
0001	Jane	Doe	(555) 555-1111	James, Mary, John
0002	John	Doe	(555) 555-2222	Peter
0003	Jane	Smith	(555) 555-3333	Liam, Sean, Collin
0004	John	Smith	(555) 555-4444	Amy, Anabel

Figure 1-2: A table that isn't a relation

1-2 is certainly a table, but it isn't a relation. Why? Because there are multiple values in some of the rows in the *Children* column. In contrast, Figure 1-1 is a legal relation.

Note: Although the official name of the two-dimensional "thing" we have been discussing is "relation," most people consider the word "table" to be synonymous and we will use both terms interchangeably throughout this book.

A relation has a name that is unique within its schema. Each column (or attribute) in a relation also has a name, but in this case, the name needs to be unique only within the table. In fact, as you will see shortly, there are times when you actually want to have columns with the same names in multiple tables.

In a well-designed relational database, each table represents an entity. We often document entities (and, as you will see, the relationships among them) in a diagram known as an *entity-relationship diagram* (ERD). There are many ways to draw ERDs, each of which can convey just about the same information. The particular style we'll be using in this book is known as the *information engineering* (IE) style. An entity is represented as a rectangle with its name in the top section and its attributes in the bottom, as you see in Figure 1-3.

A relation is both *column-order independent* and *row-order independent.* This mean that we can view the columns in any order and the rows in any order without losing the meaning of the data. The assumption is, however, that all the data in one row remain in that row.

Domains

Each column in a relation has a *domain*, an expression of the legal values for that column. In some cases, a domain is very specific. For example, if you are working with a column that stores the sizes of T-shirts, the entire domain might consist of the values S, M, L, XL, and XXL. Domains are more commonly, however, general data types, such as integer or date.[3]

Once you assign a domain to a column, the DBMS will enforce that domain, rejecting any command that attempts to enter a value into the column that isn't from the domain. This is an example of a *constraint* on a relation, a rule to which the relation must adhere.

Primary Keys

Each row in a relation must have a unique value that identifies the row. This *primary key* is made up of the values in one or more columns (the smallest number of columns needed to enforce uniqueness). A table that stores information about an order, for example, would probably use the order number as its primary key.

People are particularly difficult to identify uniquely, so we often assign each person in a table an arbitrary number. If you look back at Figure 1-3, you will see that there is a *customer_numb* attribute, representing a number that will be simply given to each customer when a row for a new customer is entered into the table. The IE diagramming method places an asterisk in front of the column or columns that make up a primary key, just as is done in Figure 1-3.

---

[3]   In fact, today's major DBMSs do not provide direct support for true relational domains. Nonetheless you will see that there are SQL constructs that simulate domains.

Customer
*customer_numb
customer_first_name
customer_last_name
customer_street
customer_city
customer_state
customer_zip
customer_phone

Figure 1-3:   A UML etity

Sometimes there is no single column that will uniquely identify each row in a table. As an example, consider the table in Figure 1-4 (*dependents*), which lists employees' dependent children. We can't use the employee number as the primary key because customer numbers repeat for each child an employee has, and many employees have more than one child. By the same token, the children's names and birthdates aren't unique. The solution is to consider the values in two columns as the primary key. In this case, the employee number and the child's name make the best primary key. Taken as a unit, the two values are unique in every row. A primary key made up of more than one column is known as a *concatenated key*.

Emp. #	Child name	Child birth date
0001	Sarah	1-15-2000
0002	John	2-12-1999
0002	Mary	6-6-2004
0002	John	4-15-2006
0003	Pamela	10-10-2004
0003	Paul	10-10-2004

Figure 1-4: A relation with a concatenated primary key

Why are unique primary keys so important? Because they ensure that you can retrieve every piece of data that you put into a database. If primary keys aren't unique, a query will retrieve one or more rows with a value you specify, but you can't be certain which is the exact row you want unless you know something that identifies just that one row. In fact, you should be able to retrieve any single data value knowing three things: the name of the table, the name of the column, and the primary key of the row.

As you will see later in this book, you specify a table's primary key when you define the table to the DBMS. The DBMS will then enforce a constraint that requires unique primary key values.

Note: It is actually possible to create a table that has no primary key, but some DBMSs won't let you put any data in it.

Nulls

Sometimes you don't put data in some columns of some rows because you don't know the appropriate data values. The empty columns don't contain a zero or a blank. Instead, they contain a special indicator known as *null*, which means "unknown."

There are two important implications of the presence of nulls in a table. First, we can't allow nulls as all or part of a primary key. If there is only one row with null for a primary key, then the property of unique primary key values is preserved. The minute we introduce a second row with a null primary key, however, the primary keys are no longer unique. A DBMS will therefore ensure that all primary keys have values, a constraint known as *entity integrity*.

Secondly, nulls can affect the result of queries. Assume, for example, that you want to retrieve the names of all employees who have a salary of more than $100,000. For all employees that have a value in the salary column, the answer to "Is the salary more than $100,000" will be either "yes" or "no." But if the salary column contains null, the DBMS doesn't know the answer to the question; the result is "maybe."

We say that a DBMS operates using *three-valued logic*: yes, no, or maybe. The question that remains is what a DBMS should do when the answer to the question it is asking is "maybe." Should it retrieve rows with null or leave them out? The relational data model doesn't specify exactly what a DBMS should do, but does require the DBMS to act consistently—either always retrieve rows with nulls or always leave them out—and that the user be aware of what is happening. We'll deal with effect of nulls at various places throughout this book.

Base versus Virtual Tables

There are two primary types of tables with which you will be working when you use SQL. The tables that contain data that are stored in the database are known as *base tables*. However, the DBMS also uses several types of temporary tables that only exist in main memory. These are *virtual tables* and by definition they are not stored in the database. Most modern DBMS use several types of virtual tables, including views, temporary tables, and query result tables. If you want to keep the data in a virtual table, then those data must be inserted into a base table.

Representing Relationships

Along with data describing entities, a database must somehow represent relationships between entities. Prior to the relational data model, databases used data structures embedded in the data to show relationships. However, the relational data model relies on it data to show relationships.

Types of Relationships

There are three types of relationships between entities that we encounter in our database environments: one-to-one, one-to-many, and many-to-many.

One-to-One Relationships

A one-to-one relationship exists between two entities when an occurrence of entity A is related to zero or one occurrences of entity B and an occurrence of entity B is related to zero or one occurrences of entity A. Although the specific occurrences involved in the relationship may change over time, there is never more than one related occurrence at any given time. For example, a car and its engine have unique serial numbers. At any one time, an engine is installed in only one car; at the same time, a car has only one engine. The engine may be in no car or it can be moved from one car to another, but it can't be in more than one place at a time. By the same token, a car can have no engine or one engine. The specific engine may change over time but there is never more than one.[4]

We include a relationship in an ERD by drawing a line between the rectangles for two related entities. The line ends identify the type of the relationship. In Figure 1-5 you can see the way in which we would diagram the one-to-one relationship between a car and its engine. The |0 at the end of the line means "zero or one."

If the relationship is required (mandatory), then the |0 at the end of the line changes to || (one and only one). We use mandatory relationships when we don't want an occurrence of an entity to be store in the database unless it is related to an occurrence of the entity at the other end of the relationship. For example, if we didn't want an engine in the database unless that engine was in a car, the end of the line next to the *car* entity would be ||.

One-to-many Relationships

True one-to-one relationships are very uncommon, but database environments are full of one-to-many relationships. When a one-to-many relationship exists between two entities, one occurrence of entity A is related to zero, one, or more occurrences of entity B; each occurrence of entity B is related to at most one occurrence of entity A. If, for example, we add car owners to our car database, then there will be a one-to-many

---

[4]   Yes, there is at least one exception to the statement that a car has only one engine: hybrids have a gasoline engine and an electric engine. There are exceptions to just about every scenario in this book, so please take them in the spirit in which they were intended: as examples.

relationship between an owner and a car. At any time, a person can own zero, one, or more cars and a car belongs to zero or one owners.

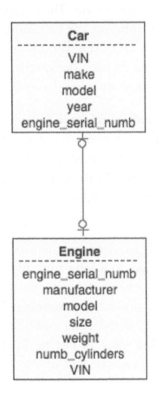

Figure 1-5: A one-to-one relationship

In an ERD, the line between the related entities has |0 or ||
at one end, representing the zero, one, or more end of the
relationship (or one and only one in the case of a mandatory
relatioship). The end of the line at the "many" side of the re-
lationship is marked with >0 or >|, representing zero, one, or
more (or in the case of a mandatory relationship, one or more).
In Figure 1-6, the *owner* entity is at the "one" end of the relationship and the *car* entity is at the "many" end.

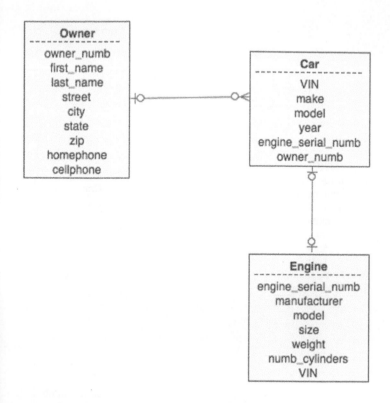

Figure 1-6: Adding a one-to-many relationship

The third type of relationship between entities, a many-to-many relationship, is also very common. When two entities are related in that way, one occurrence of entity A can be related to many occurrences of entity B (zero, one, or more) and one occurrence of entity B can be related to many occurrences of entity A. To demonstrate, let's add an entity for a Web site to the car database, indicating which cars are advertised on which Web sites. A car can be advertised on many Web sites and a site can advertise many cars.

The many-to-many relationship has been diagrammed in Figure 1-7. Notice that each end of the line connecting the Web site and *Car* entities has the "many" symbol, >0.

Many-to-many Relationships

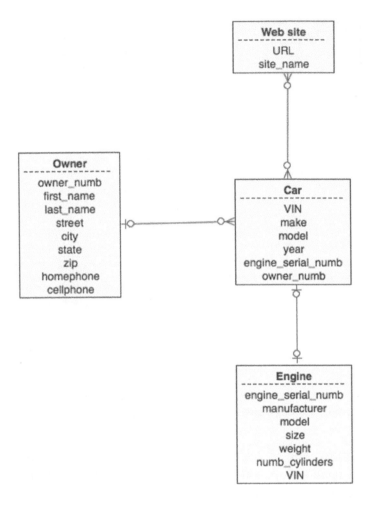

Figure 1-7: Adding a many-to-many relationship

While many-to-many relationships are common, they are also a major problem: The relational data model cannot represent them directly, which means that they must be removed from the design and replaced with one-to-many relationships. In Figure 1-8 we have introduced an entity called a *Listing*. It represents one car being listed on one Web site.

The *listing* entity is what we call a *composite entity*. It's purpose is to represent the relationship between two other entities. Notice in Figure 1-8 that its primary key is the concatenation of the primary key's of its parent entities (*car* and *Web site*).

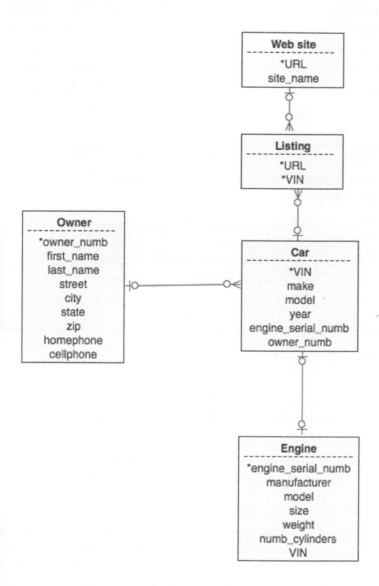

Figure 1-8: Removing many-to-many relationships

Foreign Keys and Referential Integrity

If you look back at Figure 1-8, you'll notice that some attributes appear in more than one entity. For example, you can see that the *engine* entity contains the VIN of the car into which it is inserted. This is how a relational database shows data relationships. When *VIN* in the *engine* entity has a value, it represents the relationship with a specific occurrence of *car*. Any attribute in an entity that is the same as the entire primary key of another entity is known as a *foreign key*. Table 1-1 lists all the foreign keys in the car database we have been developing.

Table containing the foreign key	Foreign key attributes	Table referenced by foreign key
Engine	VIN	Car
Car	engine_serial_numb	Engine
	owner_numb	Owner
Listing	URL	Web site
	VIN	Car

Table 1-1: Foreign keys in the database design in Figure 1-8

A foreign key can be null. For example, if an engine isn't installed in a car, then the *VIN* attribute in the Engine entity will be null. However, foreign keys that are part of a primary key, such as the *URL* and *VIN* attributes in the *listing* entity, must have values to satisfy entity integrity.

When foreign keys are non-null, a matching primary key value must exist in the table referenced by the foreign key. When a car has an owner, for example, a row with the matching *owner_numb* must exist in the *Owner* table. Otherwise, it will be impossible to find information about that owner. This property is known as *referential integrity*: Every non-null foreign key value must reference an existing primary key value. As you will see throughout this book, much of what you do with SQL involves retrieving matching data using primary key–foreign key relationships.

Foreign keys are not limited to single columns; they can be concatenated, just like primary keys. As an example, consider a part of the database design for a very small accounting firm in Figure 1-9. Because the firm is so small, the database designer decides that employee numbers aren't necessary and instead uses the accountants' first and last names as the primary key of the *accountant* table. The *project* table, used to gather data about one accountant preparing one year's tax returns for one customer, uses the tax year and the customer number as its primary key. However, it has three foreign keys. (We'll get to those in a moment.) The *form* table that stores data about the forms that are part of a specific tax return uses the concatenation of the form's ID and the primary key of the project table for its primary key.

A foreign key is the same as the *complete* primary key of another table. Therefore, the *acct_first_name* attribute by itself in the project table is not a foreign key; neither is the *acc_last_name* attribute. If you concatenate them, however, then they are the same as the primary key of the *accountant* table and, in fact, this is the unit with which referential integrity should be enforced.

Assume that "Jane Johnson" is working on customer 10100's 2014 tax return. It's not enough to ensure that "Jane" appears somewhere in the first name column in the *accountant* table and "Johnson" appears anywhere in the *last name* column in the *accountant* table. There could be many people named "Jane" and many with the last name of "Johnson." What we need to ensure is that there is one person named "Jane Johnson" in the *accountant* table, the concatenation of the two attributes that make up the primary key.

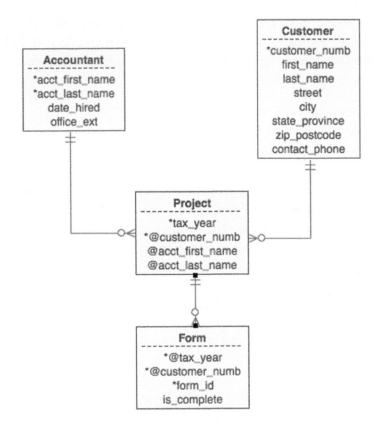

Figure 1-9: A part of a database design with concatenated foreign keys

The same holds true for the concatenated foreign key in the *form* table: the tax year and the customer number. A row with a matching pair must exist in the *project* table before referential integrity is satisfied.

Views

Users don't necessarily work directly with base tables. Instead, they use *views*, which present a subset of the database. A view can be constructed from one or more tables and/or views, using one or more columns and one or more rows.

Views are stored in the database as SQL query expressions. Each has a name. When someone uses the name of the view, either from the command line or in an application program, the DBMS executes the query and assembles a virtual table in main memory. The user can then see the view's data, query the view, and in some cases, use it for updates.

There are two main reasons for using views. First, they let you store complex queries in the database. The user then doesn't need to type the entire query, but can use the view's name. Second, views provide a security mechanism. Users are prohibited from accessing base tables directly but instead work with views that present the portions of the database to which they should have access.

Most of the sample queries throughout this book are taken from a portion of a relational database that supports a rare book dealer. You can find the ER diagram in Figure 1-10. The rare book dealer handles rare fiction editions and some modern fiction. Because many of the books are one-of-a-kind, he tracks each volume individually.

The portion of the database we will be using contains data on customers and the volumes that they purchase. Notice, however, that it really takes three entities to describe a volume that is sold. The *work* entity describes a text written by one author with one title. A book is a specific published version of a work; it is identified by an ISBN. A volume is one copy of a book. This is the unit that is being sold.

Notice that many of the text attributes of a work/book/volume are represented by numeric codes that act as foreign keys. For example, a book has a *work_id* that connects it to the work. It also has a *publisher_id* that connects to a table that contains the text of publisher names. Why design the database this way? Because it is very easy to make mistakes when typing text; data that are repeated may become inconsistent, resulting in queries

The Design of the Sample Database

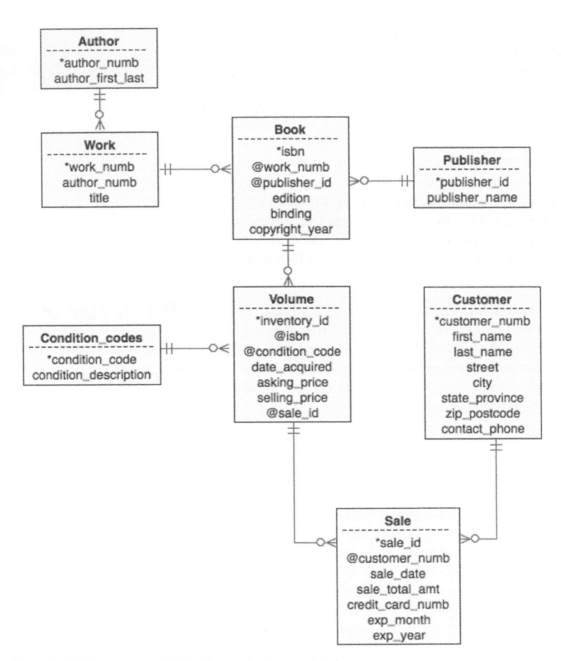

Figure 1-10: The complete ERD for the rare book store database

that don't retrieve all appropriate rows. Therefore, we store the text just once and relate it to works/books/volumes using integer codes.

The data that we will be using appear in Tables 1-2 through 1-9.[5] With the exception of work authors and titles, the data are fictional, made up just for use in this book.

```
publisher_id  |          publisher_name
--------------+------------------------------------
           1 | Wiley
           2 | Simon & Schuster
           3 | Macmillan
           4 | Tor
           5 | DAW
```

Table 1-2: Publisher

```
author_numb  |         author_last_first
-------------+------------------------------------
           1 | Bronte, Charlotte
           2 | Doyle, Sir Arthur Conan
           3 | Twain, Mark
           4 | Stevenson, Robert Louis
           5 | Rand, Ayn
           6 | Barrie, James
           7 | Ludlum, Robert
           8 | Barth, John
           9 | Herbert, Frank
          10 | Asimov, Isaac
          11 | Funke, Cornelia
          12 | Stephenson, Neal
```

Table 1-3: Author

---

[5] Some column names have been abbreviated so the data will fit on the printed page.

```
condition_code  |   condition_description
----------------+-----------------------
             1 | New
             2 | Excellent
             3 | Fine
             4 | Good
             5 | Poor
```

Table 1-4: Condition codes

```
work_numb  | author_numb |                     title
-----------+-------------+------------------------------------------------
         1 |           1 | Jane Eyre
         2 |           1 | Villette
         3 |           2 | Hound of the Baskervilles
         4 |           2 | Lost World, The
         5 |           2 | Complete Sherlock Holmes
         7 |           3 | Prince and the Pauper
         8 |           3 | Tom Sawyer
         9 |           3 | Adventures of Huckleberry Finn, The
         6 |           3 | Connecticut Yankee in King Arthur's Court, A
        13 |           5 | Fountainhead, The
        14 |           5 | Atlas Shrugged
        15 |           6 | Peter Pan
        10 |           7 | Bourne Identity, The
        11 |           7 | Matarese Circle, The
        12 |           7 | Bourne Supremacy, The
        16 |           4 | Kidnapped
        17 |           4 | Treasure Island
        18 |           8 | Sot Weed Factor, The
        19 |           8 | Lost in the Funhouse
        20 |           8 | Giles Goat Boy
        21 |           9 | Dune
        22 |           9 | Dune Messiah
        23 |          10 | Foundation
        24 |          10 | Last Foundation
        25 |          10 | I, Robot
        26 |          11 | Inkheart
        27 |          11 | Inkdeath
        28 |          12 | Anathem
        29 |          12 | Snow Crash
        30 |           5 | Anthem
        31 |          12 | Cryptonomicon
```

Table 1-5: Work

isbn	work_numb	publisher_id	edition	binding	copyright_year
978-1-11111-111-1	1	1	2	Board	1857
978-1-11111-112-1	1	1	1	Board	1847
978-1-11111-113-1	2	4	1	Board	1842
978-1-11111-114-1	3	4	1	Board	1801
978-1-11111-115-1	3	4	10	Leather	1925
978-1-11111-116-1	4	3	1	Board	1805
978-1-11111-117-1	5	5	1	Board	1808
978-1-11111-118-1	5	2	19	Leather	1956
978-1-11111-120-1	8	4	5	Board	1906
978-1-11111-119-1	6	2	3	Board	1956
978-1-11111-121-1	8	1	12	Leather	1982
978-1-11111-122-1	9	1	12	Leather	1982
978-1-11111-123-1	11	2	1	Board	1998
978-1-11111-124-1	12	2	1	Board	1989
978-1-11111-125-1	13	2	3	Board	1965
978-1-11111-126-1	13	2	9	Leather	2001
978-1-11111-127-1	14	2	1	Board	1960
978-1-11111-128-1	16	2	12	Board	1960
978-1-11111-129-1	16	2	14	Leather	2002
978-1-11111-130-1	17	3	6	Leather	1905
978-1-11111-131-1	18	4	6	Board	1957
978-1-11111-132-1	19	4	1	Board	1962
978-1-11111-133-1	20	4	1	Board	1964
978-1-11111-134-1	21	5	1	Board	1964
978-1-11111-135-1	23	5	1	Board	1962
978-1-11111-136-1	23	5	4	Leather	2001
978-1-11111-137-1	24	5	4	Leather	2001
978-1-11111-138-1	23	5	4	Leather	2001
978-1-11111-139-1	25	5	4	Leather	2001
978-1-11111-140-1	26	5	1	Board	2001
978-1-11111-141-1	27	5	1	Board	2005
978-1-11111-142-1	28	5	1	Board	2008
978-1-11111-143-1	29	5	1	Board	1992
978-1-11111-144-1	30	1	1	Board	1952
978-1-11111-145-1	30	5	1	Board	2001
978-1-11111-146-1	31	5	1	Board	1999

Table 1-6: Books

inventory_id	isbn	condition_code	date_acquired	asking_price	selling_price	sale_id
1	978-1-11111-111-1	3	12-JUN-12 00:00:00	175.00	175.00	1
2	978-1-11111-131-1	4	23-JAN-12 00:00:00	50.00	50.00	1
7	978-1-11111-137-1	2	20-JUN-12 00:00:00	80.00		
3	978-1-11111-133-1	2	05-APR-11 00:00:00	300.00	285.00	1
4	978-1-11111-142-1	1	05-APR-11 00:00:00	25.95	25.95	2
5	978-1-11111-146-1	2	05-APR-11 00:00:00	22.95	22.95	2
6	978-1-11111-144-1	3	15-MAY-12 00:00:00	80.00	76.10	2
8	978-1-11111-137-1	1	20-JUN-12 00:00:00	50.00		
9	978-1-11111-136-1	2	20-DEC-11 00:00:00	75.00		
10	978-1-11111-136-1	1	15-DEC-11 00:00:00	50.00		
11	978-1-11111-143-1	1	05-APR-12 00:00:00	25.00	25.00	3
12	978-1-11111-132-1	3	12-JUN-12 00:00:00	15.00	15.00	3
13	978-1-11111-133-1	2	20-APR-12 00:00:00	18.00	18.00	3
15	978-1-11111-121-1	2	20-APR-12 00:00:00	110.00	110.00	5
14	978-1-11111-121-1	2	20-APR-12 00:00:00	110.00	110.00	4
16	978-1-11111-121-1	2	20-APR-12 00:00:00	110.00		
17	978-1-11111-124-1	1	12-JAN-13 00:00:00	75.00		
18	978-1-11111-146-1	2	11-MAY-12 00:00:00	30.00	30.00	6
19	978-1-11111-122-1	2	06-MAY-12 00:00:00	75.00	75.00	6
20	978-1-11111-130-1	2	20-APR-12 00:00:00	150.00	120.00	6
21	978-1-11111-126-1	2	20-APR-12 00:00:00	10.00	110.00	6
22	978-1-11111-139-1	2	16-MAY-12 00:00:00	200.00	170.00	6
23	978-1-11111-125-1	3	16-MAY-12 00:00:00	45.00	45.00	7
24	978-1-11111-131-1	2	20-APR-12 00:00:00	35.00	35.00	7
25	978-1-11111-126-1	3	16-NOV-12 00:00:00	75.00	75.00	8
26	978-1-11111-133-1	1	16-NOV-12 00:00:00	35.00	55.00	8
27	978-1-11111-141-1	1	06-NOV-12 00:00:00	24.95		
28	978-1-11111-141-1	1	06-NOV-12 00:00:00	24.95		
29	978-1-11111-141-1	1	06-NOV-12 00:00:00	24.95		
30	978-1-11111-145-1	1	06-NOV-12 00:00:00	27.95		
31	978-1-11111-145-1	1	06-NOV-12 00:00:00	27.95		
32	978-1-11111-145-1	2	06-NOV-12 00:00:00	27.95		
33	978-1-11111-139-1	1	06-OCT-12 00:00:00	75.00	50.00	9
34	978-1-11111-133-1	1	16-NOV-12 00:00:00	125.00	125.00	10
35	978-1-11111-126-1	1	06-OCT-12 00:00:00	75.00	75.00	11

Table 1-7:   Volume (continued on next page)

#	ISBN		Date	Time	Amount	Amount	
36	978-1-11111-130-1	3	06-DEC-11	00:00:00	50.00	50.00	
37	978-1-11111-136-1	3	06-DEC-11	00:00:00	75.00	75.00	11
38	978-1-11111-130-1	2	06-APR-12	00:00:00	200.00	150.00	12
39	978-1-11111-132-1	3	06-APR-12	00:00:00	75.00	75.00	12
40	978-1-11111-129-1	1	06-APR-12	00:00:00	25.95	25.95	13
41	978-1-11111-141-1	1	16-MAY-12	00:00:00	40.00	40.00	14
42	978-1-11111-141-1	1	16-MAY-12	00:00:00	40.00	40.00	14
43	978-1-11111-132-1	1	12-NOV-12	00:00:00	17.95		
44	978-1-11111-138-1	1	12-NOV-12	00:00:00	75.95		
45	978-1-11111-138-1	1	12-NOV-12	00:00:00	75.95		
46	978-1-11111-131-1	3	12-NOV-12	00:00:00	15.95		
47	978-1-11111-140-1	3	12-NOV-12	00:00:00	25.95		
48	978-1-11111-123-1	2	16-AUG-12	00:00:00	24.95		
49	978-1-11111-127-1	2	16-AUG-12	00:00:00	27.95		
50	978-1-11111-127-1	2	06-JAN-13	00:00:00	50.00	50.00	15
51	978-1-11111-141-1	2	06-JAN-13	00:00:00	50.00	50.00	15
52	978-1-11111-141-1	2	06-JAN-13	00:00:00	50.00	50.00	16
53	978-1-11111-123-1	2	06-JAN-13	00:00:00	40.00	40.00	16
54	978-1-11111-127-1	2	06-JAN-13	00:00:00	40.00	40.00	16
55	978-1-11111-133-1	2	06-FEB-13	00:00:00	60.00	60.00	17
56	978-1-11111-127-1	2	16-FEB-12	00:00:00	40.00	40.00	17
57	978-1-11111-135-1	2	16-FEB-12	00:00:00	40.00	40.00	18
59	978-1-11111-127-1	2	25-FEB-13	00:00:00	35.00	35.00	18
58	978-1-11111-131-1	2	16-FEB-13	00:00:00	25.00	25.00	18
60	978-1-11111-128-1	2	16-DEC-12	00:00:00	50.00	45.00	19
61	978-1-11111-136-1	3	22-OCT-12	00:00:00	50.00	50.00	19
62	978-1-11111-115-1	2	22-OCT-12	00:00:00	75.00	75.00	20
63	978-1-11111-130-1	2	16-JUL-12	00:00:00	500.00		
64	978-1-11111-136-1	2	06-MAR-12	00:00:00	125.00		
65	978-1-11111-136-1	2	06-MAR-12	00:00:00	125.00		
66	978-1-11111-137-1	2	06-MAR-12	00:00:00	125.00		
67	978-1-11111-137-1	2	06-MAR-12	00:00:00	125.00		
68	978-1-11111-138-1	2	06-MAR-12	00:00:00	125.00		
69	978-1-11111-138-1	2	06-MAR-12	00:00:00	125.00		
70	978-1-11111-139-1	2	06-MAR-12	00:00:00	125.00		
71	978-1-11111-139-1	2	06-MAR-12	00:00:00	125.00		

Table 1-7:   Volume (continued)

cust # numb	first_ name	last_ name	street	city	state prov.	zip_ post	contact_ phone
1	Janice	Jones	125 Center Road	Anytown	NY	11111	518-555-1111
2	Jon	Jones	25 Elm Road	Next Town	NJ	18888	209-555-2222
3	John	Doe	821 Elm Street	Next Town	NJ	18888	209-555-3333
4	Jane	Doe	852 Main Street	Anytown	NY	11111	518-555-4444
5	Jane	Smith	1919 Main Street	New Village	NY	13333	518-555-5555
6	Janice	Smith	800 Center Road	Anytown	NY	11111	518-555-6666
7	Helen	Brown	25 Front Street	Anytown	NY	11111	518-555-7777
8	Helen	Jerry	16 Main Street	Newtown	NJ	18886	518-555-8888
9	Mary	Collins	301 Pine Road, Apt. 12	Newtown	NJ	18886	518-555-9999
10	Peter	Collins	18 Main Street	Newtown	NJ	18886	518-555-1010
11	Edna	Hayes	209 Circle Road	Anytown	NY	11111	518-555-1110
12	Franklin	Hayes	615 Circle Road	Anytown	NY	11111	518-555-1212
13	Peter	Johnson	22 Rose Court	Next Town	NJ	18888	209-555-1212
14	Peter	Johnson	881 Front Street	Next Town	NJ	18888	209-555-1414
15	John	Smith	881 Manor Lane	Next Town	NJ	18888	209-555-1515

Table 1-8: Customers

sale_id	customer_numb	sale_date	sale_total_amt	credit_card_numb	exp_month	exp_year
3	1	15-JUN-13 00:00:00	58.00	1234 5678 9101 1121	10	18
4	4	30-JUN-13 00:00:00	110.00	1234 5678 9101 5555	7	17
5	6	30-JUN-13 00:00:00	110.00	1234 5678 9101 6666	12	17
6	12	05-JUL-13 00:00:00	505.00	1234 5678 9101 7777	7	16
7	8	05-JUL-13 00:00:00	80.00	1234 5678 9101 8888	8	16
8	5	07-JUL-13 00:00:00	90.00	1234 5678 9101 9999	9	15
9	8	07-JUL-13 00:00:00	50.00	1234 5678 9101 8888	8	16
10	11	10-JUL-13 00:00:00	125.00	1234 5678 9101 1010	11	16
11	9	10-JUL-13 00:00:00	200.00	1234 5678 9101 0909	11	15
12	10	10-JUL-13 00:00:00	200.00	1234 5678 9101 0101	10	15
13	2	10-JUL-13 00:00:00	25.95	1234 5678 9101 2222	2	15
14	6	10-JUL-13 00:00:00	80.00	1234 5678 9101 6666	12	17
15	11	12-JUL-13 00:00:00	75.00	1234 5678 9101 1231	11	17
16	2	25-JUL-13 00:00:00	130.00	1234 5678 9101 2222	2	15
17	1	25-JUL-13 00:00:00	100.00	1234 5678 9101 1121	10	18
18	5	22-AUG-13 00:00:00	100.00	1234 5678 9101 9999	9	15
2	1	05-JUN-13 00:00:00	125.00	1234 5678 9101 1121	10	18
1	1	29-MAY-13 00:00:00	510.00	1234 5678 9101 1121	10	18
19	6	01-SEP-13 00:00:00	95.00	1234 5678 9101 7777	7	16
20	2	01-SEP-13 00:00:00	75.00	1234 5678 9101 2222	2	15

Table 1-9: Sale

Relational Algebra

When we use SQL to manipulate data in a database, we are actually using something known as the *relational calculus,* a method for using a single command to instruct the DBMS to perform one or more actions. The DBMS must then break down the SQL command into a set of operations that it can perform one after the other to produce the requested result. These single operations are taken from the *relational algebra.*

Note: Don't panic. Although both the relational calculus and the relational algebra can be expressed in the notation of formal logic, there is no need for us to do so. You won't see anything remotely like mathematic notation in this chapter.

In this chapter we will look at seven relational algebra operations. The first five—restrict,[1] project, join, union, and difference—are fundamental to SQL operations. In fact, any DBMS that supports them is said to be *relationally complete.* The remaining operations (product and intersect) are useful for helping us understand how SQL processes queries.

---

1   Restrict is a renaming of the operation that was originally called "select." However, because SQL's main retrieval command is SELECT, restrict was introduced by C. J. Date (one of today's most respected database design theorists) for the relational algebra operation to provide clarity. It is used in this book to help avoid confusion.

It is possible to use SQL without understanding much about relational algebra. However, you will find it easier to formulate effective efficient queries if you have an understanding of what the SQL syntax is asking the DBMS to do. There is often more than one way to write a SQL command to obtain a specific result. The commands will often differ in the underlying relational algebra operations required to generate results and therefore may differ significantly in performance.

Note: The bottom line is: You really do need to read this chapter.

The most important thing to understand about relational algebra is that each operation does one thing. For example, one operation extracts columns while another extracts rows. The DBMS must do the operations one at a time, in a step-by-step sequence. We therefore say that relational algebra is *procedural*. SQL, on the other hand, lets us formulate our queries in a logical way without necessarily specifying the order in which relational operations should be performed. SQL is therefore *non-procedural*.

There is no official syntax for relational algebra. What you will see in this chapter, however, is a relatively consistent way of expressing the operations without resorting to mathematical symbols. In general each command has the following format:

```
OPERATION parameters FROM source_table_name(s)
      GIVING result_table_name
```

The parameters vary depending on the specific operation. They may specify a second table that is part of the operation, or they may specify which attributes are to be included in the result.

The result of every relational algebra operation is another table. In most cases the table will be a relation, but some operations—such as the outer join—may have nulls in primary key columns (preventing the table from having a unique primary key) and therefore will not be legal relations. The result tables are virtual tables that can be used as input to another relational algebra operation.

A *projection* of a relation is a new relation created by copying one or more the columns from the original relation into a new table. As an example, consider Figure 2-1. The result table (arbitrarily called *Names_and_numbers*) is a projection of the customer relation with the attributes *customer_numb, first_name*, and *last_name*.

Making Vertical Subsets: Project

Using the syntax for relational algebra, the projection in Figure 2-1 is written:

```
PROJECT customer_rows, first_name, last_name
     FROM customer GIVING Names_and_numbers
```

The order of the columns in the result table is based on the order in which the column names appear in the project statement; the order in which they are defined in the source table has no effect on the result. Rows appear in the order in which they are stored in the source table; project does not include sorting or ordering the data in any way. As with all relational algebra operations, duplicate rows are removed.

Note: It is important to keep in mind that relational algebra is first and foremost a set of theoretical operations. A DBMS may not implement an operation the same way that it is described in theory. For example, most DBMSs don't remove duplicate rows from result tables unless the user requests it explicitly. Why? Because to remove duplicates the DBMS must sort the result table by every column (so that duplicate rows will be next to one another) and then scan the table from top to bottom looking for the duplicates. This can be a very slow process if the result table is large.

Whenever you issue a SQL command that asks for specific columns—just about every retrieval command—you are asking the DBMS to perform the *project* operation. Project is a very

customer_numb	first_name	last_name	street	city	state_province	zip_postcode	contact_phone
1	Janice	Jones	125 Center Road	Anytown	NY	11111	518-555-1111
2	Jon	Jones	25 Elm Road	Next Town	NJ	18888	209-555-2222
3	John	Doe	821 Elm Street	Next Town	NJ	18888	209-555-3333
4	Jane	Doe	852 Main Street	Anytown	NY	11111	518-555-4444
5	Jane	Smith	1919 Main Street	New Village	NY	13333	518-555-5555
6	Janice	Smith	800 Center Road	Anytown	NY	11111	518-555-6666
7	Helen	Brown	25 Front Street	Anytown	NY	11111	518-555-7777
8	Helen	Jerry	16 Main Street	Newtown	NJ	18886	518-555-8888
9	Mary	Collins	301 Pine Road, Apt. 12	Newtown	NJ	18886	518-555-9999
10	Peter	Collins	18 Main Street	Newtown	NJ	18886	518-555-1010
11	Edna	Hayes	209 Circle Road	Anytown	NY	11111	518-555-1110
12	Franklin	Hayes	615 Circle Road	Anytown	NY	11111	518-555-1212
13	Peter	Johnson	22 Rose Court	Next Town	NJ	18888	209-555-1212
14	Peter	Johnson	881 Front Street	Next Town	NJ	18888	209-555-1414

```
PROJECT customer_numb, first_name, last_name
FROM customer GIVING Names_and_numbers
```

customer_numb	first_name	last_name
1	Janice	Jones
2	Jon	Jones
3	John	Doe
4	Jane	Doe
5	Jane	Smith
6	Janice	Smith
7	Helen	Brown
8	Helen	Jerry
9	Mary	Collins
10	Peter	Collins
11	Edna	Hayes
12	Franklin	Hayes
13	Peter	Johnson
14	Peter	Johnson

Figure 2-1: Taking a projection

fast operation because the DBMS does not need to evaluate any of the data in the table.

There is one issue with project with which you need to be concerned. A DBMS will project any columns that you request. It makes no judgment as to whether the selected columns produce a meaningful result. For example, consider the following operation:

```
PROJECT sale_total_amt, exp_month FROM sale
     GIVING invalid
```

In theory, there is absolutely nothing wrong with this project. However, it probably doesn't mean much to associate a dollar amount with a credit card expiration month. Notice in Figure 2-2 that because there is more than one sale with the same total cost (for example, $110), the same sale value is associated with more than one expiration month. We could create a concatenated primary key for the result table using both columns, but that still wouldn't make the resulting table meaningful in the context of the database environment. There is no set of rules as to what constitutes a meaningful projection. Judgments as to the usefulness of projections depend solely on the meaning of the data the database is trying to capture.

Making Horizontal Subsets: Restrict

The *restrict* operation asks a DBMS to choose rows that meet some logical criteria. As defined in the relational algebra, restrict copies rows from the source relation into a result table. Restrict copies all attributes; it has no way to specify which attributes should be included in the result table.

Restrict identifies which rows are to be included in the result table with a logical expression known as a *predicate*. The operation therefore takes the following general form:

```
RESTRICT FROM source_table_name WHERE predicate
     GIVING result_table_name
```

sale_id	customer_numb	sale_date	sale_total_amt	credit_card_numb	exp_month	exp_year
3	1	15-JUN-13	58.00	1234 5678 9101 1121	10	18
4	4	30-JUN-13	110.00	1234 5678 9101 5555	7	17
5	6	30-JUN-13	110.00	1234 5678 9101 6666	12	17
6	12	05-JUL-13	505.00	1234 5678 9101 7777	7	16
7	8	05-JUL-13	80.00	1234 5678 9101 8888	8	16
8	5	07-JUL-13	90.00	1234 5678 9101 9999	9	15
9	8	07-JUL-13	50.00	1234 5678 9101 8888	8	16
10	11	10-JUL-13	125.00	1234 5678 9101 1010	11	15
11	9	10-JUL-13	200.00	1234 5678 9101 0909	11	15
12	10	10-JUL-13	200.00	1234 5678 9101 0101	10	15
13	2	10-JUL-13	25.95	1234 5678 9101 2222	2	17
14	6	10-JUL-13	80.00	1234 5678 9101 6666	12	17
15	11	12-JUL-13	75.00	1234 5678 9101 1231	11	15
16	2	25-JUL-13	130.00	1234 5678 9101 2222	2	15
17	1	25-JUL-13	100.00	1234 5678 9101 1121	10	18
18	5	22-AUG-13	100.00	1234 5678 9101 9999	9	15
2	1	05-JUN-13	125.00	1234 5678 9101 1121	10	18
1	1	29-MAY-13	510.00	1234 5678 9101 1121	10	18
19	6	01-SEP-13	95.00	1234 5678 9101 7777	7	16
20	2	01-SEP-13	75.00	1234 5678 9101 2222	2	15

```
PROJECT sale_total_amt, exp_month
FROM sale GIVING invalid
```

sale_total_amt	exp_month
58.00	10
110.00	7
110.00	12
505.00	7
80.00	8
90.00	9
50.00	8
125.00	11
200.00	11
200.00	10
25.95	2
80.00	12
75.00	11
130.00	2
100.00	10
100.00	9
125.00	10
510.00	10
95.00	7
75.00	2

Figure 2-2: An invalid projection

For example, suppose we want to retrieve data about customers who live in zipcode 11111. The operation might be expressed as

```
RESTRICT FROM customer WHERE zip_postcode =
    '11111' GIVING one_zip
```

The result appears in Figure 2-3. The result table includes the entire row for each customer that has a value of 11111 in the zip_postcode column.

Note: There are many operators that can be used to create a restrict predicate, some of which are unique to SQL. You will begin to read about constructing predicates in Chapter 4.

As we said at the beginning of this chapter, most SQL queries require more than one relational algebra operation. We might, for example, want to see just the names of the customers that live in zipcode 11111. Because such a query requires both a restrict and a project, it takes two steps:

1. Restrict the rows to those with customers that live in zipcode 1111.

2. Project the first and last name columns.

In some cases the order of the restrict and project may not matter. However, in this particular example the restrict must be performed first. Why? Because the project removes the column needed for the restrict predicate from the intermediate result table, which would make it impossible to perform the restrict.

It is up to a DBMS to determine the order in which it will perform relational algebra operations to obtain a requested result. A *query optimizer* takes care of making the decisions. When more than one series of operations will generate the same result, the query optimizer attempts to determine which

Choosing Columns and Rows: Restrict and Then Project

customer_ numb	first_ name	last_ name	street	city	state_ province	zip_ postcode	contact_ phone
1	Janice	Jones	125 Center Road	Anytown	NY	11111	518-555-1111
2	Jon	Jones	25 Elm Road	Next Town	NJ	18888	209-555-2222
3	John	Doe	821 Elm Street	Next Town	NJ	18888	209-555-3333
4	Jane	Doe	852 Main Street	Anytown	NY	11111	518-555-4444
5	Jane	Smith	1919 Main Street	New Village	NY	13333	518-555-5555
6	Janice	Smith	800 Center Road	Anytown	NY	11111	518-555-6666
7	Helen	Brown	25 Front Street	Anytown	NY	11111	518-555-7777
8	Helen	Jerry	16 Main Street	Newtown	NJ	18886	518-555-8888
9	Mary	Collins	301 Pine Road, Apt. 12	Newtown	NJ	18886	518-555-9999
10	Peter	Collins	18 Main Street	Newtown	NJ	18886	518-555-1010
11	Edna	Hayes	209 Circle Road	Anytown	NY	11111	518-555-1110
12	Franklin	Hayes	615 Circle Road	Anytown	NY	11111	518-555-1212
13	Peter	Johnson	22 Rose Court	Next Town	NJ	18888	209-555-1212
14	Peter	Johnson	881 Front Street	Next Town	NJ	18888	209-555-1414

RESTRICT FROM customer WHERE zip_postcode = '11111'
GIVING one_zip

⟶

customer_ numb	first_ name	last_ name	street	city	state_ province	zip_ postcode	contact_ phone
1	Janice	Jones	125 Center Road	Anytown	NY	11111	518-555-1111
4	Jane	Doe	852 Main Street	Anytown	NY	11111	518-555-4444
6	Janice	Smith	800 Center Road	Anytown	NY	11111	518-555-6666
7	Helen	Brown	25 Front Street	Anytown	NY	11111	518-555-7777
11	Edna	Hayes	209 Circle Road	Anytown	NY	11111	518-555-1110
12	Franklin	Hayes	615 Circle Road	Anytown	NY	11111	518-555-1212

Figure 2-3:   Restricting rows from a relation

will provide the best performance and will then execute that strategy.

Note: There is a major tradeoff for a DBMS when it comes to query optimization. Picking the most efficient query strategy can result in the shortest query execution time, but it is also possible for the DBMS to spend so much time figuring out which strategy is best that it consumes any performance advantage that might be had by executing the best strategy. Therefore, the query strategy used by a DBMS may not be the theoretically most efficient strategy, but it is the most efficient strategy that can be identified relatively quickly.

Union

The *union* operation creates a new table by placing all rows from two source tables into a single result table, placing the rows on top of one another. As an example of how a union works, assume that you have the two tables at the top of Figure 2-4. The operation

```
in_print_books UNION out_of_print_books GIVING
    union_result
```

produces the result table at the bottom of Figure 2-4.

For a union operation to be possible, the two source tables must be *union compatible.* In the relational algebra sense, this means that their columns must be defined over the same domains. The tables must have the same columns, but the columns do not necessarily need to be in the same order or be the same size.

In practice, however, the rules for union compatibility are stricter. The two source tables on which the union is performed must have columns with the same data types and sizes, in the same order. As you will see, in SQL the two source tables are actually virtual tables created by two independent retrieval statements, which are then combined by the union operation.

in_print_books

isbn	author_name	title
0-153-2345-0	Jones, Harold	My Life
0-154-2020-X	Smith, Kathryn	Autobiographical Tales
0-456-2946-0	Johnson, Mark	About Me

out_of_print_books

isbn	author_name	title
0-391-3847-2	Jones, Harold	Growing Up
0-381-4819-X	Jones, Harold	My Childhood
0-149-3857-5	Clark, Maggie	Horrible Teen Years, The

in_print_books UNION out_of_print_books GIVING union_result

isbn	author_name	title
0-149-3857-5	Clark, Maggie	Horrible Teen Years, The
0-153-2345-0	Jones, Harold	My Life
0-154-2020-X	Smith, Kathryn	Autobiographical Tales
0-381-4819-X	Jones, Harold	My Childhood
0-391-3847-2	Jones, Harold	Growing Up
0-456-2946-0	Johnson, Mark	About Me

Figure 2-4: *Thee union operation*

Join

Join is arguably the most useful relational algebra operations because it combines two tables into one, usually via a primary key–foreign key relationship. Unfortunately, a join can also be an enormous drain on database performance.

A Non-Database Example

To help you understand how a *join* works, we will begin with an example that has absolutely nothing to do with relations. Assume that you have been given the task of creating manufacturing part assemblies by connecting two individual parts. The parts are classified as either A parts or B parts.

There are many types of A parts (A1 through An, where n is the total number of types of A parts) and many types of B parts (B1 through Bn). Each B is to be matched to the A part with the same number; conversely, an A part is to be matched to a B part with the same number.

The assembly process requires four bins. One contains the A parts, one contains the B parts, and one will hold the completed assemblies. The remaining bin will hold parts that cannot be matched. (The unmatched parts bin is not strictly necessary; it is simply for your convenience.)

You begin by extracting a part from the B bin. You look at the part to determine the A part to which it should be connected. Then, you search the A bin for the correct part. If you can find a matching A part, you connect the two pieces and toss them into the completed assemblies bin. If you cannot find a matching A part, then you toss the unmatched B part into the bin that holds unmatched B parts. You repeat this process until the B bin is empty. Any unmatched A parts will be left in their original location.

Note: You could just as easily have started with the bin containing the A parts. The contents of the bin holding the completed assemblies will be the same.

As you might guess, the A bins and B bins are analogous to tables that have a primary to foreign key relationships. This matching of part numbers is very much like the matching of data that occurs when you perform a *join*. The completed assembly bin corresponds to the result table of the operation. As you read about the operation of a *join*, keep in mind that the parts that could not be matched were left out of the completed assemblies bin.

The Equi-Join

In its most common form, a join forms new rows when data in the two source tables match. Because we are looking for rows with equal values, this type of join is known as an *equi-join* (or a *natural equi-join*). It is also often called an *inner join*. As an example, consider the join in Figure 2-5.

Notice that the *customer_numb* column is the primary key of the *customer_data* table and that the same column is a foreign key in the *sale_data* table. The *customer_numb* column in *sale_data* therefore serves to relate sales to the customers to which they belong.

Assume that you want to see the names of the customers who placed each order. To do so, you must join the two tables, creating combined rows wherever there is a matching *customer_ numb*. In database terminology, we are joining the two tables *over customer_numb*. The result table, *joined_table,* can be found at the bottom of Figure 2-5.

An equi-join can begin with either source table. (The result should be the same regardless of the direction in which the join is performed.) The join compares each row in one source table with the rows in the second. For each row in the first source table that matches data in the second source table in the column or columns over which the join is being performed, a new row is placed in the result table.

customer_data

customer_numb	first_name	last_name
1	Janice	Jones
2	Jon	Jones
3	John	Doe
4	Jane	Doe
5	Jane	Smith
6	Janice	Smith
7	Helen	Brown
8	Helen	Jerry
9	Mary	Collins
10	Peter	Collins
11	Edna	Hayes
12	Franklin	Hayes
13	Peter	Johnson
14	Peter	Johnson
15	John	Smith

sale_data

sale_id	customer_numb	sale_date	sale_total_amt
3	1	15-JUN-13 00:00:00	58.00
4	4	30-JUN-13 00:00:00	110.00
5	6	30-JUN-13 00:00:00	110.00
6	12	05-JUL-13 00:00:00	505.00
7	8	05-JUL-13 00:00:00	80.00
8	5	07-JUL-13 00:00:00	90.00
9	8	07-JUL-13 00:00:00	50.00
10	11	10-JUL-13 00:00:00	125.00
11	9	10-JUL-13 00:00:00	200.00
12	10	10-JUL-13 00:00:00	200.00
13	2	10-JUL-13 00:00:00	25.95
14	6	10-JUL-13 00:00:00	80.00
15	11	12-JUL-13 00:00:00	75.00
16	2	25-JUL-13 00:00:00	130.00
17	5	25-JUL-13 00:00:00	100.00
18	1	22-AUG-13 00:00:00	100.00
1	2	05-JUN-13 00:00:00	125.00
19	1	29-MAY-13 00:00:00	510.00
2	6	01-SEP-13 00:00:00	95.00
20	2	01-SEP-13 00:00:00	75.00

JOIN customer_data TO sale_data OVER customer_numb GIVING joined_table

joined_table

customer_numb	first_name	last_name	sale_id	sale_date	sale_total_amt
1	Janice	Jones	3	15-JUN-13 00:00:00	58.00
4	Jane	Doe	4	30-JUN-13 00:00:00	110.00
6	Janice	Smith	5	30-JUN-13 00:00:00	110.00
12	Franklin	Hayes	6	05-JUL-13 00:00:00	505.00
8	Helen	Jerry	7	05-JUL-13 00:00:00	80.00
5	Jane	Smith	8	07-JUL-13 00:00:00	90.00
8	Helen	Jerry	9	07-JUL-13 00:00:00	50.00
11	Edna	Hayes	10	10-JUL-13 00:00:00	125.00
9	Mary	Collins	11	10-JUL-13 00:00:00	200.00
10	Peter	Collins	12	10-JUL-13 00:00:00	200.00
2	Jon	Jones	13	10-JUL-13 00:00:00	25.95
6	Janice	Smith	14	10-JUL-13 00:00:00	80.00
11	Edna	Hayes	15	12-JUL-13 00:00:00	75.00
2	Jon	Jones	16	25-JUL-13 00:00:00	130.00
1	Janice	Jones	17	25-JUL-13 00:00:00	100.00
5	Jane	Smith	18	22-AUG-13 00:00:00	100.00
2	Janice	Jones	1	05-JUN-13 00:00:00	125.00
1	Janice	Jones	19	29-MAY-13 00:00:00	510.00
6	Janice	Smith	2	01-SEP-13 00:00:00	95.00
2	Jon	Jones	20	01-SEP-13 00:00:00	75.00

Figure 2-5: An *equi-join*

Assume that we are using the *customer_data* table as the first source table, producing the result table in Figure 2-5 might therefore proceed conceptually as follows:

1. Search *sale_data* for rows with a *customer_numb* of 1. There are four matching rows in *sale_data*. Create four new rows in the result table, placing the same customer information in each row along with the data from *sale_data*.

2. Search *sale_data* for rows with a *customer_numb* of 2. Because there are three rows for customer 2 in *sale_data*, add three rows to the result table.

3. Search *sale_data* for rows with a customer_numb of 3. Because there are no matching rows in *sale_data*, do not place a row in the result table.

4. Continue as established until all rows from *customer_data* have been compared to *sale_data*.

If the *customer_numb* column does not appear in both tables, then no row is placed in the result table. This behavior categorizes this type of join as an *inner join*. (Yes, there is such a thing as an outer join. You will read about it shortly.)

What's Really Going On: Product and Restrict

From a relational algebra point of view, a join can be implemented using two other operations: product and restrict. As you will see, this sequence of operations requires the manipulation of a great deal of data and, if implemented by a DBMS, can result in slow query performance. Many of today's DBMSs therefore use alternative techniques for processing joins. Nonetheless, the concept of using product followed by restrict underlies the original SQL join syntax.

The *product* operation (the mathematical Cartesian product) makes every possible pairing of rows from two source tables. The product of the tables in Figure 2-5 produces a result table with 300 rows (the 15 rows in *customer_data* times the 20 rows in *sale_data*), the first 60 of which appear in Figure 2-6.

Note: Although 300 rows may not seem like a lot, consider the size of a product table created from tables with 10,000 and 100,000 rows! The manipulation of a table of this size can tie up a lot of disk I/O and CPU time.

Notice first that the *customer_numb* is included twice in the result table, once from each source table. Second, notice that in some rows, the *customer_numb* is the same. These are the rows that would have been included in a *join*. We can therefore apply a *restrict* predicate (a *join condition*) to the product table to end up with same table provided by the *join* you saw earlier. The predicate can be written:

```
customer.customer_numb = sale.customer_numb
```

The rows that are selected by this predicate from the first 60 rows in the product table appear in black in Figure 2-7; those eliminated by the predicate are gray.

Note: The "dot notation" that you see in the preceding join condition is used throughout SQL. The table name is followed by a dot, which is followed by the column name. This makes it possible to have the same column name in more than one table and yet be able to distinguish among them.

It is important that you keep in mind the implication of this sequence to two relational algebra operations when you are writing SQL joins. If you are using the traditional SQL syntax for a join (the first join syntax we'll be discussing) and you forget the predicate for the join condition, you will end up with a product. The product table contains bad information; it implies facts that are not actually stored in the database. It is therefore potentially harmful, in that a user who does not

customer_numb	first_name	last_name	sale_id	customer_numb	sale_date	sale_total_amt
1	Janice	Jones	3	1	15-JUN-13 00:00:00	58.00
2	Jon	Jones	3	1	15-JUN-13 00:00:00	58.00
3	John	Doe	3	1	15-JUN-13 00:00:00	58.00
4	Jane	Doe	3	1	15-JUN-13 00:00:00	58.00
5	Jane	Smith	3	1	15-JUN-13 00:00:00	58.00
6	Janice	Smith	3	1	15-JUN-13 00:00:00	58.00
7	Helen	Brown	3	1	15-JUN-13 00:00:00	58.00
8	Helen	Jerry	3	1	15-JUN-13 00:00:00	58.00
9	Mary	Collins	3	1	15-JUN-13 00:00:00	58.00
10	Peter	Collins	3	1	15-JUN-13 00:00:00	58.00
11	Edna	Hayes	3	1	15-JUN-13 00:00:00	58.00
12	Franklin	Hayes	3	1	15-JUN-13 00:00:00	58.00
13	Peter	Johnson	3	1	15-JUN-13 00:00:00	58.00
14	Peter	Johnson	3	1	15-JUN-13 00:00:00	58.00
15	John	Smith	3	1	15-JUN-13 00:00:00	58.00
1	Janice	Jones	4	4	30-JUN-13 00:00:00	110.00
2	Jon	Jones	4	4	30-JUN-13 00:00:00	110.00
3	John	Doe	4	4	30-JUN-13 00:00:00	110.00
4	Jane	Doe	4	4	30-JUN-13 00:00:00	110.00
5	Jane	Smith	4	4	30-JUN-13 00:00:00	110.00
6	Janice	Smith	4	4	30-JUN-13 00:00:00	110.00
7	Helen	Brown	4	4	30-JUN-13 00:00:00	110.00
8	Helen	Jerry	4	4	30-JUN-13 00:00:00	110.00
9	Mary	Collins	4	4	30-JUN-13 00:00:00	110.00
10	Peter	Collins	4	4	30-JUN-13 00:00:00	110.00
11	Edna	Hayes	4	4	30-JUN-13 00:00:00	110.00
12	Franklin	Hayes	4	4	30-JUN-13 00:00:00	110.00
13	Peter	Johnson	4	4	30-JUN-13 00:00:00	110.00
14	Peter	Johnson	4	4	30-JUN-13 00:00:00	110.00
15	John	Smith	4	4	30-JUN-13 00:00:00	110.00
1	Janice	Jones	5	6	30-JUN-13 00:00:00	110.00
2	Jon	Jones	5	6	30-JUN-13 00:00:00	110.00
3	John	Doe	5	6	30-JUN-13 00:00:00	110.00
4	Jane	Doe	5	6	30-JUN-13 00:00:00	110.00
5	Jane	Smith	5	6	30-JUN-13 00:00:00	110.00
6	Janice	Smith	5	6	30-JUN-13 00:00:00	110.00
7	Helen	Brown	5	6	30-JUN-13 00:00:00	110.00
8	Helen	Jerry	5	6	30-JUN-13 00:00:00	110.00
9	Mary	Collins	5	6	30-JUN-13 00:00:00	110.00
10	Peter	Collins	5	6	30-JUN-13 00:00:00	110.00
11	Edna	Hayes	5	6	30-JUN-13 00:00:00	110.00
12	Franklin	Hayes	5	6	30-JUN-13 00:00:00	110.00
13	Peter	Johnson	5	6	30-JUN-13 00:00:00	110.00
14	Peter	Johnson	5	6	30-JUN-13 00:00:00	110.00
15	John	Smith	5	6	30-JUN-13 00:00:00	110.00
1	Janice	Jones	6	12	05-JUL-13 00:00:00	505.00
2	Jon	Jones	6	12	05-JUL-13 00:00:00	505.00
3	John	Doe	6	12	05-JUL-13 00:00:00	505.00
4	Jane	Doe	6	12	05-JUL-13 00:00:00	505.00
5	Jane	Smith	6	12	05-JUL-13 00:00:00	505.00
6	Janice	Smith	6	12	05-JUL-13 00:00:00	505.00
7	Helen	Brown	6	12	05-JUL-13 00:00:00	505.00
8	Helen	Jerry	6	12	05-JUL-13 00:00:00	505.00
9	Mary	Collins	6	12	05-JUL-13 00:00:00	505.00
10	Peter	Collins	6	12	05-JUL-13 00:00:00	505.00
11	Edna	Hayes	6	12	05-JUL-13 00:00:00	505.00
12	Franklin	Hayes	6	12	05-JUL-13 00:00:00	505.00
13	Peter	Johnson	6	12	05-JUL-13 00:00:00	505.00
14	Peter	Johnson	6	12	05-JUL-13 00:00:00	505.00
15	John	Smith	6	12	05-JUL-13 00:00:00	505.00

Figure 2-6: The first 60 rows of a 300 row product table

understand how the result table came to be might assume that it is correct and make business decision based on the bad data.

The joins you have seen so far have used a single-column primary key and a single-column foreign key. There is no reason, however, that the values used in a *join* can't be concatenated. As an example, let's look again at *the* accounting firm example from Chapter 1. The design of the portion of the database that we used was

Equi-Joins over Concatenated Keys

```
accountant (acct first name, acct last name,
    date_hired, office_ext)

customer (customer numb, first_name,
    last_name, street, city, state_province,
    zip_postcode, contact_phone)

project (tax year, customer numb,
    acct_first_name, acct_last_name)

form (tax year, customer numb, form id,
    is_complete)
```

Suppose we want to see all the forms and the year that the forms were completed for the customer named Peter Jones by the accountant named Edgar Smith. The sequence of relational operations would go something like this:

1. Restrict from the customer table to find the single row for Peter Jones. Because some customers have duplicated names, the *restrict* predicate would probably contain the name and the phone number.

2. Join the table created in Step 1 to the *project* table over the customer number.

3. Restrict from the table created in Step 2 to find the projects for Peter Jones that were handled by the accountant Edgar Smith.

```
customer_numb | first_name | last_name | sale_id | customer_numb |      sale_date      | sale_total_amt
--------------+------------+-----------+---------+---------------+---------------------+----------------
          1 | Janice     | Jones     |    3 |          1 | 15-JUN-13 00:00:00 |          58.00
          2 | Jon        | Jones     |    3 |          1 | 15-JUN-13 00:00:00 |          58.00
          3 | John       | Doe       |    3 |          1 | 15-JUN-13 00:00:00 |          58.00
          4 | Jane       | Doe       |    3 |          1 | 15-JUN-13 00:00:00 |          58.00
          5 | Jane       | Smith     |    3 |          1 | 15-JUN-13 00:00:00 |          58.00
          6 | Janice     | Smith     |    3 |          1 | 15-JUN-13 00:00:00 |          58.00
          7 | Helen      | Brown     |    3 |          1 | 15-JUN-13 00:00:00 |          58.00
          8 | Helen      | Jerry     |    3 |          1 | 15-JUN-13 00:00:00 |          58.00
          9 | Mary       | Collins   |    3 |          1 | 15-JUN-13 00:00:00 |          58.00
         10 | Peter      | Collins   |    3 |          1 | 15-JUN-13 00:00:00 |          58.00
         11 | Edna       | Hayes     |    3 |          1 | 15-JUN-13 00:00:00 |          58.00
         12 | Franklin   | Hayes     |    3 |          1 | 15-JUN-13 00:00:00 |          58.00
         13 | Peter      | Johnson   |    3 |          1 | 15-JUN-13 00:00:00 |          58.00
         14 | Peter      | Johnson   |    3 |          1 | 15-JUN-13 00:00:00 |          58.00
         15 | John       | Smith     |    3 |          1 | 15-JUN-13 00:00:00 |          58.00
          1 | Janice     | Jones     |    4 |          4 | 30-JUN-13 00:00:00 |         110.00
          2 | Jon        | Jones     |    4 |          4 | 30-JUN-13 00:00:00 |         110.00
          3 | John       | Doe       |    4 |          4 | 30-JUN-13 00:00:00 |         110.00
          4 | Jane       | Doe       |    4 |          4 | 30-JUN-13 00:00:00 |         110.00
          5 | Jane       | Smith     |    4 |          4 | 30-JUN-13 00:00:00 |         110.00
          6 | Janice     | Smith     |    4 |          4 | 30-JUN-13 00:00:00 |         110.00
          7 | Helen      | Brown     |    4 |          4 | 30-JUN-13 00:00:00 |         110.00
          8 | Helen      | Jerry     |    4 |          4 | 30-JUN-13 00:00:00 |         110.00
          9 | Mary       | Collins   |    4 |          4 | 30-JUN-13 00:00:00 |         110.00
         10 | Peter      | Collins   |    4 |          4 | 30-JUN-13 00:00:00 |         110.00
         11 | Edna       | Hayes     |    4 |          4 | 30-JUN-13 00:00:00 |         110.00
         12 | Franklin   | Hayes     |    4 |          4 | 30-JUN-13 00:00:00 |         110.00
         13 | Peter      | Johnson   |    4 |          4 | 30-JUN-13 00:00:00 |         110.00
         14 | Peter      | Johnson   |    4 |          4 | 30-JUN-13 00:00:00 |         110.00
         15 | John       | Smith     |    4 |          4 | 30-JUN-13 00:00:00 |         110.00
          1 | Janice     | Jones     |    5 |          6 | 30-JUN-13 00:00:00 |         110.00
          2 | Jon        | Jones     |    5 |          6 | 30-JUN-13 00:00:00 |         110.00
          3 | John       | Doe       |    5 |          6 | 30-JUN-13 00:00:00 |         110.00
          4 | Jane       | Doe       |    5 |          6 | 30-JUN-13 00:00:00 |         110.00
          5 | Jane       | Smith     |    5 |          6 | 30-JUN-13 00:00:00 |         110.00
          6 | Janice     | Smith     |    5 |          6 | 30-JUN-13 00:00:00 |         110.00
          7 | Helen      | Brown     |    5 |          6 | 30-JUN-13 00:00:00 |         110.00
          8 | Helen      | Jerry     |    5 |          6 | 30-JUN-13 00:00:00 |         110.00
          9 | Mary       | Collins   |    5 |          6 | 30-JUN-13 00:00:00 |         110.00
         10 | Peter      | Collins   |    5 |          6 | 30-JUN-13 00:00:00 |         110.00
         11 | Edna       | Hayes     |    5 |          6 | 30-JUN-13 00:00:00 |         110.00
         12 | Franklin   | Hayes     |    5 |          6 | 30-JUN-13 00:00:00 |         110.00
         13 | Peter      | Johnson   |    5 |          6 | 30-JUN-13 00:00:00 |         110.00
         14 | Peter      | Johnson   |    5 |          6 | 30-JUN-13 00:00:00 |         110.00
         15 | John       | Smith     |    5 |          6 | 30-JUN-13 00:00:00 |         110.00
          1 | Janice     | Jones     |    6 |         12 | 05-JUL-13 00:00:00 |         505.00
          2 | Jon        | Jones     |    6 |         12 | 05-JUL-13 00:00:00 |         505.00
          3 | John       | Doe       |    6 |         12 | 05-JUL-13 00:00:00 |         505.00
          4 | Jane       | Doe       |    6 |         12 | 05-JUL-13 00:00:00 |         505.00
          5 | Jane       | Smith     |    6 |         12 | 05-JUL-13 00:00:00 |         505.00
          6 | Janice     | Smith     |    6 |         12 | 05-JUL-13 00:00:00 |         505.00
          7 | Helen      | Brown     |    6 |         12 | 05-JUL-13 00:00:00 |         505.00
          8 | Helen      | Jerry     |    6 |         12 | 05-JUL-13 00:00:00 |         505.00
          9 | Mary       | Collins   |    6 |         12 | 05-JUL-13 00:00:00 |         505.00
         10 | Peter      | Collins   |    6 |         12 | 05-JUL-13 00:00:00 |         505.00
         11 | Edna       | Hayes     |    6 |         12 | 05-JUL-13 00:00:00 |         505.00
         12 | Franklin   | Hayes     |    6 |         12 | 05-JUL-13 00:00:00 |         505.00
         13 | Peter      | Johnson   |    6 |         12 | 05-JUL-13 00:00:00 |         505.00
         14 | Peter      | Johnson   |    6 |         12 | 05-JUL-13 00:00:00 |         505.00
         15 | John       | Smith     |    6 |         12 | 05-JUL-13 00:00:00 |         505.00
```

Figure 2-7: The four rows of the product in Figure 2-6 that are returned by the join condition in a restrict predicate

4. Now we need to get the data about which forms appear on the projects identified in Step 3. We therefore need to join the table created in Step 3 to the *form* table. The foreign key in the *form* table is the concatenation of the tax year and customer number, which just happens to match the primary key of the *project* table. The join is therefore over the concatenation of the tax year and customer number rather than over the individual values. When making its determination whether to include a row in the result table, the DBMS puts the tax year and customer number together for each row and treats the combined value as if it were one.

5. Project the tax year and form ID to present the specific data requested in the query.

To see why treating a concatenated foreign key as a single unit when comparing to a concatenated foreign key is required, take a look at Figure 2-8. The two tables at the top of the illustration are the original *project* and *form* tables created for this example. We are interested in customer number 18 (our friend Peter Jones), who has had projects handled by Edgar Smith in 2006 and 2007.

Result table (a) is what happens if you join the tables (without restricting for customer 18) only over the tax year. This invalid join expands the 10 row *form* table to 20 rows. The data imply that the same customer had the same form prepared by more than one accountant in the same year.

Result table (b) is the result of joining the two tables just over the customer number. This time the invalid result table implies that in some cases the same form was completed in two years.

```
project                                                         form

 tax_year | customer_numb | acct_first_name | acct_last_name    tax_year | custome
---------+---------------+-----------------+---------------     ---------+-------
    2006 |            12 | Jon             | Johnson               2006 |
    2007 |            18 | Edgar           | Smith                 2006 |
    2006 |            18 | Edgar           | Smith                 2006 |
    2007 |             6 | Edgar           | Smith                 2007 |
                                                                  2007 |
                                                                  2007 |
                                                                  2006 |
                                                                  2006 |
                                                                  2007 |
                                                                  2007 |



(a) project JOIN form OVER tax_year GIVING invalid_1

 tax_year | customer_numb | acct_first_name | acct_last_name   | tax_year | customer_
---------+---------------+-----------------+-----------------+----------+---------
    2006 |            18 | Edgar           | Smith            |    2006 |
    2006 |            12 | Jon             | Johnson          |    2006 |
    2006 |            18 | Edgar           | Smith            |    2006 |
    2006 |            12 | Jon             | Johnson          |    2006 |
    2006 |            18 | Edgar           | Smith            |    2006 |
    2006 |            12 | Jon             | Johnson          |    2006 |
    2007 |             6 | Edgar           | Smith            |    2007 |
    2007 |            18 | Edgar           | Smith            |    2007 |
    2007 |             6 | Edgar           | Smith            |    2007 |
    2007 |            18 | Edgar           | Smith            |    2007 |
    2007 |             6 | Edgar           | Smith            |    2007 |
    2007 |            18 | Edgar           | Smith            |    2007 |
    2006 |            18 | Edgar           | Smith            |    2006 |
    2006 |            12 | Jon             | Johnson          |    2006 |
    2006 |            18 | Edgar           | Smith            |    2006 |
    2006 |            12 | Jon             | Johnson          |    2006 |
    2007 |             6 | Edgar           | Smith            |    2007 |
    2007 |            18 | Edgar           | Smith            |    2007 |
    2007 |             6 | Edgar           | Smith            |    2007 |
    2007 |            18 | Edgar           | Smith            |    2007 |
```

Figure 2-8: Joining using concatenated keys (continued on facing page)

The correct *join* appears in result table (c) in Figure 2-8. It has the correct 10 rows, one for each form. Notice that *both* the tax year and customer number are the same in each row, as we intended them to be.

Note: The examples you have seen so far involve two concatenated columns. There is no reason, however, that the concatenation cannot involve more than two columns if necessary.

```
(b) project JOIN form OVER tax_year GIVING invalid_2

tax_year | customer_numb | acct_first_name | acct_last_name  | tax_year | customer_numb | form_id | is_complete
---------+---------------+-----------------+-----------------+----------+---------------+---------+------------
  2006   |      12 | Jon  | Johnson         |   2006   |      12 | 1040    | t
  2006   |      12 | Jon  | Johnson         |   2006   |      12 | Sch. A  | t
  2006   |      12 | Jon  | Johnson         |   2006   |      12 | Sch. B  | t
  2006   |      18 | Edgar| Smith           |   2007   |      18 | 1040    | t
  2007   |      18 | Edgar| Smith           |   2007   |      18 | 1040    | t
  2006   |      18 | Edgar| Smith           |   2007   |      18 | Sch. A  | t
  2007   |      18 | Edgar| Smith           |   2007   |      18 | Sch. A  | t
  2006   |      18 | Edgar| Smith           |   2007   |      18 | Sch. B  | t
  2007   |      18 | Edgar| Smith           |   2007   |      18 | Sch. B  | t
  2006   |      18 | Edgar| Smith           |   2006   |      18 | 1040    | t
  2007   |      18 | Edgar| Smith           |   2006   |      18 | 1040    | t
  2006   |      18 | Edgar| Smith           |   2006   |      18 | Sch. A  | t
  2007   |      18 | Edgar| Smith           |   2006   |      18 | Sch. A  | t
  2007   |       6 | Edgar| Smith           |   2007   |       6 | 1040    | t
  2007   |       6 | Edgar| Smith           |   2007   |       6 | Sch. A  | t
```

```
(c) project JOIN form OVER tax_year + customer_numb GIVING correct_result

tax_year | customer_numb | acct_first_name | acct_last_name  | tax_year | customer_numb | form_id | is_complete
---------+---------------+-----------------+-----------------+----------+---------------+---------+------------
  2006   |      12 | Jon  | Johnson         |   2006   |      12 | 1040    | t
  2006   |      12 | Jon  | Johnson         |   2006   |      12 | Sch. A  | t
  2006   |      12 | Jon  | Johnson         |   2006   |      12 | Sch. B  | t
  2006   |      18 | Edgar| Smith           |   2006   |      18 | 1040    | t
  2006   |      18 | Edgar| Smith           |   2006   |      18 | Sch. A  | t
  2007   |      18 | Edgar| Smith           |   2007   |      18 | Sch. B  | t
  2007   |      18 | Edgar| Smith           |   2007   |      18 | 1040    | t
  2007   |      18 | Edgar| Smith           |   2007   |      18 | Sch. A  | t
  2007   |       6 | Edgar| Smith           |   2007   |       6 | 1040    | t
  2007   |       6 | Edgar| Smith           |   2007   |       6 | Sch. A  | t
```

Figure 2-8 (continued): Joining using concatenated keys

Θ-Joins

An equi-join is a specific example of a more general class of join known as a Θ-*join* (*theta-join*). A Θ-join combines two tables on some condition, which may be equality or may be something else. To make it easier to understand why you might want to join on something other than equality and how such joins work, assume that you're on vacation at a resort that offers both biking and hiking. Each outing runs a half day, but the times at which the outings start and end differ. The tables that hold the outing schedules appear in Figure 2-9. As you look at the data, you'll see that some ending and starting times overlap, which means that if you want to engage in two outings on the same day, only some pairings of hiking and biking will work.

```
hiking                                    biking

tour_numb | start_time | end_time        tour_numb | start_time | end_time
----------+------------+----------        ----------+------------+----------
        6 | 01:00:00   | 16:00:00                 1 | 09:00:00   | 12:00:00
        8 | 09:00:00   | 11:30:00                 2 | 09:00:00   | 11:30:00
        9 | 10:00:00   | 14:00:00                 3 | 09:00:00   | 12:30:00
       10 | 09:00:00   | 12:00:00                 4 | 12:00:00   | 15:00:00
        7 | 12:00:00   | 15:30:00                 5 | 13:00:00   | 17:00:00
```

Figure 2-9: Source tables for the Θ-join examples

To determine which pairs of outings you could do on the same day, you need to find pairs of outings that satisfy either of the following conditions:

```
hiking.end_time < biking.start_time

biking.end_time < hiking.start_time
```

A Θ-*join* over either of those conditions will do the trick, producing the result tables in Figure 2-10. The top result table contains pairs of outings where hiking is done first; the middle result table contains pairs of outings where biking is done first. If you want all the possibilities in the same table, a union operation will combine them, as in the bottom result table. Another way to generate the combined table is to use a complex *join* condition in the Θ-*join*:

```
hiking.end_time < biking.start_time OR
        biking.end_time < hiking.start_time
```

Note: As with the more restrictive equi-join, the "start" table for a Θ-join does not matter. The result will be the same either way.

Outer Joins

An *outer join* (as opposed to the inner joins we have been considering so far) is a join that includes rows in a result table even though there may not be a match between rows in the two tables being joined. Wherever the DBMS can't match rows, it

```
hiking JOIN biking OVER hiking.end_time < biking.start_time GIVING hiking_first

 tour_numb | start_time | end_time | tour_numb | start_time | end_time
-----------+------------+----------+-----------+------------+----------
         4 | 12:00:00   | 15:00:00 |         8 | 09:00:00   | 11:30:00
         5 | 13:00:00   | 17:00:00 |         8 | 09:00:00   | 11:30:00
         5 | 13:00:00   | 17:00:00 |        10 | 09:00:00   | 12:00:00



hiking JOIN biking OVER biking.end_time < hiking.start_time gIVING biking_first

 tour_numb | start_time | end_time | tour_numb | start_time | end_time
-----------+------------+----------+-----------+------------+----------
         2 | 09:00:00   | 11:30:00 |         7 | 12:00:00   | 15:30:00
```

Figure 2-10: The results of Θ-joins of the tables in Figure 2-9

places nulls in the columns for which no data exist. The result may therefore not be a legal relation, because it may not have a primary key. However, because the query's result table is a virtual table that is never stored in the database, having no primary key does not present a data integrity problem.

Why might someone want to perform an outer join? An employee of the rare book store, for example, might want to see the names of all customers along with the books ordered in the last week. An inner join of customer to sale would eliminate those customers who had not purchased anything during the previous week. However, an outer join will include all customers, placing nulls in the sale data columns for the customers who have not ordered. An outer join therefore not only shows you matching data but also tells you where matching data *do not* exist.

There are really three types of outer join, which vary depending the table or tables from which you want to include rows that have no matches.

The Left Outer Join

The left outer join includes all rows from the first table in the join expression

```
Table1 LEFT OUTER JOIN table2 GIVING
    result_table
```

For example, if we use the data from the tables in Figure 2-5 and perform the left outer join as

```
customer LEFT OUTER JOIN sale GIVING
    left_outer_join_result
```

then the result will appear as in Figure 2-11: There is a row for every row in customer. For the rows that don't have orders, the columns that come from sale have been filled with nulls.

The Right Outer Join

The right outer join is the precise opposite of the left outer join. It includes all rows from the table on the right of the outer join operator. If you perform

```
customer RIGHT OUTER JOIN sale GIVING
    right_outer_join_result
```

using the data from Figure 2-5, the result will be the same as an inner join of the two tables. This occurs because there are no rows in sale that don't appear in customer. However, if you reverse the order of the tables, as in

```
sale RIGHT OUTER JOIN customer GIVING
    right_outer_join_result
```

you end up with the same data as Figure 2-11.

Choosing a Right versus Left Outer Join

As you have just read, outer joins are directional: the result depends on the order of the tables in the command. (This is in direct contrast to an inner join, which produces the same result regardless of the order of the tables.) Assuming that you are performing an outer join on two tables that have a primary key–foreign key relationship, then the result of left and right outer joins on those tables is predictable (see Table 2-1). Referential integrity ensures that no rows from a table containing a

customer_numb	first_name	last_name	sale_id	customer_numb	sale_date	sale_total_amt
1	Janice	Jones	1	1	29-MAY-13 00:00:00	510.00
1	Janice	Jones	2	1	05-JUN-13 00:00:00	125.00
1	Janice	Jones	17	1	25-JUL-13 00:00:00	100.00
1	Janice	Jones	3	1	15-JUN-13 00:00:00	58.00
2	Jon	Jones	20	2	01-SEP-13 00:00:00	75.00
2	Jon	Jones	16	2	25-JUL-13 00:00:00	130.00
2	Jon	Jones	13	2	10-JUL-13 00:00:00	25.95
3	John	Doe	null	null	null	null
4	Jane	Doe	4	4	30-JUN-13 00:00:00	110.00
5	Jane	Smith	18	5	22-AUG-13 00:00:00	100.00
5	Jane	Smith	8	5	07-JUL-13 00:00:00	90.00
6	Janice	Smith	19	6	01-SEP-13 00:00:00	95.00
6	Janice	Smith	14	6	10-JUL-13 00:00:00	80.00
6	Janice	Smith	5	6	30-JUN-13 00:00:00	110.00
7	Helen	Brown	null	null	null	null
8	Helen	Jerry	9	8	07-JUL-13 00:00:00	50.00
8	Helen	Jerry	7	8	05-JUL-13 00:00:00	80.00
9	Mary	Collins	11	9	10-JUL-13 00:00:00	200.00
10	Peter	Collins	12	10	10-JUL-13 00:00:00	200.00
11	Edna	Hayes	15	11	12-JUL-13 00:00:00	75.00
11	Edna	Hayes	10	11	10-JUL-13 00:00:00	125.00
12	Franklin	Hayes	6	12	05-JUL-13 00:00:00	505.00
13	Peter	Johnson	null	null	null	null
14	Peter	Johnson	null	null	null	null
15	John	Smith	null	null	null	null

Figure 2-11: The result of a left outer join

Table 2-1 The effect of left and right outer joins on tables with a primary key–foreign key relationship

Outer Join Format	Outer Join Result
`primary_key_table LEFT OUTER JOIN foreign_key_table`	All rows from primary key table retained
`foreign_key_table LEFT OUTER JOIN primary_key_table`	Same as inner join
`primary_key_table RIGHT OUTER JOIN foreign_key_table`	Same as inner join
`foreign_key_table RIGHT OUTER JOIN primary_key_table`	All rows from primary key table retained

foreign key will ever be omitted from a join with the table that contains the referenced primary key. Therefore, a left outer join where the foreign key table is on the left of the operator and a right outer join where the foreign key table is on the right of the operator are no different from an inner join.

The Full Outer Join

When choosing between a left and a right outer join, you therefore need to pay attention to which table will appear on which side of the operator. If the outer join is to produce a result different from that of an inner join, then the table containing the primary key must appear on the side that matches the name of the operator.

A full outer join includes all rows from both tables, filling in rows with nulls where necessary. If the two tables have a primary key–foreign key relationship, then the result will be the same as that of either a left outer join when the primary key table is on the left of the operator or a right outer join when the primary key table is on the right side of the operator. In the case of the full outer join, it does not matter on which side of the operator the primary key table appears; all rows from the primary key table will be retained.

Valid versus Invalid Joins

To this point, all of the joins you have seen have involved tables with a primary key–foreign key relationship. These are

the most typical types of join and always produce valid result tables. In contrast, most joins between tables that do not
have a primary key–foreign key relationship are not valid. This
means that the result tables contain information that is not
represented in the database, conveying misinformation to the
user. Invalid joins are therefore far more dangerous than mean-
ingless projections.

As an example, let's temporarily add a table to the rare book
store database. The purpose of the table is to indicate the
source from which the store acquired a volume. Over time, the
same book (different volumes) may come from more than one
source. The table has the following structure:

```
book_sources (isbn, source name)
```

Someone looking at this table and the *book* table might con-
clude that because the two tables have a matching column
(*isbn*) it makes sense to join the tables to find out the source
of every volume that the store has ever had in inventory. Unfortunately, this is not the information that the result table will
contain.

To keep the result table to a reasonable length, we'll work with
an abbreviated *book_sources* table that doesn't contain sources
for all volumes (Figure 2-12). Let's assume that we go ahead
and join the tables over the ISBN. The result table (without
columns that aren't of interest to the join itself) can be found
in Figure 2-13.

If the store has ever obtained volumes with the same ISBN
from different sources, there will be multiple rows for that
ISBN in the *book_sources* table. Although this doesn't give us a
great deal of meaningful information, in and of itself the table
is valid. However, when we look at the result of the join with
the volume table, the data in the result table contradict what
is in *book_sources*. For example, the first two rows in the result table have the same inventory ID number, yet come from

```
       isbn          |       source_name
---------------------+--------------------------
978-1-11111-111-1 | Tom Anderson
978-1-11111-111-1 | Church rummage sale
978-1-11111-118-1 | South Street Market
978-1-11111-118-1 | Church rummage sale
978-1-11111-118-1 | Betty Jones
978-1-11111-120-1 | Tom Anderson
978-1-11111-120-1 | Betty Jones
978-1-11111-126-1 | Church rummage sale
978-1-11111-126-1 | Betty Jones
978-1-11111-125-1 | Tom Anderson
978-1-11111-125-1 | South Street Market
978-1-11111-125-1 | Hendersons
978-1-11111-125-1 | Neverland Books
978-1-11111-130-1 | Tom Anderson
978-1-11111-130-1 | Hendersons
```

Figure 2-12: The *book_sources* table

different sources. How can the same volume come from two places? That is physically impossible. This invalid join therefore implies facts that simply cannot be true.

The reason this join is invalid is that the two columns over which the join is performed are not in a primary key–foreign key relationship. In fact, in both tables the *isbn* column is a foreign key that references the primary key of the *book* table.

Are joins between tables that do not have a primary key–foreign key relationship ever valid? On occasion, they are, in particular if you are joining two tables with the same primary key. You will see an example of this type of join when we discuss joining a table to itself when a predicate requires that multiple rows exist before any are placed in a result table.

For another example, assume that you want to create a table to store data about your employees:

```
inventory_id |         isbn          | sale_id |     source_name
-------------+-----------------------+---------+---------------------
           1 | 978-1-11111-111-1 |       1 | Church rummage sale
           1 | 978-1-11111-111-1 |       1 | Tom Anderson
          20 | 978-1-11111-130-1 |       6 | Hendersons
          20 | 978-1-11111-130-1 |       6 | Tom Anderson
          21 | 978-1-11111-126-1 |       6 | Betty Jones
          21 | 978-1-11111-126-1 |       6 | Church rummage sale
          23 | 978-1-11111-125-1 |       7 | Neverland Books
          23 | 978-1-11111-125-1 |       7 | Hendersons
          23 | 978-1-11111-125-1 |       7 | South Street Market
          23 | 978-1-11111-125-1 |       7 | Tom Anderson
          25 | 978-1-11111-126-1 |       8 | Betty Jones
          25 | 978-1-11111-126-1 |       8 | Church rummage sale
          35 | 978-1-11111-126-1 |      11 | Betty Jones
          35 | 978-1-11111-126-1 |      11 | Church rummage sale
          36 | 978-1-11111-130-1 |      11 | Hendersons
          36 | 978-1-11111-130-1 |      11 | Tom Anderson
          38 | 978-1-11111-130-1 |      12 | Hendersons
          38 | 978-1-11111-130-1 |      12 | Tom Anderson
          63 | 978-1-11111-130-1 |         | Hendersons
          63 | 978-1-11111-130-1 |         | Tom Anderson
```

Figure 2-13: An invalid join result

```
employees (id numb, first_name, last_name,
     department, job_title, salary, hire_date)
```

Some of the employees are managers. For those individuals, you also want to store data about the project they are currently managing and the date they began managing that project. (A manager handles only one project at a time.) You could add the columns to the employees table and let them contain nulls for employees who are not managers. An alternative is to create a second table just for the managers:

```
managers (id numb, current_project,
     project_start_date)
```

When you want to see all the information about a manager, you must join the two tables over the id_numb column. The result table will contain rows only for the manager because employees without rows in the managers table will be left out of the join. There will be no spurious rows such as those we got when we joined the volume and *book_sources* tables. This join therefore is valid.

Note: Although the id_numb column in the managers table technically is not a foreign key referencing employees, most databases using such a design would nonetheless include a constraint that forced the presence of a matching row in employees for every manager.

The bottom line is that you need to be very careful when performing joins between tables that do not have a primary key–foreign key relationship. Although such joins are not always invalid, in most cases they will be.

Difference

Among the most powerful database queries are those phrased in the negative, such as "show me all the customers who have not purchased from us in the past year." This type of query is particularly tricky because it asking for data that are not in the database. The rare book store has data about customers who *have* purchased, but not those who have not. The only way to perform such a query is to request the DBMS to use the *difference* operation.

Difference retrieves all rows that are in one table but not in another. For example, if you have a table that contains all your products and another that contains products that have been purchased the expression—

```
all_products MINUS products_that_have_been_
     purchased GIVING not_purchased
```

—is the products that have *not* been purchased. When you remove the products that *have* been purchased from all products, what are left are the products that *have not* been purchased.

The difference operation looks at entire rows when it makes the decision whether to include a row in the result table. This means that the two source tables must be union compatible. Assume that the *all_products* table has two columns—*prod_numb* and *product_name*—and the *products_that_have_been_purchased* table also has two columns—*prod_numb* and *order_numb*. Because they don't have the same columns, the tables aren't union-compatible.

As you can see from Figure 2-14, this means that a DBMS must first perform two projections to generate the union-compatible tables before it can perform the difference. In this case, the operation needs to retain the product number. Once the projections into union-compatible tables exist, the DBMS can perform the difference.

As mentioned earlier in this chapter, to be considered relationally complete a DBMS must support restrict, project, join, union, and difference. Virtually every query can be satisfied using a sequence of those five operations. However, one other operation is usually included in the relational algebra specification: *intersect*.

In one sense, the intersect operation is the opposite of union. Union produces a result containing all rows that appear in either relation, while *intersect* produces a result containing all rows that appear in both relations. Intersection can therefore only be performed on two union-compatible relations.

Assume, for example, that the rare book store receives data listing volumes in a private collection that are being offered for sale. We can find out which volumes are already in the store's inventory using an *intersect* operation:

```
books_in_inventory INTERSECT books_for_sale
    GIVING already_have
```

Intersect

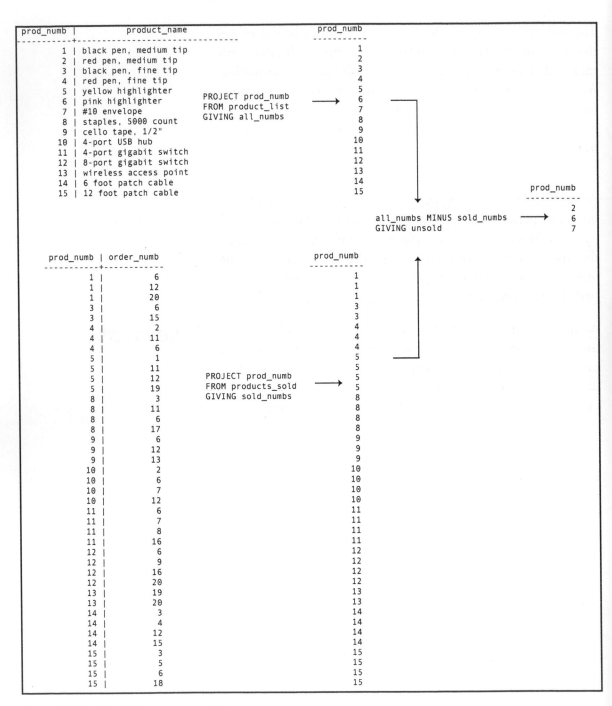

Figure 2-14: The difference operation

As you can see in Figure 2-15, the first step in the process is to use the project operation to create union-compatible operations. Then an intersect will provide the required result. (Columns that are not a part of the operation have been omitted so that the tables will fit on the book page.)

Note: A join over the concatenation of all the columns in the two tables produces the same result as an intersect.

An eighth relational algebra operation—*divide*—is often included with the operations you have seen in this chapter. It can be used for queries that need to have multiple rows in the same source table for a row to be included in the result table. Assume, for example, that the rare book store wants a list of sales on which two specific volumes have appeared.

There are many forms of the divide operation, all of which except the simplest are extremely complex. To set up the simplest form you need two relations, one with two columns (a *binary* relation) and one with a single column (a *unary* relation). The binary relation has a column that contains the values that will be placed in the result of the query (in our example, a sale ID) and a column for the values to be queried (in our example, the ISBN of the volume). This relation is created by taking a projection from the source table (in this case, the *volume* table).

The unary relation has the column being queried (the ISBN). It is loaded with a row for each value that must be matched in the binary table. A sale ID will be placed in the result table for all sales that contain ISBNs that match all of the values in the unary table. If there are two ISBNs in the unary table, then there must be a row for each of them with the same sale ID in the binary table to include the sale ID in the result. If we were to load the unary table with three ISBNs, then three matching rows would be required.

Divide

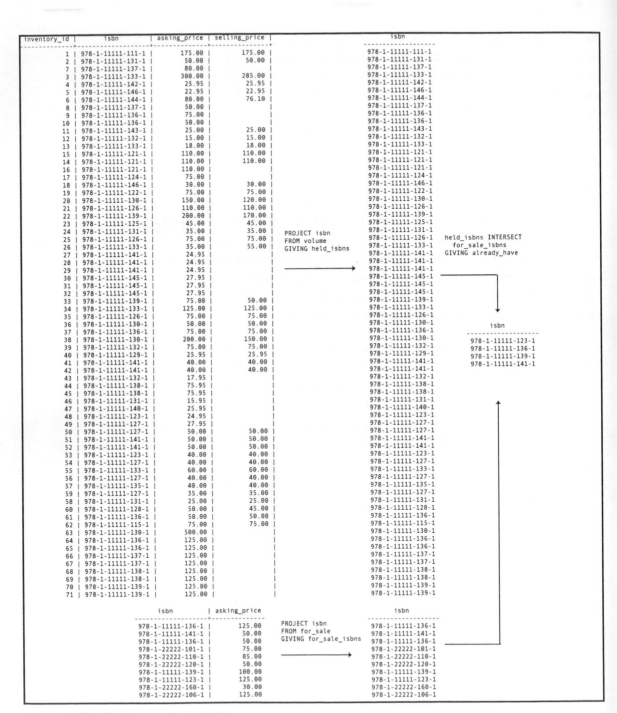

Figure 2-15: The intersect operation

You can get the same result as a divide using multiple restricts and joins. In our example, you would restrict the volume table twice, once for the first ISBN and once for the second. Then you would join the tables over the sale ID. Only those sales that had rows in both of the tables being joined would end up in the result table.

Because divide can be performed fairly easily with restrict and join, DBMSs generally do not implement it directly.

Introduction to SQL

SQL[1] is a database manipulation language that has been implemented by virtually every relational database management system (DBMS) intended for multiple users, partly because it has been accepted by ANSI (the American National Standards Institute) and ISO (International Standards Organization) as a standard query language for relational databases.

The chapter presents an overview of the environment in which SQL exists. We will begin with a bit of SQL history, so you will know where it came from and where it is heading. Next, you will be introduced to the design of the database that is used for sample queries throughout this book. Finally, you will read about the way in which SQL commands are processed and the software environments in which they function.

A Bit of SQL History

SQL was developed by IBM at its San Jose Research Laboratory in the early 1970s. Presented at an ACM conference in 1974, the language was originally named SEQUEL

---

1   Whether you say "sequel" or "S-Q-L" depends on how long you've been working with SQL. Those of us who have been working in this field for longer than we'd like to admit often say "sequel," which is what I do. When I started using SQL, there was no other pronunciation. That is why you'll see "a SQL" (a sequel) rather than "an SQL" (an es-que-el) throughout this book. Old habits die hard! However, many people do prefer the acronym.

(Structured English Query Language) and pronounced "sequel." The language's name was later shortened to SQL.

Although IBM authored SQL, the first SQL implementation was provided by Oracle Corporation (then called Relational Software Inc.). Early commercial implementations were concentrated on midsized UNIX-based DBMSs, such as Oracle, Ingres, and Informix. IBM followed in 1981 with SQL/DS, the forerunner to DB2, which debuted in 1983.

ANSI published the first SQL standard (SQL-86) in 1986. An international version of the standard issued by ISO appeared in 1987. A significant update to SQL-86 was released in 1989 (SQL-89). Virtually all relational DBMSs that you encounter today support most of the 1989 standard.

In 1992, the standard was revised again (SQL-92), adding more capabilities to the language. Because SQL-92 was a superset of SQL-89, older database application programs ran under the new standard with minimal modifications. In fact, until October 1996, DBMS vendors could submit their products to NIST (National Institute for Standards and Technology) for verification of SQL standard compliance. This testing and certification process provided significant motivation for DBMS vendors to adhere to the SQL standard. Although discontinuing standard compliance testing saves vendors money, it also makes it easier for products to diverge from the standard.

The SQL-92 standard was superseded by SQL:1999, which was once again a superset of the preceding standard. The primary new features of SQL:1999 supported the object-relational data model, which is discussed in Chapters 18 and 19 of this book.

The SQL:1999 standard also adds extension to SQL to allow methods/functions/procedures to be written in SQL or to be written in another programming language such as C++ or Java and then invoked from within another SQL statement. As a result,

SQL becomes less "relational," a trend decried by some relational purists.

Note: Regardless of where you come down on the relational theory argument, you will need to live with the fact that the major commercial DBMSs, such as Oracle and DB/2, have provided support for the object-relational (or post-relational) data model for several years now. The object-relational data model is a fact of life, although there certainly is no rule that says that you must use those features should you choose not to do so.

Even the full SQL:1999 standard does not turn SQL into a complete, stand-alone programming language. In particular, SQL lacks I/O statements. This makes perfect sense, since SQL should be implementation and operating system independent. However, the full SQL:1999 standard does include operations such as selection and iteration that make it *computationally complete*. These language features, which are more typical of general-purpose programming languages, are used when writing stored procedures and triggers. (See Chapter 14.)

The SQL standard has been updated three times since the appearance of SQL:1999 in versions named SQL:2003, SQL:2006, and SQL:2008. As well as fleshing out the capabilities of the core relational features and extending object-relational support, these revisions have added support for XML (Extended Markup Language). XML is a platform-independent method for representing data using text files. SQL's XML features are introduced in Chapter 17.

This book is based on the more recent versions of the SQL standard (SQL:2003 through SQL:2008). However, keep in mind that SQL:2008 (or whatever version of the language you are considering) is simply a standard, not a mandate. Various DBMSs exhibit different levels of conformance to the standard. In addition, the implementation of language features usually

Conformance Levels

lags behind the standard. Therefore, although SQL:2008 may be the latest version of the standard, no DBMS meets the entire standard and most are based on earlier versions.[2]

Conformance to early versions of the standard (SQL-92 and earlier) was measured by determining whether the portion of the language required for a specific level of conformance was supported. Each feature in the standard was identified by a *leveling rule*, indicating at which conformance level it was required. At the time, there were three conformance levels:

◊ Full SQL-92 conformance: All features in the SQL-92 standard are supported.

◊ Intermediate SQL-92 conformance: All features required for intermediate conformance are supported.

◊ Entry SQL-92: conformance: All features required for entry level conformance are supported.

In truth, most DBMSs were only entry level compliant and some supported a few of the features at higher conformance levels. The 2006 and 2008 standards define conformance in a different way, however.

The standard itself is documented in nine parts (parts 1, 2, 3, 4, 9, 10, 11, 13, 14). Core conformance is defined as supporting the basic SQL features (Part 2, Core/Foundation) as well as features for definition and information schemas (Part 11, SQL/Schemata). A DBMS can claim conformance to any of the remaining parts individually as long as the product meets the conformance rules presented in the standard.

---

2   In one sense, the SQL standard is a moving target. Just as DBMSs look like they're going to catch up to the most recent standard, the standard is updated. DBMS developers scurry to implement new features and as soon as they get close, the standard changes again.

In addition to language features specified in the standard, there are some features from earlier standard that, although not mentioned in the 2006 and 2008 standards, are widely implemented. This includes, for example, support for indexes. (See Chapter 10.)

There are two general ways in which you can issue a SQL command to a database:

◊ Interactive SQL, in which a user types a single command and sends it immediately to the database. The result of an interactive query is a table in main memory (a *virtual table*). In mainframe environments, each user has one result table at a time, which is replaced each time a new query is executed; PC environments sometimes allow several. Result tables may not be legal relations—because of nulls they may have no primary key—but that is not a problem because they are not part of the database but exist only in main memory.

◊ Embedded SQL, in which SQL statements are placed in an application program. The interface presented to the user may be form-based or command-line based. Embedded SQL may be *static*, in which case the entire command is specified at the time the program is written. Alternatively, it may be *dynamic*, in which case the program builds the statement using user input and then submits it to the database.

The basic syntaxes of interactive SQL and the static embedded SQL are very similar. We will therefore spend the first portion of this book looking at interactive syntax and then turn to adapting and extending that syntax for embedding it in a program. Once you understand static embedded SQL syntax, you will be ready to look at preparing dynamic SQL statements for execution.

SQL Environments

Interactive SQL Command Processors

In addition to the two methods for writing SQL syntax, there are also a number of graphic query builders. These provide a way for a user who may not know the SQL language to "draw" the elements of a query. Many of these programs are report writers (for example, Crystal Reports[3]) and are not intended for data modification or for maintaining the structure of a database.

At the most general level, we can describe working with an interactive SQL command processor in the following way:

◊ Type the SQL command.

◊ Send the command to the database and wait for the result.

In this era of the graphic user interface (GUI), command line environments like that in Figure 3-1 seem rather primitive. Nonetheless, the SQL command line continues to provide basic access to relational databases and is used extensively when developing a database.

A command line environment also provides support for *ad hoc queries*, queries that arise at the spur of the moment and are not likely to be issued with any frequency. Experienced SQL users can usually work faster at the command line than with any other type of SQL command processor.

The down side to the traditional command line environment is that it is relatively unforgiving. If you make a typing error or an error in the construction of a command, it may be difficult to get the processor to recall the command so that it can be edited and resubmitted to the database. In fact, you may have no other editing capabilities except the backspace key.

---

3   For more information, see www.crystalreports.com.

```
  ○ ○ ○                            Terminal — edb-psql — 127×23
edb=#
edb=#
edb=# select * from customer;
 customer_numb | first_name | last_name |        street        |    city     | state_province | zip_postcode | contact_phone
---------------+------------+-----------+----------------------+-------------+----------------+--------------+---------------
             1 | Janice     | Jones     | 125 Center Road      | Anytown     | NY             | 11111        | 518-555-1111
             2 | Jon        | Jones     | 25 Elm Road          | Next Town   | NJ             | 18888        | 209-555-2222
             3 | John       | Doe       | 821 Elm Street       | Next Town   | NJ             | 18888        | 209-555-3333
             4 | Jane       | Doe       | 852 Main Street      | Anytown     | NY             | 11111        | 518-555-4444
             5 | Jane       | Smith     | 1919 Main Street     | New Village | NY             | 13333        | 518-555-5555
             6 | Janice     | Smith     | 800 Center Road      | Anytown     | NY             | 11111        | 518-555-6666
             7 | Helen      | Brown     | 25 Front Street      | Anytown     | NY             | 11111        | 518-555-7777
             8 | Helen      | Jerry     | 16 Main Street       | Newtown     | NJ             | 18886        | 518-555-8888
             9 | Mary       | Collins   | 301 Pine Road, Apt. 12 | Newtown   | NJ             | 18886        | 518-555-9999
            10 | Peter      | Collins   | 18 Main Street       | Newtown     | NJ             | 18886        | 518-555-1010
            11 | Edna       | Hayes     | 209 Circle Road      | Anytown     | NY             | 11111        | 518-555-1110
            12 | Franklin   | Hayes     | 615 Circle Road      | Anytown     | NY             | 11111        | 518-555-1212
            13 | Peter      | Johnson   | 22 Rose Court        | Next Town   | NJ             | 18888        | 209-555-1212
            14 | Peter      | Johnson   | 881 Front Street     | Next Town   | NJ             | 18888        | 209-555-1414
            15 | John       | Smith     | 881 Manor Lane       | Next Town   | NJ             | 18888        | 209-555-1515
(15 rows)

edb=#
```

Figure 3-1: A typical SQL command line environment

The SQL command examples that you will see throughout this book were all tested in a command line environment. As you are learning to create your own queries, this is, in most cases, the environment in which you will be working.

GUI Environments

There are actually two strategies used by GUI environments to provide access to a SQL database. The first is to simply provide a window into which you can type a command, just as you would do from the command line (for example, Figure 3-2). Such environments usually make it easier to edit the command, supporting recall of the command and full-screen editing features.

Note: The Windows "DOS prompt" is not a complete stand-alone command processor. If you are using Windows, you will need some type of application that provides a command line to interact with your database. (Most database servers designed for a Windows environment provide such a tool, although third-party products are also available, depending on the DBMS.) UNIX variants (such as

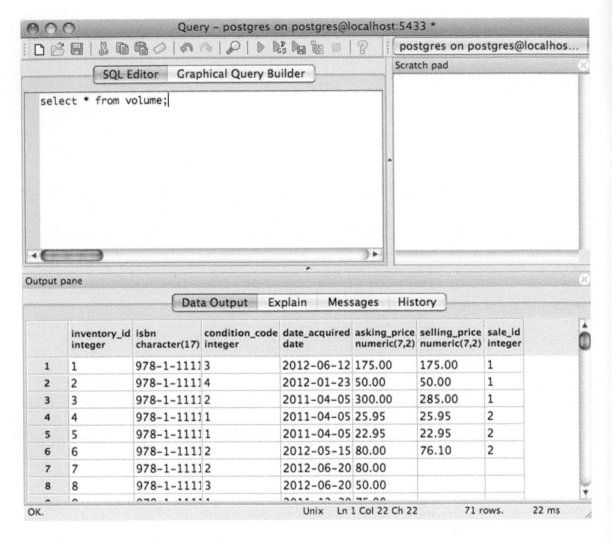

Figure 3-2: Typing a SQL command into a window

Linux and Mac OS X) provide complete command line environments and in most cases, can interact directly with a database from any shell prompt. (This assumes that the database server is running and that the user has the right to access that database.)

The other strategy is to provide a "query builder," an environment in which the user is guided through the construction of the query (for example, Figure 3-3). The query builder presents the user with lists of the legal command elements. Those lists change as the query is built so that the user also constructs legal syntax. The query builder type of SQL command environment makes it much easier for many users to construct correct SQL statements, but it is also slower than working directly at the command line.

The Embedded SQL Dilemma

Embedding SQL in a general-purpose programming language presents an interesting challenge. The host languages (for example, Java, C++, or COBOL) have compilers that don't recognize SQL. The solution is to provide SQL support through an application library that can be linked to a program. Program source code is passed through a precompiler that changes SQL commands into library routines. The modified source code will then be acceptable to a host language compiler.

In addition to the problem of actually compiling an embedded SQL program, there is a fundamental mismatch between SQL and a general-purpose programming language: Programming languages are designed to process data one row at a time while SQL is designed to handle many rows at a time. As you will see in Chapter 15, SQL includes some special elements so that it can process one row at a time when a query has returned multiple rows.

Elements of a SQL Statement

There are certainly many options for creating a SQL command. However, they are all made up of the same elements:

◊ Keywords: Each SQL command begins with a keyword—such as SELECT, INSERT, or UPDATE—that tells the command processor the type of operation that is to be performed. The remainder of the keywords precede the tables from which data are to be taken, indicate specific operations that are to be performed on the data, and so on.

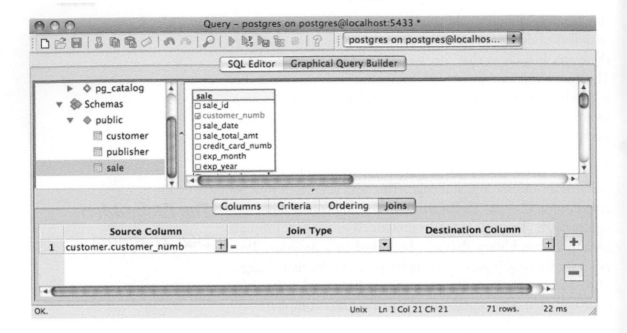

Figure 3-3: A "query builder" environment

◊ Tables: A SQL command includes the names of the tables on which the command is to operate.

◊ Columns: A SQL command includes the names of the columns that the command is to affect.

◊ Functions: A *function* is a small program that is built into the SQL language. Each function does one thing. For example, the AVG function computes the average of numeric data values. You will see a number of SQL functions discussed throughout this book.

Keywords and tables are required for all SQL commands. Columns may be optional, depending on the type of operation being preformed. Functions are never required for a legal SQL statement, but in some cases may be essential to obtaining a desired result.

Part II
Interactive SQL

4 Simple SQL Retrieval

It may seem a bit backwards to talk about retrieval before creating a database or entering data, but much of SQL's data modification syntax relies on finding data to be changed. You will therefore find it easier to work with modification statements if you are first familiar with retrieving data. We are therefore going to assume that someone else has created a database and loaded it with data for our use.

SQL has one command for retrieving data: SELECT. This is nowhere as restrictive as it might seem. SELECT contains syntax for choosing columns, choosing rows, combining tables, grouping data, and performing some simple calculations. In fact, a single SELECT statement can result in a DBMS performing any or all of the relational algebra operations.

The basic syntax of the SELECT statement has the following general structure:

```
SELECT column1, column2 …
FROM
table1, table2 …
WHERE predicate
```

The SELECT clause specifies the columns you want to see. You specify the tables used in the query in the FROM clause. The operational WHERE clause can contain a wide variety of criteria that identify which rows you want to retrieve.

Note: Most SQL command processors are not case sensitive when it comes to parts of a SQL statement. SQL keywords, table names, column names, and so on can be in any case you choose. However, most DBMSs are case sensitive when it comes to matching data values. Therefore, whenever you place a value in quotes for SQL to match, you must match the case of the stored data. In this book, SQL keywords will appear in uppercase letters; database components such as column and table names will appear in lowercase letters.

In addition to these basic clauses, SELECT has many other syntax options. Rather than attempt to summarize them all in a single general statement, you will learn to build the parts of a SELECT gradually throughout this and the next few chapters of this book.

Note: The SQL queries you see throughout the book are terminated by a semi-colon (;). This is not part of the SQL standard, but is used by many DBMSs so that you can type a command on multiple lines. The SQL command processor doesn't execute the query until it encounters the semi-colon.

Choosing Columns

One of the characteristics of a relation is that you can view any of the columns in any order you choose. SQL therefore lets you specify the columns you want to see and the order in which you want to see them, using the relational algebra *project* to produce the final result table.

Retrieving All Columns

To retrieve all the columns in a table, viewing the columns in the order in which they were defined when the table was created, you can use an asterisk (*) rather than listing each column. For example, to see all the works that the rare book store has handled, you would use

```
SELECT *
FROM work;
```

Because this query is requesting all rows in the table, there is no WHERE clause. As you can see in Figure 4-1, the result table labels each column with its name.

Note: The layout of the printed output of many SQL queries in this book has been adjusted so that it will fit across the width of the pages. When you actually view listings on the screen, each row

```
work_numb | author_numb |                     title
----------+-------------+--------------------------------------------------
        1 |           1 | Jane Eyre
        2 |           1 | Villette
        3 |           2 | Hound of the Baskervilles
        4 |           2 | Lost World, The
        5 |           2 | Complete Sherlock Holmes
        7 |           3 | Prince and the Pauper
        8 |           3 | Tom Sawyer
        9 |           3 | Adventures of Huckleberry Finn, The
        6 |           3 | Connecticut Yankee in King Arthur's Court, A
       13 |           5 | Fountainhead, The
       14 |           5 | Atlas Shrugged
       15 |           6 | Peter Pan
       10 |           7 | Bourne Identity, The
       11 |           7 | Matarese Circle, The
       12 |           7 | Bourne Supremacy, The
       16 |           4 | Kidnapped
       17 |           4 | Treasure Island
       18 |           8 | Sot Weed Factor, The
       19 |           8 | Lost in the Funhouse
       20 |           8 | Giles Goat Boy
       21 |           9 | Dune
       22 |           9 | Dune Messiah
       23 |          10 | Foundation
       24 |          10 | Last Foundation
       25 |          10 | I, Robot
       26 |          11 | Inkheart
       27 |          11 | Inkdeath
       28 |          12 | Anathem
       29 |          12 | Snow Crash
       30 |           5 | Anthem
       31 |          12 | Cryptonomicon
```

Figure 4-1: Viewing all columns in a table

will be in a single horizontal line. If a listing is too wide to fit on the screen or a terminal program's window, you will need to scroll.

Using the * operator to view all columns is a convenient shorthand for interactive SQL when you want a quick overview of data. However, it can be troublesome when used in embedded SQL .If the columns in the table are changed. In particular, if a column is added to the table and the application is not modified to handle the new column, then the application may not work properly.

Retrieving Specific Columns

In most SQL queries, you will want to specify exactly which column or columns you want retrieved. To specify columns, you list them following SELECT in the order in which you want to see them. For example, a query to view the names and phone numbers of all of our store's customers is written

```
SELECT first_name,last_name,contact_phone
FROM customer;
```

The result (see Figure 4-2) shows all rows in the table for just the three columns specified in the query. The order of the columns in the result table matches the order in which the columns appeared after the SELECT keyword.

Removing Duplicates

Unique primary keys ensure that relations have no duplicate rows. However, when you view only a portion of the columns in a table, you may end up with duplicates. For example, executing the following query produced the result in Figure 4-3:

```
SELET customer_numb, credit_card_numb
FROM sale;
```

Duplicates appear because the same customer uses the same credit card umber for more than one purchase. Keep in mind that although this table with duplicate rows is not a legal relation, that doesn't present a problem for the database because it is not stored in the database.

```
first_name | last_name | contact_phone
-----------+-----------+----------------
Janice     | Jones     | 518-555-1111
Jon        | Jones     | 209-555-2222
John       | Doe       | 209-555-3333
Jane       | Doe       | 518-555-4444
Jane       | Smith     | 518-555-5555
Janice     | Smith     | 518-555-6666
Helen      | Brown     | 518-555-7777
Helen      | Jerry     | 518-555-8888
Mary       | Collins   | 518-555-9999
Peter      | Collins   | 518-555-1010
Edna       | Hayes     | 518-555-1110
Franklin   | Hayes     | 518-555-1212
Peter      | Johnson   | 209-555-1212
Peter      | Johnson   | 209-555-1414
John       | Smith     | 209-555-1515
```

Figure 4-2: Choosing specific columns

```
customer_numb |   credit_card_numb
--------------+-----------------------
            1 | 1234 5678 9101 1121
            1 | 1234 5678 9101 1121
            1 | 1234 5678 9101 1121
            1 | 1234 5678 9101 1121
            2 | 1234 5678 9101 2222
            2 | 1234 5678 9101 2222
            2 | 1234 5678 9101 2222
            4 | 1234 5678 9101 5555
            5 | 1234 5678 9101 9999
            5 | 1234 5678 9101 9999
            6 | 1234 5678 9101 6666
            6 | 1234 5678 9101 7777
            6 | 1234 5678 9101 6666
            8 | 1234 5678 9101 8888
            8 | 1234 5678 9101 8888
            9 | 1234 5678 9101 0909
           10 | 1234 5678 9101 0101
           11 | 1234 5678 9101 1231
           11 | 1234 5678 9101 1010
           12 | 1234 5678 9101 7777
```

Figure 4-3: A result table with duplicate rows

To remove duplicates from a result table, you insert the keyword DISTINCT following SELECT:

```
SELECT DISTINCT customer_numb, credit_card_numb
FROM sale;
```

The result is a table without the duplicate rows (see Figure 4-4). Although a legal relation has no duplicate rows, most DBMS vendors have implemented SQL so that it leaves the duplicates. As you read in Chapter 2, the primary reason is performance. To remove duplicates, a DBMS must sort the result table by every column in the table. It must then scan the table from top to bottom, looking at every "next" row to identify duplicate rows that are next to one another. If a result table is large, the sorting and scanning can significantly slow down the query. It is therefore up to the user to decide whether to request unique rows.

Ordering the Result Table

The order in which rows appear in the result table may not be what you expect. In some cases, rows will appear in the order in which they are physically stored. However, if the query optimizer uses an index to process the query, then the rows will appear in index key order. If you want row ordering to be

```
customer_numb |    credit_card_numb
--------------+---------------------
            1 | 1234 5678 9101 1121
            2 | 1234 5678 9101 2222
            4 | 1234 5678 9101 5555
            5 | 1234 5678 9101 9999
            6 | 1234 5678 9101 6666
            6 | 1234 5678 9101 7777
            8 | 1234 5678 9101 8888
            9 | 1234 5678 9101 0909
           10 | 1234 5678 9101 0101
           11 | 1234 5678 9101 1010
           11 | 1234 5678 9101 1231
           12 | 1234 5678 9101 7777
```

Figure 4-4: The result table in Figure 4-3 with the duplicates removed

consistent and predictable, you will need to specify how you want the rows to appear.

When you want to control the order of rows in a result table you add an ORDER BY clause to your SELECT statement.

For example, if you issue the query

```
SELECT *
FROM author;
```

you will see the unordered listing in Figure 4-5. Adding the ORDER BY clause sorts the result in alphabetical order (see Figure 4-6):

```
SELECT *
FROM author
ORDER BY author_last_first;
```

The keywords ORDER BY are followed by the column or columns on which you want to sort the result table. When you include more than one column, the first column represents the outer sort, the next column a sort within it. For example, assume that you issue the query

```
author_numb |                author_last_first
------------+------------------------------------------
          1 | Bronte, Charlotte
          2 | Doyle, Sir Arthur Conan
          3 | Twain, Mark
          4 | Stevenson, Robert Louis
          5 | Rand, Ayn
          6 | Barrie, James
          7 | Ludlum, Robert
          8 | Barth, John
          9 | Herbert, Frank
         10 | Asimov, Isaac
         11 | Funke, Cornelia
         12 | Stephenson, Neal
```

Figure 4-5: An unordered result table

```
author_numb |               author_last_first
------------+------------------------------------------
--------------------
         10 | Asimov, Isaac
          6 | Barrie, James
          8 | Barth, John
          1 | Bronte, Charlotte
          2 | Doyle, Sir Arthur Conan
         11 | Funke, Cornelia
          9 | Herbert, Frank
          7 | Ludlum, Robert
          5 | Rand, Ayn
         12 | Stephenson, Neal
          4 | Stevenson, Robert Louis
          3 | Twain, Mark
```

Figure 4-6: The result table from Figure 4-6 sorted in alphabetical order by author name

```
SELECT zip_postcode, last_name, first_name
FROM customer
ORDER BY zip_postcode, last_name;
```

The result (see Figure 4-7) first orders by the zipcode and then sorts by the customer's last name within each zipcode. If we reverse the order of the columns on which the output is to be sorted, as in

```
SELECT zip_postcode, last_name, first_name
FROM customer
ORDER BY last_name, zip_postcode;
```

the output (see Figure 4-8) then sorts first by last name and then by zipcode within each last name.

Choosing Rows

As well as viewing any columns from a relation, you can also view any rows you want. We specify row selection criteria in a SELECT statement's WHERE clause.

In its simplest form, a WHERE clause contains a logical expression against which each row in a table is evaluated. If a row meets the criteria in the expression, then it becomes a part of the result table. If the row does not meet the criteria, then it

```
zip_postcode | last_name | first_name
-------------+-----------+------------
 11111       | Brown     | Helen
 11111       | Doe       | Jane
 11111       | Hayes     | Edna
 11111       | Hayes     | Franklin
 11111       | Jones     | Janice
 11111       | Smith     | Janice
 13333       | Smith     | Jane
 18886       | Collins   | Mary
 18886       | Collins   | Peter
 18886       | Jerry     | Helen
 18888       | Doe       | John
 18888       | Johnson   | Peter
 18888       | Johnson   | Peter
 18888       | Jones     | Jon
 18888       | Smith     | John
```

Figure 4-7: Sorting output by two columns

```
zip_postcode | last_name | first_name
-------------+-----------+------------
 11111       | Brown     | Helen
 18886       | Collins   | Peter
 18886       | Collins   | Mary
 11111       | Doe       | Jane
 18888       | Doe       | John
 11111       | Hayes     | Franklin
 11111       | Hayes     | Edna
 18886       | Jerry     | Helen
 18888       | Johnson   | Peter
 18888       | Johnson   | Peter
 11111       | Jones     | Janice
 18888       | Jones     | Jon
 11111       | Smith     | Janice
 13333       | Smith     | Jane
 18888       | Smith     | John
```

Figure 4-8: Reversing the sort order of the query in Figure 4-8

is omitted. The trick to writing row selection criteria—one example of the predicates to which you were introduced in Chapter 2—is therefore knowing how to create logical expressions against which data can be evaluated.

Predicates

As you read in Chapter 2, a logical expression that follows WHERE is known as a predicate. It uses a variety of operators to represent row selection criteria. If a row meets the criteria in a predicate (in other words, the criteria evaluate as true), then the row is included in the result table. If the row doesn't meet the criteria (the criteria evaluate as false), then the row is excluded.

Relationship Operators

In Table 4-1 you can see the six operators used to express data relationships.[1] To write an expression using one of the operators, you surround it with two values. In database queries, such expression have either a column name on one side and a literal value on the other, as in

```
cost > 1.95
```

or column names on both sides:

```
numb_on_hand <= reorder_point
```

The first expression asks the question "Is the cost of the item greater than 1.95?" The second asks "Is the number of items in stock less than or equal to the reorder point?"

The way in which you enter literal values into a logical expression depends on the data type of the column to which you are comparing the value:

◊ Numbers: Type numbers without any formatting. In other words, leave out dollar signs, commas, and so on. You should, however, put decimal points in the appropriate place in a number with a factional portion.

◊ Characters: Type characters surrounded by quotation marks. Most DBMSs accept pairs of either single or

---

1   The symbol used for the "not equal to" operator varies from one DBMS to another. Check the documentation that accompanies your software to determine whether the "not equal to" operator is != or < >.

Table 4-1: The relationship operators

Operator	Meaning	Examples
=	Equal to	cost = 1.95
		numb_in_stock = reorder_point
<	Less than	cost < 1.95
		numb_in_stock < reorder_point
<=	Less than or equal to	cost <= 1.95
		numb_in_stock <= reorder_point
>	Greater than	cost > 1.95
		numb_in_stock > reorder_point
>=	Greater than or equal to	cost >= 1.95
		numb_in_stock >= reorder_point
!= or < >	Not equal to	cost != 1.95
		numb_in_stock != reorder_point

double quotes. If your characters include an apostrophe
(a single quote), then you should use double quotes.
Otherwise, use single quotes.

◊ Dates: Type dates in the format used to store them in
the database. This will vary from one DBMS to another.

◊ Times: Type times in the format used to store them in
the database. This will vary from one DBMS to another.

When you are using two column names, keep in mind that
the predicate is applied to each row in the table individually.
The DBMS substitutes the values stored in the columns in the
same row when making its evaluation of the criteria. You can
therefore use two column names when you need to examine
data that are stored in the same row but in different columns.

However, you cannot use a simple logical expression to compare the same column in two or more rows.

The DBMS also bases the way it evaluates data on the type of data:

◊ Comparisons involving numeric data are based on numerical order.

◊ Comparisons involving character data are based on alphabetical order.

◊ Comparisons involving dates and times are based on chronological order.

Logical Operators

Sometimes a simple logical expression is not enough to identify the rows you want to retrieve; you need more than one criterion. In that case, you can chain criteria together with logical operators. For example, assume that you want to retrieve volumes that you have in stock that cost more than $75 and that are in excellent condition. The predicate you need is therefore made up of two simple expressions:

```
condition_code = 2
asking_price > 75
```

A row must meet both of these criteria to be included in the result table. You therefore connect the two expressions with the logical operator AND into a single complex expression:

```
condition_code = 2 AND asking_price >75
```

Whenever you connect two simple expressions with AND, a row must meet *all* of the conditions to be included in the result.

You can use the AND operators to create a predicate that includes a range of dates. For example, if you want to find all sales that were made in August and September of 2013, the predicate would be written:

Table 4-2: AND truth table

AND	True	False
True	True	False
False	False	False

```
sale_date >= '01-Aug-2013'
     AND sale_date <= '31-Sep-2013'
```

To be within the interval, a sale date must meet *both* individual criteria.[2]

You will find a summary of the action of the AND operators in Table 4-2. The labels in the columns and rows represent the result of evaluating the single expressions on either side of the AND. As you can see, the only way to get a true result for the entire expression is for both simple expressions to be true.

If you want to create an expression from which a row needs to meet only one condition, then you connect simple expressions with the logical operator OR. For example, if you want to retrieve volumes that cot more than $125 or less than $50, you would use the predicate

```
asking_price > 100 OR asking_price < 50
```

Whenever you connect two simple expressions with OR, a row needs to meet only one of the conditions to be included in the result of the query. When you want to create a predicate that looks for dates outside an interval, you use the OR operator. For example, to see sales that occurred prior to March 1, 2013 or after December 31, 2013, the predicate is written

```
sale_date < '01-Mar-2013'
     OR sale_date > '31-Dec-2013'
```

---

2   The date format used in the sample queries is a fairly generic one that is recognized by most DBMSs. However, you should consult the documentation for your DBMS to determine exactly what will work with your product.

Table 4-3: OR truth table

OR	True	False
True	True	True
False	True	False

You can find a summary of the OR operation in Table 4-3. Notice that the only way to get a false result is for both simple expression surrounding OR to be false.

There is no limit to the number of simple expression you can connect with AND and OR. For example, the following expression is legal:

```
condition_code >= 3
    AND selling_price < asking_price
    AND selling_price > 75
```

Negation

The logical operator NOT (or !) inverts the result of logical expression. If a row meets the criteria in a predicate, then placing NOT in front of the criteria *excludes* the row from the result. By the same token, if a row does not meet the criteria in a predicate, then placing NOT in front of the expression *includes* the row in the result. For example,

```
NOT (asking_price <= 50)
```

retrieves all rows where the cost is not less than or equal to $50 (in other words, greater than $50). First the DBMS evaluates the value in the *asking_price* column against the expression *asking_price <= 50*. If the row meets the criteria, then the DBMS does nothing. If the row does not meet the criteria, it includes the row in the result.

The parentheses in the preceding example group the expression to which NOT is to be applied. In the following example, the NOT operator applies only to the expression *asking_price <= 50*.

```
NOT (asking_price <= 50)
    AND selling_price < asking_price
```

NOT can be a bit tricky when it is applied to complex expressions As an example, consider this expression:

```
NOT (asking_price <= 50
    AND selling_price < asking_price)
```

Rows that have both an asking price of less than or equal to $50 and a selling price that was less than the asking price will meet the criteria within parentheses. However, the NOT operator excludes them from the result. Those rows that have either an asking price of more than $50 or a selling price greater than or equal to the asking price will fail the criteria within the parentheses, but will be included in the result by the NOT. This means that the expression is actually the same as

```
asking_price > 50
    OR selling_price >= asking_price
```

or

```
NOT (asking_price <= 50)
    OR NOT (selling_price < asking_price)
```

Precedence and Parentheses

When you create an expression with more than one logical operation, the DBMS must decide on the order in which it will process the simple expressions. Unless you tell it otherwise, a DBMS uses a set of default *rules of precedence*. In general, a DBMS evaluates simple expressions first, followed by the logical expression. When there is more than one operator of the same type, evaluation proceeds from left to right.

As a first example, consider this expression:

```
asking_price < 50
    OR condition_code = 2
    selling_price > asking_price
```

If the asking price of a book is $25, its condition code is 3, and the selling price was $20, the DBMS will exclude the row from the result. The first simple expression is true; the second is false. An OR between the first two produces a true result because at least one of the criteria is true. Then the DBMS performs an AND between the true result of the first portion and the result of the third simple expression (false). Because we are combining a true result and a false result with AND, the overall result is false. The row is therefore excluded from the result.

We can change the order in which the DBMS evaluates the logical operators, and coincidentally, the result of the expression, by using parentheses to group the expressions that are to have higher precedence:

```
asking_price < 50 OR (condition_code = 2
    AND selling_price > asking_price)
```

A DBMS gives highest precedence to the parts of the expression within parentheses. Using the same sample data from the preceding paragraph, the expression within parentheses is false (both simple expressions are false). However, the OR with the first simple expression produces true, because the first simple expression is true. Therefore, the row is included in the result.

Special Operators

SQL predicates can include a number of special operators that make writing logical criteria easier. These include BETWEEN, LIKE, IN, and IS NULL.

Note: There are additional operators that are used primarily with subqueries, SELECT statements in which you embed one complete SELECT within another. You will be introduced to them in Chapter 5.

The BETWEEN operator simplifies writing predicates that look for values that lie within an interval. Remember the example you saw earlier in this chapter using AND to generate a date interval? Using the BETWEEN operator, you could rewrite that predicate as

```
sale_date BETWEEN '01-Aug-2013'
    AND '31-Sep-2013'
```

Any row with a sale date of August 1, 2013 through September 31, 2013 will be included in the result.

If you negate the BETWEEN operator, the DBMS returns all rows that are outside the interval. For example,

```
sale_date NOT BETWEEN '01-Aug-2013'
    AND '31-Sep-2013'
```

retrieves all rows with dates *prior* to August 1, 2013 and *after* September 31, 2013. It does not include the 01-Aug-2013 or 31-Sep-2013. NOT BETWEEN is therefore a shorthand for the two simple expressions linked by OR that you saw earlier in this chapter.

LIKE

The LIKE operator provides a measure of character string pattern matching by allowing you to use placeholders (wildcards) for one or more characters. Although you may find that the wildcards a different in your particular DBMS, in most case, % stands for zero, one, or more characters and _ stands for zero or one character.

The way in which the LIKE operator works is summarized in Table 4-4. As you can see, you can combine the two wildcards to produce a variety of begins with, ends with, and contains expressions.

As with BETWEEN you can negate the LIKE operator:

```
last_name NOT LIKE 'Sm%'
```

Rows that are like the pattern are therefore excluded from the result.

One of the problems you may run into when using LIKE is that you need to include the wildcard characters as part of your

Table 4-4: Using the LIKE operator

Expression	Meaning
LIKE 'Sm%'	Begins with *Sm*
LIKE '%ith'	Ends with *ith*
LIKE '%ith%'	Contains *ith*
LIKE 'Sm_'	Begins with *Sm* and is followed by at most one character
LIKE '_ith'	Ends with *ith* and is preceded by at most one character
LIKE '_ith_'	Contains *ith* and begins and ends with at most one additional character
LIKE '%ith_'	Contains *ith*, begins with any number of characters, and ends with at most one additional character
LIKE '_ith%'	Contains *ith*, begins with at most one additional character, and ends with any number of characters

data. For example, what can you do if you want rows that contain 'nd_by'? The expression you want is

```
column_name LIKE '%nd_by%'
```

The problem is that the DBMS will see the _ as a wildcard, rather than as characters in your search string. The solution was introduced in SQL-9s, providing you with the ability to designate an *escape character*.

An escape character removes the special meaning of the character that follows. Because many programming languages use \ as the escape character, it is a logical choice for pattern matching, although it can be any character that is not part of your data. To establish the escape character, you add the keyword ESCAPE, followed by the escape character, to your expression:

```
column_name LIKE '%nd\_by%' ESCAPE '\'
```

The IN operator compares the value in a column against a set **IN** of values. IN returns true if the value is within the set. For example, assume that a store employee is checking the selling price of a book and wants to know if it is either $25, $50, or $60. Using the IN operator, the expression would be written:

```
selling_price IN (25,50,60)
```

This is shorthand for

```
selling_price = 25 OR selling_price = 50
    OR selling_price = 60
```

Therefore, any row whose price is one of those three values will be included in the result. Conversely, if you write the predicate

```
selling_price NOT IN (25,50,60)
```

the DBMS will return the rows with pries other than those in the set of values. The preceding expression is therefore the same as

```
selling_price != 25 AND selling_price != 50
    AND selling_price !=60
```

or

```
NOT (selling_price = 25 OR selling_price = 50
    OR selling_price = 60)
```

Note: The most common use of IN and NOT IN is with a sub-query, where the set of values to which data are compared are generated by an embedded SELECT. You will learn about this in Chapter 5.

As you know, null is a specific indicator in a database. Al- **IS NULL** though columns that contain nulls appear empty when you view them, the database actually stores a value that represents null so that an unknown value can be distinguished from, for example, a string value containing a blank. As a user, however, you will rarely know exactly what a DBMS is using internally for null. This means that you need some special way to identify null in a predicate so you can retrieve rows containing nulls. That is where the IS NULL operator comes in.

For example, an expression to identify all rows for volumes that have not been sold is written as

```
sale_date IS NULL
```

Conversely, to find all volumes that have been sold, you could use

```
sale_date IS NOT NULL
```

Performing Row Selection Queries

To perform SQL queries that select specific rows, you place a predicate after the SQL keyword WHERE. Depending on the nature of the predicate, the intention of the query may be to retrieve one or more rows. In this section you will therefore see some SELECT examples that combine a variety of row selection criteria. You will also see how those criteria are combined in queries with column selection and with sorting of the output.

Using a Primary Key Expression to Retrieve One Row

A common type of SQL retrieval query uses a primary key expression in its predicate to retrieve exactly one row. For example, if someone at the rare book store wants to see the name and telephone number of customer number 6, then the query is written

```
SELECT first_name, last_name, contact_phone
FROM customer
WHERE customer_numb = 6;
```

The result is the single row requested by the predicate.

```
first_name | last_name | contact_phone
-----------+-----------+---------------
Janice     | Smith     | 518-555-6666
```

If a table has a concatenated primary key, such as the employee number and child name for the *dependents* table you saw in Chapter 1, then a primary key expression needs to include a complex predicate in which each column of the primary key appears in its own simple logical expression. For example, if you wanted to find the birthdate of employee number 0002's son John, you would use following query:

```
SELECT child_birth_date
FROM dependents
WHERE employee_number = '0002'
     AND child_name = 'John';
```

In this case, the result is simply

```
child_birth_date
----------------
2-Dec-1999
```

Although queries with primary key expressions are written with the intention of retrieving only one row, more commonly SQL queries are designed to retrieve multiple rows.

Retrieving Multiple Rows

When you want to retrieve data based on a value in a single column, you construct a predicate that includes just a simple logical expression. For example, to see all the books ordered on sale number 6, someone at the store would use

Using Simple Predicates

```
SELECT isbn
FROM volume
WHERE sale_id = 6;
```

The output (see Figure 4-9) displays a single column for rows where the sale_id is six.

When you want to see rows that meet two or more simple conditions, you use a complex predicate in which the simple conditions are connected by AND or OR. For example, if someone wanted to see the books on order number 6 that sold for less than the asking price, the query would be written

Using Complex Predicates

```
isbn
------------------
 978-1-11111-146-1
 978-1-11111-122-1
 978-1-11111-130-1
 978-1-11111-126-1
 978-1-11111-139-1
```

Figure 4-9: Displaying a single column from multiple rows using a

```
SELECT isbn
FROM volume
WHERE sale_id = 6
    AND selling_price < asking_price;
```

Only two rows meet the criteria:

```
isbn
------------------
978-1-11111-130-1
978-1-11111-139-1
```

By the same token, if you wanted to see all sales that took place prior to August 1, 2013 and for which the total amount of the sale was less than $100, the query would be written

```
SELECT sale_id, sale_total_amt
FROM sale
WHERE sale_date < '1-Aug-2012'
    AND sale_total_amt < 100;
```

It produces the result in Figure 4-10.

Note: Don't forget that the date format required by your DBMS may be different from the one used in examples in this book.

Alternatively, if you needed information about all sales that occurred prior to or on August 1, 2013 that totaled more than 100 along with sales that occurred after August 1, 2013 that totaled less than 100, you would write the query

```
sale_id | sale_total_amt
--------+---------------
      3 |          58.00
      7 |          80.00
      8 |          90.00
      9 |          50.00
     13 |          25.95
     14 |          80.00
     15 |          75.00
```

Figure 4-10: Retrieving rows using a complex predicate including a date

```
SELECT sale_id, sale_date, sale_total_amt
FROM sale
WHERE (sale_date <= '1-Aug-2013'
    AND sale_total_amt > 100)
    OR (sale_date > '1-Aug-2013'
    AND sale_total_amt < 100);
```

Notice that although the AND operator has precedence over OR and therefore the parentheses are not strictly necessary, the predicate in this query includes parentheses for clarity. Extra parentheses are never a problem—as long as you balance every opening parenthesis with a closing parenthesis—and you should feel free to use them whenever they help make it easier to understand the meaning of a complex predicate. The result of this query can be seen in Figure 4-11.

As an example of using one of the special predicate operators, consider a query where someone wants to see all sales that occurred between July 1, 2013 and August 31, 2013. The query would be written

Using BETWEEN and NOT BETWEEN

```
SELECT sale_id, sale_date, sale_total_amt
FROM sale
WHERE sale_date BETWEEN '1-Jul-2013' AND '31-
Aug-2013';
```

It produces the output in Figure 4-12.

```
sale_id |       sale_date        | sale_total_amt
--------+------------------------+----------------
      4 | 30-JUN-13 00:00:00     |         110.00
      5 | 30-JUN-13 00:00:00     |         110.00
      6 | 05-JUL-13 00:00:00     |         505.00
     10 | 10-JUL-13 00:00:00     |         125.00
     11 | 10-JUL-13 00:00:00     |         200.00
     12 | 10-JUL-13 00:00:00     |         200.00
     16 | 25-JUL-13 00:00:00     |         130.00
      2 | 05-JUN-13 00:00:00     |         125.00
      1 | 29-MAY-13 00:00:00     |         510.00
     19 | 01-SEP-13 00:00:00     |          95.00
     20 | 01-SEP-13 00:00:00     |          75.00
```

Figure 4-11: Using a complex predicate that includes multiple logical operators

```
sale_id |       sale_date        | sale_total_amt
--------+------------------------+----------------
      6 | 05-JUL-13 00:00:00     |         505.00
      7 | 05-JUL-13 00:00:00     |          80.00
      8 | 07-JUL-13 00:00:00     |          90.00
      9 | 07-JUL-13 00:00:00     |          50.00
     10 | 10-JUL-13 00:00:00     |         125.00
     11 | 10-JUL-13 00:00:00     |         200.00
     12 | 10-JUL-13 00:00:00     |         200.00
     13 | 10-JUL-13 00:00:00     |          25.95
     14 | 10-JUL-13 00:00:00     |          80.00
     15 | 12-JUL-13 00:00:00     |          75.00
     16 | 25-JUL-13 00:00:00     |         130.00
     17 | 25-JUL-13 00:00:00     |         100.00
     18 | 22-AUG-13 00:00:00     |         100.00
```

Figure 4-12: Using BETWEEN to retrieve rows in a date range

The inverse query retrieves all orders not placed between July 1, 2013 and August 31, 2013 is written

```
SELECT sale_id, sale_date, sale_total_amt
FROM sale
WHERE sale_date NOT BETWEEN '1-Jul-2013' AND
'31-Aug-2013';
```

and produces the output in Figure 4-13.

```
sale_id |      sale_date       | sale_total_amt
--------+----------------------+----------------
      3 | 15-JUN-13 00:00:00   |          58.00
      4 | 30-JUN-13 00:00:00   |         110.00
      5 | 30-JUN-13 00:00:00   |         110.00
      2 | 05-JUN-13 00:00:00   |         125.00
      1 | 29-MAY-13 00:00:00   |         510.00
     19 | 01-SEP-13 00:00:00   |          95.00
     20 | 01-SEP-13 00:00:00   |          75.00
```

Figure 4-13: Using NOT BETWEEN to retrieve rows outside a date range

```
sale_id |      sale_date       | sale_total_amt
--------+----------------------+----------------
      1 | 29-MAY-13 00:00:00   |         510.00
      2 | 05-JUN-13 00:00:00   |         125.00
      3 | 15-JUN-13 00:00:00   |          58.00
      5 | 30-JUN-13 00:00:00   |         110.00
      4 | 30-JUN-13 00:00:00   |         110.00
     19 | 01-SEP-13 00:00:00   |          95.00
     20 | 01-SEP-13 00:00:00   |          75.00
```

Figure 4-14: Output sorted by date

If we want output that is easier to read, we might ask the DBMS to sort the result by sale date:

```
SELECT sale_id, sale_date, sale_total_amt
FROM sale
WHERE sale_date NOT BETWEEN '1-Jul-2013'
     AND '31-Aug-2013'
ORDER BY sale_date;
```

producing the result in Figure 4-14.

The predicates you have seen to this point omit one important thing: the presence of nulls. What should a DBMS do when it encounters a row that contains null rather than a known value? As you read in Chapter 2, the relational data model doesn't have a specific rule as to what a DBMS should do, but it does require that the DBMS act consistently when it encounters nulls.

Nulls and Retrieval: Three-Valued Logic

Consider the following query as an example:

```
SELECT inventory_id, selling_price
FROM volume
WHERE selling_price < 100;
```

The result can be found in Figure 4-15. Notice that every row in the result table has a value of selling price, which means that rows for unsold items—those with null in the selling price column—are omitted. The DBMS can't ascertain what the selling price for unsold items will be: Maybe it will be less than $100 or maybe it will be greater than or equal to $100.

The policy of most DBMSs is to exclude rows with nulls from the result. For rows with null in the selling price column, the *maybe* answer to "Is selling price less than 100" becomes *false*. This seems pretty straightforward, but what happens when you have a complex logical expression of which one portion returns *maybe*? The operation of AND, OR, and NOT must be expanded to take into account that they may be operating on a *maybe*.

The three-valued logic table for AND can be found in Table 4-5. Notice that something important hasn't changed: The only way to get a true result is for both simple expressions linked by AND to be true. Given that most DBMSs exclude rows where the predicate evaluates to *maybe*, the presence of nulls in the data will not change what an end user sees.

The same is true when you look at the three-valued truth table for OR (see Table 4-6). As long as one simple expression is true, it does not matter whether the second returns true, false, or maybe. The result will always be true.

If you negate an expression that returns maybe, the NOT operator has no effect. In other words, NOT (MAYBE) is still *maybe*.

```
inventory_id | selling_price
-------------+--------------
           2 |         50.00
           4 |         25.95
           5 |         22.95
           6 |         76.10
          11 |         25.00
          12 |         15.00
          13 |         18.00
          18 |         30.00
          19 |         75.00
          23 |         45.00
          24 |         35.00
          25 |         75.00
          26 |         55.00
          33 |         50.00
          35 |         75.00
          36 |         50.00
          37 |         75.00
          39 |         75.00
          40 |         25.95
          41 |         40.00
          42 |         40.00
          50 |         50.00
          51 |         50.00
          52 |         50.00
          53 |         40.00
          54 |         40.00
          55 |         60.00
          56 |         40.00
          57 |         40.00
          59 |         35.00
          58 |         25.00
          60 |         45.00
          61 |         50.00
          62 |         75.00
```

Figure 4-15: Retrieval based on a column that includes rows with nulls

To see the rows that return *maybe*, you need to add an expression to your query that uses the IS NULL operator. For example, the easiest way to see which volumes have not been sold is to write a query like:

Table 4-5: Three-valued AND truth table

AND	True	False	Maybe
True	True	False	Maybe
False	False	False	False
Maybe	Maybe	False	Maybe

Table 4-6: Three-valued OR truth table

OR	True	False	Maybe
True	True	True	True
False	True	False	Maybe
Maybe	True	Maybe	Maybe

```
SELECT inventory_id, isbn, selling_price
FROM volume
WHERE selling_price is null;
```

The result can be found in Figure 4-16. Note that the selling price column is empty in each row. (Remember that you typically can't see any special value for null.) Notice also that the rows in this result table are all those excluded from the query in Figure 4-15.

Four-Valued Logic

Codd's 330 rules for the relational data model include an enhancement to three-valued logic that he called *four-valued logic*. In four-valued logic, there are actually two types of null: "null and it doesn't matter that it's null" and "null and we've really got a problem because it's null." For example, if a company sells internationally, then it probably has a column for

```
inventory_id |         isbn          | selling_price
-------------+-----------------------+--------------
           7 | 978-1-11111-137-1 |
           8 | 978-1-11111-137-1 |
           9 | 978-1-11111-136-1 |
          10 | 978-1-11111-136-1 |
          16 | 978-1-11111-121-1 |
          17 | 978-1-11111-124-1 |
          27 | 978-1-11111-141-1 |
          28 | 978-1-11111-141-1 |
          29 | 978-1-11111-141-1 |
          30 | 978-1-11111-145-1 |
          31 | 978-1-11111-145-1 |
          32 | 978-1-11111-145-1 |
          43 | 978-1-11111-132-1 |
          44 | 978-1-11111-138-1 |
          45 | 978-1-11111-138-1 |
          46 | 978-1-11111-131-1 |
          47 | 978-1-11111-140-1 |
          48 | 978-1-11111-123-1 |
          49 | 978-1-11111-127-1 |
          63 | 978-1-11111-130-1 |
          64 | 978-1-11111-136-1 |
          65 | 978-1-11111-136-1 |
          66 | 978-1-11111-137-1 |
          67 | 978-1-11111-137-1 |
          68 | 978-1-11111-138-1 |
          69 | 978-1-11111-138-1 |
          70 | 978-1-11111-139-1 |
          71 | 978-1-11111-139-1 |
```

Figure 4-16: Using IS NULL to retrieve rows containing nulls

the country of each customer. Because it is essential to know a customer's country, a null in the *country* column would fall into the category of "null and we've really got a problem." In contrast, a missing value in a *company name* column would be quite acceptable in a customer table for rows that represented individual customers. Then the null would be "null and it doesn't matter that it's null." Four-valued logic remains purely theoretical, however, and isn't implemented in DBMSs.

5

Retrieving Data from More Than One Table

As you read in Chapter 1, logical relationships between entities in a relational database are represented by matching primary and foreign key values. Given that there are no permanent connections between tables stored in the database, a DBMS must provide some way for users to match primary and foreign key values when needed using the join operation.

In this chapter you will be introduced to the syntax for including a join in a SQL query. Throughout this chapter you will also read about the impact joins have on database performance. At the end you will see how subqueries (SELECTs within SELECTs) can be used to avoid joins and, in some cases, significantly decrease the time it takes for a DBMS to complete a query.

SQL Syntax for Inner Joins

There are two types of syntax you can use for requesting the join of two tables. The first, which we have been calling the "traditional" join syntax, is the only way to write a join in the SQL standards through SQL-89. SQL-92 added a join syntax that is both more flexible and easier to use.

Traditional SQL Joins

The traditional SQL join syntax is based on the combination of the product and restrict operations that you read about in Chapter 2. It has the following general form:

```
SELECT columns
FROM table1, table2
WHERE table1.primary_key = table2.foreign_key
```

Listing the tables to be joined after FROM requests the product. The join condition in the WHERE clause's predicate requests the restrict that identifies the rows that are part of the joined tables. Don't forget that if you leave off the join condition in the predicate, then the presence of the two tables after FROM simply generates a product table.

Note: If you really, really, really want a product, use the CROSS JOIN operator in the FROM clause.

For example, assume that someone wanted to see all the orders placed by a customer whose phone number is 518-555-1111. The phone number is part of the *customer* table; the purchase information is in the *sale* table. The two relations are related by the presence of the customer number in both (primary key of the *customer* table; foreign key in *sale*). The query to satisfy the information request therefore requires an equi-join of the two tables over the customer number, the result of which can be seen in Figure 5-1:

```
SELECT first_name, last_name, sale_id, sale_date
FROM customer, sale
WHERE customer.customer_numb = sale.customer_numb
      AND contact_phone = '518-555-1111';
```

There are two important things to notice about the preceding query:

◊ The join is between a primary key in one table and a foreign key in another. As you will remember from Chapter

first_name	last_name	sale_id	sale_date
Janice	Jones	3	15-JUN-13 00:00:00
Janice	Jones	17	25-JUL-13 00:00:00
Janice	Jones	2	05-JUN-13 00:00:00
Janice	Jones	1	29-MAY-13 00:00:00

Figure 5-1: Output from a query containing an equi-join between a primary key and a foreign key

2, equi-joins that don't meet this pattern are frequently invalid.

◊ Because the *customer_numb* column appears in more than one table in the query, it must be qualified by the name of the table from which it should be taken. To add a qualifier, precede the name of a column by its name, separating the two with a period.

Note: With some large DBMSs, you must also qualify the names of tables you did not create with the user ID of the account that did create the table. For example, if user ID DBA created the customer table, then the full name of the customer number column would be DBA.customer.customer_numb. Check your product documentation to determine whether your DBMS is one of those that require the user ID qualifier.

How might a SQL query optimizer choose to process this query? Although we cannot be certain because there is more than one order of operations that will work, it is likely that the restrict operation to choose the customer with a telephone number of 518-555-1111 will be performed first. This cuts down on the amount of data that needs to be manipulated for the join. The second step probably will be the join operation, because doing the project to select columns for display will eliminate the column needed for the join.

SQL-92 Join Syntax

The SQL-92 standard introduced an alternative join syntax that is both simpler and more flexible than the traditional join syntax. If you are performing a natural equi-join, there are three variations of the syntax you can use, depending on whether the column or columns over which you are joining have the same name and whether you want to use all matching columns in the join.

Note: Despite the length of time that has passed since the introduction of this revised join syntax, not all DBMSs support all three varieties of the syntax. You will need to consult the documentation of your particular product to determine exactly which syntax you can use.

Joins over All Columns with the Same Name

When the primary key and foreign key columns you are joining have the same name and you want to use all matching columns in the join condition, all you need to do is indicate that you want to join the tables, using the following general syntax:

```
SELECT column(s)
FROM table1 NATURAL JOIN table2
```

The query we used as an example in the preceding section could therefore be written as

```
SELECT first_name, last_name, sale_id,
    sale_date
FROM customer NATURAL JOIN sale
WHERE contact_phone = '518-555-1111';
```

Note: Because the default is a natural equi-join, you will obtain the same result if you simply use JOIN instead of NATURAL JOIN.

The SQL command processor identifies all columns in the two tables that have the same name and automatically performs the join of those columns.

Note: If you are determined to obtain a product rather than a natural join, you can do it using the SQL-92 CROSS JOIN operator.

Joins over Selected Columns

If you don't want to use all matching columns in a join condition but the columns still have the same name, you specify the names of the columns over which the join is to be made by adding a USING clause:

```
SELECT column(s)
FROM table1 JOIN table2 USING (column)
```

Using this syntax, the sample query would be written

```
SELECT first_name, last_name, sale_id,
```

```
      sale_date
FROM customer JOIN sale USING (customer_numb)
WHERE contact_phone = '518-555-1111';
```

**Joins over Columns with
Different Names**

When the columns over which you are joining table don't have the same name, then you must use a join condition similar to that used in the traditional SQL join syntax:

```
SELECT column(s)
FROM table1 JOIN table2 ON join_condition
```

In this case, the sample query will appear as

```
SELECT first_name, last_name, sale_id,
      sale_date
FROM customer JOIN sale
ON customer.customer_numb = sale.customer_numb
WHERE contact_phone = '518-555-1111';
```

All of the joins you have seen to this point have been performed using a single matching column. However, on occasion you may run into tables where you are dealing with concatenated primary and foreign keys. As an example, we'll return to the four tables from the small accounting firm database that we used in Chapter 2 when we discussed how joins over concatenated keys work:

Joining using Concatenated Keys

```
accountant (acct_first_name, acct_last_name,
      date_hired, office_ext)
```

```
customer (customer_numb, first_name, last_name,
      street, city, state_province, zip_post-
      code, contact_phone)
```

```
project (tax_year, customer_numb,
      acct_first_name, acct_last_name)
```

```
form (tax_year, customer_numb, form_id,
      is_complete)
```

To see which accountant worked on which forms during which year, a query needs to join the *project* and *form* tables, which are related by a concatenated primary key. The join condition needed is

```
project.tax_year || project.customer_numb =
    form.tax_year || form.customer_numb
```

The || operator represents concatenation in most SQL implementations. It instructs the SQL command processor to view the two columns as if they were one and to base its comparison on the concatenation rather than individual column values.

The following join condition produces the same result because it pulls rows from a product table where *both* the customer ID numbers and the tax years are the same:

```
project.tax_year = form.tax_year AND project.
    customer_numb = form.customer_numb
```

You can therefore write a query using the traditional SQL join syntax in two ways:

```
SELECT acct_first_name, acct_last_name,
    form.tax_year, form.form_ID
FROM project, form
WHERE project.tax_year
    || project.customer_numb = form.tax_year
    || form.customer_numb;
```

or

```
SELECT acct_first_name, acct_last_name,
    form.tax_year, form.form_ID
FROM project, form
project.tax_year = form.tax_year
    AND project.customer_numb =
        form.customer_numb;
```

If the columns have the same names in both tables and are the only matching columns, then the SQL-92 syntax

```
SELECT acct_first_name, acct_last_name,
    form.tax_year, form.form_ID
FROM project JOIN form;
```

has the same effect as the preceding two queries.

When the columns have the same names but aren't the only matching columns, then you must specify the columns in a USING clause:

```
SELECT acct_first_name, acct_last_name,
     form.tax_year, form.form_ID
FROM project JOIN form USING (tax_year,
     form_ID);
```

Alternatively, if the columns don't have the same name, you can use the complete join condition, just as you would if you were using the traditional join syntax:

```
SELECT acct_first_name, acct_last_name,
     form.tax_year, form.form_ID
FROM project JOIN form ON project.tax_year
     || project.customer_numb = form.tax_year
     || form.customer_numb;
```

or

```
SELECT acct_first_name, acct_last_name,
     form.tax_year, form.form_ID
FROM project JOIN form
     ON project.tax_year = form.tax_year
     AND project.customer_numb =
          form.customer_numb;
```

Notice that in all forms of the query, the tax year and form ID columns in the SELECT clause are qualified by a table name. It really doesn't matter form which the data are taken, but because the columns appear in both tables, the SQL command processor needs to be told which pair of columns to use.

What if you need to join more than two tables in the same query? For example, some at the rare book store might want to see the names of the people who have purchased a volume with the ISBN of 978-1-11111-146-1. The query that retrieves that information must join *volume* to *sale* to find the sales on which

Joining More than Two Tables

the volume was sold. Then the result of the first join must be joined again to *customer* to gain access to the names.

Using the traditional join syntax, the query is written

```
SELECT first_name, last_name
FROM customer, sale, volume
WHERE volume.sale_id = sale.sale_id
    AND sale.customer_numb =
            customer.customer_numb
    AND isbn = '978-1-11111-136-1';
```

With the simplest form of the SQL-92 syntax, the query becomes

```
SELECT first_name, last_name
FROM customer JOIN sale JOIN volume
WHERE isbn = '978-1-11111-136-1';
```

Both syntaxes produce the following result:

```
first_name | last_name
-----------+-----------
Mary       | Collins
Janice     | Smith
```

Keep in mind that the join operation can work on only two tables at a time. If you need to join more than two tables, you must join them in pairs. Therefore, a join of three tables requires two joins, a join of four tables requires three joins, and so on.

Although the SQL-92 syntax is certainly simpler than the traditional join syntax, it has another major benefit: It gives you control over the order in which the joins are performed. With the traditional join syntax, the query optimizer is in complete control of the order of the joins. However, in SQL-92, the joins are performed from left to right, following the order in which the joins are placed in the FROM clause.

This means that you sometimes can affect the performance of a query by varying the order in which the joins are performed.[1] Remember that the less data the DBMS has to manipulate, the faster a query will execute. Therefore, you want to perform the most discriminatory joins first.

As an example, consider the sample query used in the previous section. The *volume* table has the most rows, followed by *sale* and then *customer*. However, the query also contains a highly discriminatory restrict predicate that limits the rows from that table. Therefore, it is highly likely that the DBMS will perform the restrict on *volume* first. This means that the query is likely to execute faster is you write it so that *sale* is joined with *volume* first, given that this join will significantly limit the rows from *sale* that need to be joined with *customer*.

In contrast, what would happen if there was no restrict predicate in the query, and you wanted to retrieve the name of the customer for ever book ordered in the database? The query would appear as

```
SELECT first_name, last_name
FROM customer JOIN sale JOIN volume;
```

First, keep in mind that this type of query, which is asking for large amounts of data, will rarely execute as quickly as one that contains predicates to limit the number of rows. Nonetheless, if will execute a bit fast if *customers* is joined to *sale* before joining to *volume*. Why? Because the joins manipulate fewer rows in that order.

Assume that there are 20 customers, 100 sales, and 300 volumes sold. Every sold item in *volume* must have a matching

SQL-92 Syntax and Multiple-Table Join Performance

---

1   This holds true only if a DBMS has implemented the newer join syntax according to the SQL standard. A DBMS may support the syntax without its query optimizer using the order of tables in the FROM clause to determine join order.

row in *sale*. Therefore, the result from that join will be at least 300 rows long. Those 300 rows must be joined to the 20 rows in *customer*. However, if we reverse the order, then the 20 rows in *customer* are joined to 100 rows in *sale*, producing a table of 100 rows, which can then be joined to *volume*. In either case, we are stuck with a join of 100 rows to 300 rows, but when the *customer* table is handled first, the other join is 20 to 100 rows, rather than 20 to 300 rows.

Finding Multiple Rows in One Table: Joining a Table to Itself

One of the limitations of a restrict operation is that its predicate is applied to only one row in a table at a time. This means that a predicate such as

```
isbn = '0-131-4966-9' AND isbn = '0-191-4923-8'
```

and the query

```
SELECT first_name, last_name
FROM customer JOIN sale JOIN volume
WHERE isbn = '978-1-11111-146-1'
    AND isbn = '978-1-11111-122-1';
```

will always return 0 rows. No row can have more than one value in the *isbn* column!

What the preceding query is actually trying to do is locate customers who have purchased two specific books. This means that there must be at least two rows for a customer's purchases in *volume*, one for each for each of the books in question.

Given that you cannot do this type of query with a simple restrict predicate, how can you retrieve the data? The technique is to join the *volume* table to itself over the sale ID. The result table will have two columns for the book's ISBN, one for each copy of the original table. Those rows that have both the ISBNs that we want will finally be joined to the *sale* table (over the sale ID) and *customer* (over customer number) tables so that the query an project the customer's name.

Before looking at the SQL syntax, however, let's examine the relational algebra of the joins so you can see exactly what is happening. Assume that we are working with the subset of the *volume* table in Figure 5-2. (The sale ID and the ISBN are the only columns that affect the relational algebra; the rest have been left off for simplicity.) Notice first that the result of our sample query should display the first and last names of the customer who made purchase number 6. (It is the only order that contains both of the books in question.

The first step in the query is to join the table in Figure 5-7 to itself over the sale ID, producing the result table in Figure 5-3. The columns that come from the first copy have been labeled T1; those that come from the second copy are labeled T2.

The two rows in black are those that have the ISBNs for which we are searching. Therefore, we need to follow the join with a restrict that says something like

```
WHERE isbn (from table 1) = '978-1-11111-146-1'
    AND isbn (from table 2) =
          '978-1-11111-122-1'
```

The result will be a table with one row in it (the second of the two black rows in Figure 5-3.)

At this point, the query can join the table to *sale* over the sale ID to provide access to the customer number of the person who made the purchase. The result of that second join can then be joined to *customer* to obtain the customer's name (Franklin Hayes). Finally, the query projects the columns the user wants to see.

Correlation Names

The challenge facing a query that needs to work with multiple copies of a single table is to tell the SQL command processor to make the copies of the table. We do this by placing the name of the table more than once on the FROM line, associating

```
sale_id |          isbn
--------+--------------------
      1 | 978-1-11111-111-1
      1 | 978-1-11111-133-1
      1 | 978-1-11111-131-1
      2 | 978-1-11111-142-1
      2 | 978-1-11111-144-1
      2 | 978-1-11111-146-1
      3 | 978-1-11111-133-1
      3 | 978-1-11111-132-1
      3 | 978-1-11111-143-1
      4 | 978-1-11111-121-1
      5 | 978-1-11111-121-1
      6 | 978-1-11111-139-1
      6 | 978-1-11111-146-1
      6 | 978-1-11111-122-1
      6 | 978-1-11111-130-1
      6 | 978-1-11111-126-1
      7 | 978-1-11111-125-1
      7 | 978-1-11111-131-1
      8 | 978-1-11111-126-1
      8 | 978-1-11111-133-1
      9 | 978-1-11111-139-1
     10 | 978-1-11111-133-1
```

Figure 5-2: A subset of the *volume* table

```
sale_id (T1)|         isbn        | sale_id (T2)|         isbn
------------+---------------------+-------------+--------------------
          1 | 978-1-11111-111-1   |           1 | 978-1-11111-133-1
          1 | 978-1-11111-111-1   |           1 | 978-1-11111-131-1
          1 | 978-1-11111-111-1   |           1 | 978-1-11111-111-1
          1 | 978-1-11111-131-1   |           1 | 978-1-11111-133-1
          1 | 978-1-11111-131-1   |           1 | 978-1-11111-131-1
          1 | 978-1-11111-131-1   |           1 | 978-1-11111-111-1
          1 | 978-1-11111-133-1   |           1 | 978-1-11111-133-1
          1 | 978-1-11111-133-1   |           1 | 978-1-11111-131-1
          1 | 978-1-11111-133-1   |           1 | 978-1-11111-111-1
          2 | 978-1-11111-142-1   |           2 | 978-1-11111-144-1
          2 | 978-1-11111-142-1   |           2 | 978-1-11111-146-1
          2 | 978-1-11111-142-1   |           2 | 978-1-11111-142-1
          2 | 978-1-11111-146-1   |           2 | 978-1-11111-144-1
          2 | 978-1-11111-146-1   |           2 | 978-1-11111-146-1
          2 | 978-1-11111-146-1   |           2 | 978-1-11111-142-1
          2 | 978-1-11111-144-1   |           2 | 978-1-11111-144-1
          2 | 978-1-11111-144-1   |           2 | 978-1-11111-146-1
```

Figure 5-3: The result of joining the table in Figure 5-2 to itself (continued on next page)

```
 2 | 978-1-11111-144-1 |     2 | 978-1-11111-142-1
 3 | 978-1-11111-143-1 |     3 | 978-1-11111-133-1
 3 | 978-1-11111-143-1 |     3 | 978-1-11111-132-1
 3 | 978-1-11111-143-1 |     3 | 978-1-11111-143-1
 3 | 978-1-11111-132-1 |     3 | 978-1-11111-133-1
 3 | 978-1-11111-132-1 |     3 | 978-1-11111-132-1
 3 | 978-1-11111-132-1 |     3 | 978-1-11111-143-1
 3 | 978-1-11111-133-1 |     3 | 978-1-11111-133-1
 3 | 978-1-11111-133-1 |     3 | 978-1-11111-132-1
 3 | 978-1-11111-133-1 |     3 | 978-1-11111-143-1
 5 | 978-1-11111-121-1 |     5 | 978-1-11111-121-1
 4 | 978-1-11111-121-1 |     4 | 978-1-11111-121-1
 6 | 978-1-11111-146-1 |     6 | 978-1-11111-139-1
 6 | 978-1-11111-146-1 |     6 | 978-1-11111-126-1
 6 | 978-1-11111-146-1 |     6 | 978-1-11111-130-1
 6 | 978-1-11111-146-1 |     6 | 978-1-11111-122-1
 6 | 978-1-11111-146-1 |     6 | 978-1-11111-146-1
 6 | 978-1-11111-122-1 |     6 | 978-1-11111-139-1
 6 | 978-1-11111-122-1 |     6 | 978-1-11111-126-1
 6 | 978-1-11111-122-1 |     6 | 978-1-11111-130-1
 6 | 978-1-11111-122-1 |     6 | 978-1-11111-122-1
 6 | 978-1-11111-122-1 |     6 | 978-1-11111-146-1
 6 | 978-1-11111-130-1 |     6 | 978-1-11111-139-1
 6 | 978-1-11111-130-1 |     6 | 978-1-11111-126-1
 6 | 978-1-11111-130-1 |     6 | 978-1-11111-130-1
 6 | 978-1-11111-130-1 |     6 | 978-1-11111-122-1
 6 | 978-1-11111-130-1 |     6 | 978-1-11111-146-1
 6 | 978-1-11111-126-1 |     6 | 978-1-11111-139-1
 6 | 978-1-11111-126-1 |     6 | 978-1-11111-126-1
 6 | 978-1-11111-126-1 |     6 | 978-1-11111-130-1
 6 | 978-1-11111-126-1 |     6 | 978-1-11111-122-1
 6 | 978-1-11111-126-1 |     6 | 978-1-11111-146-1
 6 | 978-1-11111-139-1 |     6 | 978-1-11111-139-1
 6 | 978-1-11111-139-1 |     6 | 978-1-11111-126-1
 6 | 978-1-11111-139-1 |     6 | 978-1-11111-130-1
 6 | 978-1-11111-139-1 |     6 | 978-1-11111-122-1
 6 | 978-1-11111-139-1 |     6 | 978-1-11111-146-1
 7 | 978-1-11111-125-1 |     7 | 978-1-11111-131-1
 7 | 978-1-11111-125-1 |     7 | 978-1-11111-125-1
 7 | 978-1-11111-131-1 |     7 | 978-1-11111-131-1
 7 | 978-1-11111-131-1 |     7 | 978-1-11111-125-1
 8 | 978-1-11111-126-1 |     8 | 978-1-11111-133-1
 8 | 978-1-11111-126-1 |     8 | 978-1-11111-126-1
 8 | 978-1-11111-133-1 |     8 | 978-1-11111-133-1
 8 | 978-1-11111-133-1 |     8 | 978-1-11111-126-1
 9 | 978-1-11111 139 1 |     9 | 978-1-11111-139-1
10 | 978-1-11111-133-1 |    10 | 978-1-11111-133-1
```

Figure 5-3 (continued): The result of joining the table in Figure 5-2 to itself each instance of the name with a different alias. Such aliases for table names are known as *correlation names* and take the syntax

```
FROM table_name AS correlation_name
```

For example, to instruct SQL to use two copies of the *volume* table you might use

```
FROM volume AS T1, volume AS T2
```

The AS is optional. Therefore, the following syntax is also legal:

```
FROM volume T1, volume T2
```

In the other parts of the query, you refer to the two copies using the correlation names rather than the original table name.

Note: You can give any table a correlation name; its use is not restricted to queries that work with multiple copies of a single table. In fact, if a table name is difficult to type and appears several times in a query, you can save yourself some typing and avoid problems with typing errors by giving the table a short correlation name.

Performing the Same-Table Join

The query that performs the same-table join needs to specify all of the relational algebra operations you read about in the preceding section. It can be written using the traditional join syntax as follows:

```
SELECT first_name, last_name
FROM volume T1, volume T2, sale, customer
WHERE T1.isbn = '978-1-11111-146-1'
    AND T2.isbn = '978-1-11111-122-1'
    AND T1.sale_id = T2.sale_id
    AND T1.sale_id = sale.sale_id
    AND sale.customer_numb =
        customer.customer_numb;
```

There is one very important thing to notice about this query. Although our earlier discussion of the relational algebra indicated that the same-table join would be performed first, followed by a restrict and the other two joins, there is no way using the traditional syntax to indicate the joining of an inter-mediate result table (in this case, the same-table join). There-fore, the query syntax must join *sale* to either T1 or T2. None-theless, it is likely that the query optimizer will determine that performing the same-table join, followed by the restrict, is a more efficient way to process the query than joining *sale* to T1 first.

If you use the SQL-92 join syntax, then you have some control over the order in which the joins are performed:

```
SELECT first_name, last_name
FROM volume T1 JOIN volume T2
     ON (T1.sale_id = T2.sale_id)
     JOIN sale JOIN customer
WHERE T1.isbn = '978-1-11111-146-1'
     AND T2.isbn = '978-1-11111-122-1';
```

The SQL command processor will process the multiple joins in the FROM clause from left to right, ensuring that the same-table join is performed first.

Outer Joins

As you read in Chapter 2, an outer join is a join that includes rows in a result table even though there may not be a match between rows in the two tables being joined. Whenever the DBMS can't match rows, it places nulls in the columns for which no data exist. The result may therefore not be a legal relation, since it may not have a primary key. However, because a query's result table is a virtual table that is never stored in the database, having no primary keys doesn't present a data integrity problem.

To perform an outer join using the SQL-92 syntax, you in-dicate the type of join in the FROM clause. For example, to perform a left outer join between the *customer* and *sale* tables you could type

```
SELECT first_name, last_name, sale_id,
    sale_date
FROM customer LEFT OUTER JOIN sale;
```

Matching More than Two Rows

You can extend the same table join technique you have just read about to find as many rows in a table you need. Create one copy of the table with a correlation name for the number of rows the query needs to match in the FROM clause and join those tables together. In the WHERE clause, use a predicate that includes one restrict for each copy of the table. For example, to retrieve data that have four specified rows in a table, you need four copies of the table, three joins, and four expressions in the restrict predicate. The general format of such a query is

```
SELECT column(s)
FROM table_name T1 JOIN table_name T2
    JOIN table_name T3 JOIN table_name T4
WHERE T1.column_name = value
    AND T2.column_name = value
    AND T3.column_name = value
    AND T4.column_name = value
```

The result appears in Figure 5-4. Notice that five rows appear to be empty in the *sale_id* and *sale_date* columns. These five customers haven't made any purchases. Therefore, the columns in question are actually null. However, most DBMSs have no visible indicator for null; it looks as if the values are blank. It is the responsibility of the person viewing the result table to realize that the empty spaces represent nulls rather than blanks.

The SQL-92 outer join syntax for joins has the same options as the inner join syntax:

◊ If you use the syntax in the preceding example, the DBMS will automatically perform the outer join on all matching columns between the two tables.

◊ If you want to specify the columns over which the outer join will be performed and the columns have the same names in both tables, add a USING clause:

```
first_name  | last_name  | sale_id | sale_date
------------+------------+---------+-----------
Janice      | Jones      |       1 | 29-MAY-13
Janice      | Jones      |       2 | 05-JUN-13
Janice      | Jones      |      17 | 25-JUL-13
Janice      | Jones      |       3 | 15-JUN-13
Jon         | Jones      |      20 | 01-SEP-13
Jon         | Jones      |      16 | 25-JUL-13
Jon         | Jones      |      13 | 10-JUL-13
John        | Doe        |         |
Jane        | Doe        |       4 | 30-JUN-13
Jane        | Smith      |      18 | 22-AUG-13
Jane        | Smith      |       8 | 07-JUL-13
Janice      | Smith      |      19 | 01-SEP-13
Janice      | Smith      |      14 | 10-JUL-13
Janice      | Smith      |       5 | 30-JUN-13
Helen       | Brown      |         |
Helen       | Jerry      |       9 | 07-JUL-13
Helen       | Jerry      |       7 | 05-JUL-13
Mary        | Collins    |      11 | 10-JUL-13
Peter       | Collins    |      12 | 10-JUL-13
Edna        | Hayes      |      15 | 12-JUL-13
Edna        | Hayes      |      10 | 10-JUL-13
Franklin    | Hayes      |       6 | 05-JUL-13
Peter       | Johnson    |         |
Peter       | Johnson    |         |
John        | Smith      |         |
```

Figure 5-4: The result of an outer join

```
SELECT first_name, last_name, sale_id,
          sale_date
    FROM customer LEFT OUTER JOIN sale
          USING (customer_numb);
```

◊ If the columns over which you want to perform the
  outer join do not have the same name, then append an
  ON clause that contains the join condition:

```
SELECT first_name, last_name
    FROM customer T1
          LEFT OUTER JOIN sale T2
          ON (T1.customer_numb =
                T2.customer_numb);
```

Note: The SQL standard also includes an operation known as the UNION JOIN. It performs a FULL OUTER JOIN on two tables and then throw out the rows that match, placing all those that don't match in the result table. The UNION JOIN hasn't been widely implemented.

Table Constructors in Queries

SQL standards from SQL-92 forward allow the table on which a SELECT is performed to be a virtual table, rather than just a base table. This means that a DBMS should allow a complete SELECT (in other words, a subquery) to be used in a FROM clause to prepare the table on which the remainder of the query will operate. Expressions that create tables for use in SQL statements in this way are known as *table constructors*.

Note: When you join tables in the FROM clause you are actually generating a source for a query on the fly. What is described in this section is just an extension of that principle.

For example, the following query lists all volumes that were purchased by customers 6 and 10:

```
SELECT isbn, first_name, last_name
FROM volume JOIN (SELECT first_name,
     last_name, sale_id
FROM sale JOIN customer
WHERE customer.customer_numb = 6
     OR customer.customer_numb = 10);
```

The results can be found in Figure 5-5. Notice that the row selection is being performed in the subquery that is part of the FROM clause. This forces the SQL command processor to perform the subquery prior to performing the join in the outer query. Although this query could certainly be written in another way, using the subquery in the FROM clause gives a programmer using a DBMS with a query optimizer that uses the FROM clause order additional control over the order in which the relational algebra operations are performed.

```
       isbn           | first_name | last_name
----------------------+------------+-----------
 978-1-11111-121-1 | Janice     | Smith
 978-1-11111-130-1 | Peter      | Collins
 978-1-11111-132-1 | Peter      | Collins
 978-1-11111-141-1 | Janice     | Smith
 978-1-11111-141-1 | Janice     | Smith
 978-1-11111-128-1 | Janice     | Smith
 978-1-11111-136-1 | Janice     | Smith
```

Figure 5-5: Using a table constructor in a query's FROM clause

As we discussed earlier in this chapter, with some DBMSs you can control the order in which joins are performed by using the SQL-92 syntax and being careful with the order in which you place joins in the FROM clause. However, there is a type of SQL syntax—a *subquery*—that you can use with any DBMS to obtain the same result but often avoid performing a join altogether.[2]

A subquery (or *subselect*) is a complete SELECT statement embedded within another SELECT. The result of the inner SELECT becomes data used by the outer.

Note: Subqueries have other uses besides avoiding joins, which you will see throughout the rest of this book.

A query containing a subquery has the following general form:

```
SELECT column(s)
FROM table
WHERE operator (SELECT column(s))
      FROM table
      WHERE …);
```

There are two general types of subqueries. In an *uncorrelated subquery*, the SQL command processor is able to complete the

Avoiding Joins with Uncorrelated Subqueries

---

2   Even a subquery may not avoid joins. Some query optimizers actually replace subqueries with joins when processing a query.

Using the IN Operator

processing of the inner SELECT before moving to the outer. However, in a *correlated subquery*, the SQL command processor cannot complete the inner query without information from the outer. Correlated subqueries usually require that the inner SELECT be performed more than once and therefore can execute relatively slowly. The same is not true for uncorrelated subqueries, which can be used to replace join syntax and therefore may produce faster performance.

Note: You will see examples of correlated subqueries beginning in Chapter 6.

As a first example, consider the following query

```
SELECT sale_date, customer_numb
FROM sale JOIN volume
WHERE isbn = '978-1-11111-136-1';
```

which produces the following output:

```
     sale_date          | customer_numb
- - - - - - - - - - - - - - - - - - - - +- - - - - - - - - - - - - -
  10-JUL-13 00:00:00 |              9
  01-SEP-13 00:00:00 |              6
```

We can rewrite the query using subquery syntax as

```
SELECT sale_date, customer_numb
FROM sale
WHERE sale_id IN (SELECT sale_id
      FROM volume
      WHERE isbn = '978-1-11111-136-1');
```

The inner SELECT retrieves data from the *volume* table and produces a set of sale IDs. The outer SELECT then retrieves data from *sale* where the sale ID is in the set of values retrieved by the subquery.

The use of the IN operator is actually exactly the same as the use you read about in Chapter 4. The only difference is that rather than placing the set of values in parentheses as literals, the set is generated by a SELECT.

When processing this query, the DBMS never joins the two tables. It performs the inner SELECT first and then uses the result table from that query when processing the outer SE-LECT. In the case in which the two tables are very large, this can significantly speed up processing the query.

Note: You can also use NOT IN with subqueries. This is a very powerful syntax that you will read about in Chapter 6.

Like IN, the ANY operator searches a set of values. In its simplest form, ANY is equivalent to IN:

Using the ANY Operator

```
SELECT sale_date, customer_numb
FROM sale
WHERE sale_id = ANY (SELECT sale_id
      FROM volume
      WHERE isbn = '978-1-11111-136-1');
```

This syntax tell the DBMS to retrieve rows from *sale* where the sale ID is "equal to any" of those retrieved by the SELECT in the subquery.

What sets ANY apart from IN is that the = can be replaced with any other relationship operator (for example, < and >). For example, you could use it to create a query that asked for all customers who had purchased a book with a price greater than the average cost of a book. Because queries of this type require the use of SQL summary functions, we will leave their discussion until Chapter 7.

The SELECT that you use as a subquery can have a subquery. In fact, if you want to rewrite a query that joins more than two tables, you will need to nest subqueries in this way. As an example, consider the following query that you saw earlier in this chapter:

Nesting Subqueries

```
SELECT first_name, last_name
FROM customer, sale, volume
WHERE volume.sale_id = sale.sale_id
    AND sale.customer_numb =
        customer.customer_numb
    AND isbn = '978-1-11111-136-1';
```

It can be rewritten as

```
SELECT first_name, last_name
FROM customer
WHERE customer_numb IN
    (SELECT customer_numb
    FROM sale
    WHERE sale_id = ANY
        (SELECT sale_id
        FROM volume
        WHERE isbn = '978-1-11111-136-1'));
```

Note that each subquery is surrounded completely by parentheses. The end of the query therefore contains two closing parentheses next to each other. The rightmost) closes the outer subquery; the) to its left closes the inner subquery.

The DBMS processes the innermost subquery first, returning a set of sale IDs that contains the sales on which the ISBN in question appears. The idle SELECT (the outer subquery) returns a set of customer numbers for rows where the sale ID is any of those in the set returned by the innermost subquery. Finally, the outer query displays information about customers whose customer numbers are in the set produced by the outer subquery.

In general, the larger the tables in question (in other words, the more rows they have), the more performance benefit you will see if you assemble queries using subqueries rather than joins. How many levels deep can you nest subqueries? There is no theoretical limit. However, once a query becomes more than a few levels deep, it may become hard to keep track of what is occurring.

The same-table join that you read about earlier in this chapter can also be replaced with subqueries. As you will remember, that query required a join between *sale* and *customer* to obtain the customer name, a join between *sale* and *volume*, and a join of the *volume* table to itself to find all sales that contained two desired ISBNs. Because there were three joins in the original query, the rewrite will require one nested subquery for each join.

Replacing a Same-Table Join with Subqueries

```
SELECT last_name, first_name
FROM customer
WHERE customer_numb IN
      (SELECT customer_numb
      FROM sale
      WHERE sale_id IN
            (SELECT sale_id
            FROM volume
            WHERE isbn = '978-1-11111-146-1'
            AND sale_id IN
                  (SELECT sale_id
                  FROM volume
                  WHERE isbn =
                      '978-1-11111-122-1')));
```

The innermost subquery retrieves a set of sale IDs for the rows on which an ISBN of '978-1-11111-122-1' appears. The next level subquery above it retrieves rows from *volume* where the sale ID appears in the set retrieved by the innermost subquery and where the ISBN is '978-1-11111-146-1'. These two subqueries therefore replace the same-table join.

The set of sale IDs is then used by the outermost subquery to obtain a set of customer numbers for the sales whose numbers appear in the result set of the two innermost subqueries. Finally, the outer query displays customer information for the customers whose number are part of the outermost subquery's result set.

Notice that the two innermost subqueries are based on the same table. To process this query, the DBMS makes two passes through the *volume* table—one for each subquery—rather than joining a copy of the table to itself. When a table is very large, this syntax can significantly speed up performance because the DBMS does not need to create and manipulate a duplicate copy of the large table in main memory.

6

Advanced Retrieval Operations

To this point, the queries you have read about combine and extract data from relations in relatively straightforward ways. However, there are additional operations you can perform on relations that, for example, answer questions such as "show me that data that are not ..." or "show me the combination of data that are ...". In this chapter you will read about the implementation of additional relational algebra operations in SQL that will perform such queries as well as performing calculations and using functions that you can use to obtain information about the data you retrieve.

Union

Union is one of the few relational algebra operations whose name can be used in a SQL query. When you want to use a union, you write two individual SELECT statements, joined by the keyword UNION:

```
SELECT column(s)
FROM table(s)
WHERE predicate
UNION
SELECT column(s)
FROM table(s)
WHERE predicate
```

The columns retrieved by the two SELECT must have the same data types and sizes and be in the same order For example, the following is legal as long as the customer numbers are the

131

same data type (for example, integer) and the customer names are the same data type and length (for example, 30-character strings):

```
SELECT customer_numb, customer_first,
     customer_last
FROM some_table
UNION
SELECT cust_no, first_name, last_name
FROM some_other_table
```

Notice that the source tables of the two SELECTS don't need to be the same, nor do the columns need to have the same names. However, the following is not legal:

```
SELECT customer_first, customer_last
FROM some_table
UNION
SELECT cust_no, cust_phone
FROM some_table
```

Although both SELECTs are taken from the same table, and the two base tables are therefore union compatible, the result tables returned by the two SELECTs are *not* union compatible and the union therefore cannot be performed. The *cust_no* column has a domain of INT and therefore doesn't match the CHAR domain of the *customer_first* column.

Performing Union Using the Same Source Tables

A typical use of UNION in interactive SQL is a replacement for a predicate with an OR. As an example, consider this query:

```
SELECT first_name, last_name
FROM customer JOIN sale JOIN volume
WHERE isbn = '978-1-11111-128-1'
UNION
SELECT first_name, last_name
FROM customer JOIN sale JOIN volume
WHERE isbn = '978-1-11111-143-1';
```

It produces the following output

```
first_name | last_name
-----------+-----------
Janice     | Jones
Janice     | Smith
```

The DBMS processes the query by performing the two SE-LECTs. It then combines the two individual result tables into one, eliminating duplicate rows. To remove the duplicates, the DBMS sorts the result table by every column in the table and then scans it for matching rows placed next to one another. (That is why the rows in the result are in alphabetical order by the author's first name.) The information returned by the preceding query is the same as the following:

```
SELECT first_name, last_name
FROM customer JOIN sale JOIN volume
WHERE isbn = '978-1-11111-128-1'
    OR isbn = '978-1-11111-143-1';
```

However, there are two major differences. First, when you use the complex predicate that contains OR, most DBMSs retain the duplicate rows. In contrast, the query with the UNION operator removes them automatically.

The second difference is in how the queries are processed. The query that performs a union make two passes through the *volume* table, one for each of the individual SELECTs, making only a single comparison with the ISBN value in each row. The query that uses the OR in its predicate makes only one pass through the table but must make two comparison when testing most rows.[1]

---

[1]   Some query optimizers do not behave in this way. You will need to check with either a DBA or a system programmer (someone who knows a great deal about your DBMS) to find out for certain.

Which query will execute faster? If you include a DISTINCT in the query with an OR predicate, then it will return the same result as the query that performs a union. However, if you are using a DBMS that does not remove duplicates automatically and you can live with the duplicate rows, then the query with the OR predicate will be faster.

Note: If you want a union to retain all rows—including the duplicates—use UNION ALL instead of UNION.

Performing Union using Different Source Tables

Another common use of UNION is to pull together data from different source tables into a single result table. Suppose, for example, we wanted to obtain a list of books published by Wiley and books that have been purchased by customer number 11. A query to obtain this data can be written as

```
SELECT author_last_first, title
FROM work, book, author, publisher
WHERE work.author_numb = author.author_numb
AND work.work_numb = book.work_numb
AND book.publisher_id = publisher.publisher_id
AND publisher_name = 'Wiley'
UNION
SELECT author_last_first, title
FROM work, book, author, sale, volume
WHERE customer_numb = 11
AND work.author_numb = author.author_numb
AND work.work_numb = book.work_numb
AND book.isbn = volume.isbn
AND volume.sale_id = sale.sale_id;
```

To proess this query, the result of which appear in Figure 6-1, the DBMS performs each separate SELECT and then combines the individual result tables.

```
             author_last_first         |              title
-----------------------------------------+-------------------------------------
 Barth, John                            | Giles Goat Boy
 Bronte, Charlotte                      | Jane Eyre
 Funke, Cornelia                        | Inkdeath
 Rand, Ayn                              | Anthem
 Rand, Ayn                              | Atlas Shrugged
 Twain, Mark                            | Adventures of Huckleberry Finn, The
 Twain, Mark                            | Tom Sawyer
```

Figure 6-1: The result of a union between result tables coming from different source tables

Alternative SQL-92 Union Syntax

The SQL-92 standard introduced an alternative means of making two tables union compatible: the CORRESPONDING BY clause. This syntax can be used when the two source tables have some columns by the names. However, the two source tables need not have completely the same structure.

To use CORRESPONDING BY, you SELECT * from each of the source tables but then indicate the columns to be used for the union in the CORRESPONDING BY clause:

```
SELECT *
FROM table1
WHERE predicate
UNION CORRESPONDING BY (columns_for_union)
SELECT *
FROM table2
WHERE predicate
```

For example, the query to retrieve the names of all customers who had ordered two specific books could be rewritten

```
SELECT *
FROM volume JOIN sale JOIN customer
WHERE isbn = '978-1-11111-128-1'
UNION CORRESPONDING BY (first_name, last_name)
SELECT *
FROM volume JOIN sale JOIN customer
WHERE isbn = '978-1-11111-128-1';
```

To process this query, the DBMS performs the two SELECTs, returning all columns in the tables. However, when the time comes to perform the union, it throws away all columns except those in the parentheses following BY.

Negative Queries

Among the most powerful database queries are those phrased in the negative, such as "show me all the customers who have no made a purchase in the past year." This type of query is particularly tricky because it is asking for data that are not in the database. (The bookstore has data about customers who *have* purchased, but not those who have not.) The only way to perform such a query is to request the DBMS to use the difference operation.

Traditional SQL Negative Queries

The traditional way to perform a query that requires a difference is to use subquery syntax with the NOT IN operator. To do so, the query takes the following general format:

```
SELECT column(s)
FROM table(s)
WHERE column NOT IN (SELECT column
     FROM table(s)
     WHERE predicate)
```

The outer query retrieves a list of all things of interest; the subquery retrieves those that meet the necessary criteria. The NOT IN operator then acts to include all those from the list of all things that *are not* in the set of values returned by the subquery.

As a first example, consider the query that retrieves all books that are not in stock (no rows exist in *volume*):

```
SELECT title
FROM book, work
WHERE book.work_numb = work.work_numb
AND isbn NOT IN (SELECT isbn
     FROM volume);
```

The outer query selects those rows in *books* (the list of all things) whose ISBNs are not in *volume* (the list of things that *are*). The result in Figure 6-2 contains the nine books that do not appear at least once in the *volume* table.

As a second example, we will retrieve the titles of all books for which we don't have a new copy in stock, the result of which can be found in Figure 6-3:

```
SELECT title
FROM work, book
WHERE work.work_numb = book.work_numb
AND book.isbn NOT IN (SELECT isbn
        FROM volume
        WHERE condition_code = 1);
```

In this case, the subquery contains a restrict predicate in its WHERE clause, limiting the rows retrieved by the subquery to new volumes (those with a condition code value of 1). The outer query then copies a book to the result table if the ISBN is *not* in the result of the subquery.

Notice that in both of the sample queries there is no explicit syntax to make the two tables union compatible, something required by the relational algebra *difference* operation. However, the outer query's WHERE clause contains a predicate that

```
title
- - - - - - - - - - - - - - - - - - - - - - - - - - - - - - - - - - - - - - - - - - - - - - - - -
 Jane Eyre
 Villette
 Hound of the Baskervilles
 Lost World, The
 Complete Sherlock Holmes
 Complete Sherlock Holmes
 Tom Sawyer
 Connecticut Yankee in King Arthur's Court, A
 Dune
```

Figure 6-2: *The result of the first SELECT that uses a NOT IN subquery*

```
title                                           |      isbn
------------------------------------------------+------------------
  Jane Eyre                                     | 978-1-11111-111-1
  Jane Eyre                                     | 978-1-11111-112-1
  Villette                                      | 978-1-11111-113-1
  Hound of the Baskervilles                     | 978-1-11111-114-1
  Hound of the Baskervilles                     | 978-1-11111-115-1
  Lost World, The                               | 978-1-11111-116-1
  Complete Sherlock Holmes                      | 978-1-11111-117-1
  Complete Sherlock Holmes                      | 978-1-11111-118-1
  Tom Sawyer                                    | 978-1-11111-120-1
  Connecticut Yankee in King Arthur's Court, A  | 978-1-11111-119-1
  Tom Sawyer                                    | 978-1-11111-121-1
  Adventures of Huckleberry Finn, The           | 978-1-11111-122-1
  Matarese Circle, The                          | 978-1-11111-123-1
  Bourne Supremacy, The                         | 978-1-11111-124-1
  Fountainhead, The                             | 978-1-11111-125-1
  Atlas Shrugged                                | 978-1-11111-127-1
  Kidnapped                                     | 978-1-11111-128-1
  Treasure Island                               | 978-1-11111-130-1
  Sot Weed Factor, The                          | 978-1-11111-131-1
  Dune                                          | 978-1-11111-134-1
  Foundation                                    | 978-1-11111-135-1
  Last Foundation                               | 978-1-11111-137-1
  I, Robot                                      | 978-1-11111-139-1
  Inkheart                                      | 978-1-11111-140-1
  Anthem                                        | 978-1-11111-144-1
```

Figure 6-3: The result of the second SELECT that uses a NOT IN subquery

compares a column taken from the result of the outer query with the same column taken from the result of the subquery. These two columns represent the union compatible tables.

As a final example, consider a query that retrieves the names of all customers who have not made a purchase after 1-Aug-2013. When you are putting together a query of this type, your first thought might be to write the query as follows:

```
SELECT first_name, last_name
FROM customer JOIN sale
WHERE sale_date < '1-Aug-2013';
```

```
first_name   | last_name
-------------+-----------
 Janice      | Jones
 John        | Doe
 Jane        | Doe
 Helen       | Brown
 Helen       | Jerry
 Mary        | Collins
 Peter       | Collins
 Edna        | Hayes
 Franklin    | Hayes
 Peter       | Johnson
 Peter       | Johnson
 John        | Smith
```

Figure 6-4: The result of the third query using a NOT IN subquery

This query, however, won't work as you intend. First of all, the join eliminates all customers who have no purchases in the *sale* table, even though they should be included in the result. Second, the retrieval predicate identifies those customers who placed orders prior to 1-Aug-2013 but says nothing about who may or may not have made a purchase after that date. Customers may have made a purchase prior to 1-Aug-2013, on 1-Aug-2013, after 1-Aug-2013, or any combination of the preceding.

The typical way to perform this query correctly is to use a difference: the difference between all customers and those who *have* made a purchase after 1-Aug-2013. The query—the result of which can be found in Figure 6-4—appears as follows:

```
SELECT first_name, last_name
FROM customer
WHERE customer_numb NOT IN
    (SELECT customer_numb
     FROM sale
     WHERE sale_date >= '1-Aug-2013')
```

Negative Queries using the EXCEPT Operator

The SQL-92 standard added an operator—EXCEPT—that performs a difference operation directly between two union compatible tables. Queries using EXCEPT look very much like a union:

```
SELECT first_name, last_name
FROM customer
EXCEPT
SELECT first_name, last_name
FROM customer, sale
WHERE customer.customer_numb =
            sale.customer_numb
    AND sale_date >= '1-Aug-2013';
```

or

```
SELECT *
FROM customer
EXCEPT CORRESPONDING BY (first_name, last_name)
SELECT *
FROM customer, sale
WHERE customer.customer_numb =
            sale.customer_numb
    AND sale_date >= '1-Aug-2013';
```

Using the first syntax you include two complete SELECT statements that are joined by the keyword EXCEPT. The SELECTs must return union compatible tables. The first SELECT retrieves a list of all things (in this example, all customers); the second retrieves the things that *are* (in this example, customers with sales after 1-Aug-2013). The EXCEPT operator then removes all rows from the first table that appear in the second.

The second syntax retrieves all columns from both sources but uses the CORRESPONDING BY clause to project the columns to make the two tables union compatible.

The EXISTS Operator

The EXISTS operator check the number of rows returned by a subquery. If the subquery contains one or more rows, then the result is true and a row is placed in the result table; otherwise, the result is false and no row is added to the result table.

For example, suppose the online bookstore wants to see the titles of books that have been sold. To write the query using EXISTS, you would use

```
SELECT title
FROM book t1, work
WHERE t1.work_numb = work.work_numb
AND EXISTS (SELECT *
      FROM volume
      WHERE t1.isbn = volume.isbn
      AND selling_price > 0);
```

The preceding is a *correlated subquery*. Rather than completing the entire subquery and then turning to the outer query, the DBMS processes the query in the following manner:

1. Look at a row in *book*.

2. Use the ISBN from that row in the subquery's WHERE clause.

3. If the subquery finds at least one row in *volume* with the same ISBN, place a row in the intermediate result table. Otherwise, do nothing.

4. Repeat steps 1 through 3 for all rows in the *book* table.

5. Join the intermediate result table to *work*.

6. Project the *title* column.

The important thing to recognize here is that the DBMS repeats the subquery for every row in *book*. It is this repeated execution of the subquery that makes this a correlated subquery.

*Note: Depending on your DBMS, you may get better performance using 1 instead of *. This holds true for DB2, and just might work with others.*

When you are using the EXISTS operator, it doesn't matter what follows SELECT in the subquery. EXISTS is merely checking to determine whether any rows are present in the subquery's result table. Therefore, it is easiest simply to use * rather than to specify individual columns. How will this query perform? It will probably perform better than a query that joins *book* and *volume*, especially if the two tables are large. If you were to write the query using an IN subquery—

```
SELECT title
FROM work, book
WHERE work.work_numb = book.work_numb
AND isbn IN (SELECT isbn
      FROM volume);
```

—you would be using an uncorrelated subquery that returned a set of ISBNs that the outer query searches. The more rows returned by the uncorrelated subquery, the closer the performance of the EXISTS and IN queries will be. However, if the uncorrelated subquery returns only a few rows, it will probably perform better than the query containing the correlated subquery.

The INTERSECT Operator

INTERSECT operates on the results of two independent tables and must be performed on union compatible tables. In most cases, the two source tables are each generated by a SELECT. INTERSECT is the relational algebra intersect operation, which returns all rows the two tables have in common. It is the exact opposite of EXCEPT,

As a first example, let's prepare a query that lists all of the rare book store's customers *except* those who have made purchases with a total cost of more than $500. One way to write this query is

```
SELECT first_name, last_name
FROM customer
EXCEPT
SELECT first_name, last_name
FROM customer JOIN sale
WHERE sale_total_amt > 500;
```

Note that those customers who have made multiple purchases, some of which are less than $500 and some of which are greater than $500 will be excluded from the result.

If we replace the EXCEPT with an INTERSECT—

```
SELECT first_name, last_name
FROM customer
INTERSECT
SELECT first_name, last_name
FROM customer JOIN sale
WHERE sale_total_amt > 500;
```

—the query returns the names of those who *have* made a purchase of over $500. As you can see in Figure 6-5, the query results are quite different.

Although SQL is not a complete programming language, it can perform some calculations. SQL recognizes simple arithmetic expressions involving column names and literal values. (When you are working with embedded SQL, you can also use host language variables.) For example, if you wanted to compute a discounted price for a volume, the computation could be written

Performing Arithmetic

```
asking_price *.9
```

Output from the query using EXCEPT	Output from the query using INTERSECT
`first_name	last_name`	`first_name	last_name`
`------------+----------`	`------------+----------`
` Edna	Hayes`	` Franklin	Hayes`
` Helen	Jerry`	` Janice	Jones`
` Jane	Doe`	
` Jane	Smith`	
` Janice	Smith`	
` Jon	Jones`	
` Mary	Collins`	
` Peter	Collins`	

Figure 6-5: Output of queries using EXCEPT and INTERSECT

UNION vs. EXCEPT vs. INTERSET

One way to compare the operation of UNION, EXCEPT, and INTERSECT is to look at graphic representations, as in Figure 6-6. Each circle represents a table of data; the dark areas where the images overlap represent the rows returned by a query using the respective operation. As you can see, INTERSECT returns the area of overlap, EXCEPT returns everything *except* the overlap, and UNION returns everything.

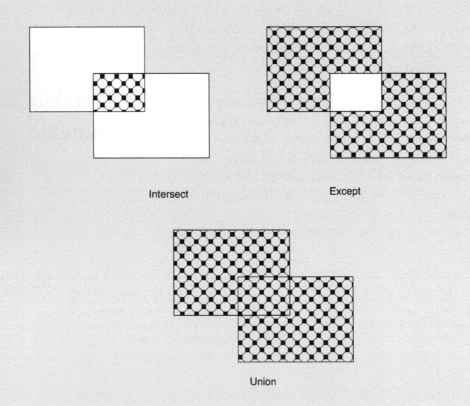

Figure 6-6: Operation of the SQL INTERSECT, EXCEPT, and UNION operators

```
       isbn        | asking_price | discounted_price
-------------------+--------------+-----------------
 978-1-11111-146-1 |        30.00 |           27.000
 978-1-11111-122-1 |        75.00 |           67.500
 978-1-11111-130-1 |       150.00 |          135.000
 978-1-11111-126-1 |       110.00 |           99.000
 978-1-11111-139-1 |       200.00 |          180.000
```

Figure 6-7: Output of a query that includes a computed column

You could then incorporate this into a query as

```
SELECT isbn, asking_price,
     asking_price * .9 AS discounted_price
FROM volume
WHERE sale_id = 6;
```

The result of the preceding query can be found in Figure 6-7.

SQL recognizes the arithmetic operators in Table 6-1. Compared with a general-purpose programming language, this list is fairly limited. For example, there are no operators for exponentiation or modulo division. This means that if you need more sophisticated arithmetic manipulations, you will probably need to use embedded SQL to retrieve the data into host language variables, and perform the arithmetic using the host programming language.

Arithmetic Operators

Table 6-1: SQL arithmetic operations

Operator	Meaning	Example
+	Unary +: Preserve the sign of the value	+balance
-	Unary -: Change the sign of the value	-balance
*	Multiplication: Multiply two values	balance * tax_rate
/	Division: Divide one value by another	balance / numb_items
+	Addition: Add two values	balance + new_charge

Operator Precedence

The rows in Table 6-1 appear in the general order of the operators' *precedence*. (Both unary operators have the same precedence, followed by multiplication and division. Addition and subtraction have the lowest precedence.) This means when multiple operations appear in the same expression, the DBMS evaluates them according to their predetermined order. For example, because the unary operators have the same precedence, for the expression

```
-balance * tax_rate
```

the DBMS will first change the sign of the value in the *balance* column and then multiply it by the value in the *tax_rate* column.

When more than one operator of the same precedence appears in the same expression, they are evaluated from left to right. Therefore, in the expression

```
balance + new_charges - payments
```

the DBMS will first add the new charges to the balance and then subtract the payments from the sum.

Sometimes the default precedence can produced unexpected results. Assume that you want to evaluate the expression

```
12 / 3 * 2
```

When the operators are evaluated from left to right, the DBMS divides 12 by 3 and then multiplies the 4 by 2, producing an 8. However, what if you really wanted to perform the multiplication first, followed by the division? (The result would be 2.)

To change the order of evaluation, you use parentheses to surround the operations that should be performed first:

```
12 / (3 * 2)
```

Just as it does when you use parentheses to change the order of evaluation of logical operators, whenever the DBMS sees a set of parentheses, it knows to evaluate what is inside the parentheses first, regardless of the precedence of the operators.

Keep in mind that you can nest one set of parentheses within another:

```
12 / (3 * (1 + 2))
```

In this example, the DBMS evaluates the innermost parentheses first (the addition), moves to the outer set of parentheses (the multiplication), and finally evaluates the division.

There is no limit to how deep you can nest parentheses. However, be sure that each opening parenthesis is paired with a closing parenthesis.

The SQL core standard contains one operator and several functions for manipulating character strings.

String Manipulation
Concatenation

As you saw in Chapter 2 when we were discussing joins using concatenated foreign keys, the concatenation operator—||—pastes one string on the end of another. It can be used for format output as well as concatenate keys for searching. For example, the rare book store could get an alphabetical list of customer names formatted as *last, first* (see Figure 6-8) with:

```
SELECT last_name || ', ' || first_name
     AS cat_name
FROM customer
ORDER BY last_name, first_name;
```

Notice that the concatenation includes a literal string to place the comma and space between the last and first names. The concatenation operation knows nothing about normal English spacing; it simply places one string on the end of another. Therefore, it is up to the user to include any necessary spacing and punctuation.

```
cat_name
----------------
 Brown, Helen
 Collins, Mary
 Collins, Peter
 Doe, Jane
 Doe, John
 Hayes, Edna
 Hayes, Franklin
 Jerry, Helen
 Johnson, Peter
 Johnson, Peter
 Jones, Janice
 Jones, Jon
 Smith, Jane
 Smith, Janice
 Smith, John
```

Figure 6-8: The result of a concatenation

UPPER and LOWER

When a DBMS evaluates a literal string against stored data, it performs a case-sensitive search. This means that upper- and lowercase letters are different: 'JONES' is not the same as 'Jones.' You can get around such problems using the UPPER and LOWER functions to convert stored data to a single case.

For example, assume that someone at the rare book store is not certain of the case in which customer names are stored. To perform a case-insensitive search for customers with a specific last name, the person could use

```
SELECT customer_numb, first_name, last_name
FROM customer
WHERE UPPER(last_name) = 'SMITH';
```

The result—

```
customer_numb | first_name | last_name
---------------+------------+----------
            5 | Jane       | Smith
            6 | Janice     | Smith
           15 | John       | Smith
```

—includes rows for customers whose last names are made up of the characters S-M-I-T-H, regardless of case. The UPPER function converts the data stored in the database to uppercase before making the comparison in the WHERE predicate. You obtain the same effect by using LOWER instead of UPPER.

The TRIM function removes leading and/or trailing characters from a string. The various syntaxes for this function and their effects are summarized in Table 6-2.

TRIM

You can place TRIM in any expression that contains a string. For example, if you are using characters to store a serial number with leading 0s (for example, 0012), you can strip those 0s when performing a search:

```
SELECT item_description
FROM items
WHERE TRIM (Leading '0' FROM item_numb) = '25'
```

The SUBSTRING function extracts portions of a string. It has the following general syntax:

SUBSTRING

```
SUBSTRING (source_string, FROM starting_posi-
    tion FOR number_of_characters)
```

Table 6-2: The various forms of the SQL TRIM function

Function	Result	Comments
TRIM (' word ')	'word'	Default: removes both leading and trailing blanks
TRIM (BOTH ' ' FROM ' word ')	'word '	Removes leading and trailing blanks
TRIM (LEADING ' ' FROM ' word ')	'word '	Removes leading blanks
TRIM (TRAILING ' ' FROM ' word ')	' word'	Removes trailing blanks
TRIM (BOTH '*' FROM '*word*')	'word'	Removes leading and trailing *

Mixed versus Single Case in Stored Data

There is always the temptation to require that text data be stored as all uppercase letters to avoid the need to use UPPER and LOWER in queries. For the most part, this isn't a good idea. First, text in all uppercase is difficult to read. Consider the following two lines of text:

```
WHICH IS EASIER TO READ? ALL CAPS OR MIXED
CASE?
```

```
Which is easier to read? All caps or mixed
case?
```

Our eyes have been trained to read mixed upper- and lower-case letters. In English, for example, we use letter case cues to locate the start of sentences and to identify proper nouns. Text in all caps removes those cues, making the text more difficult to read. The "sameness" of all uppercase also makes it more difficult to differentiate letters and thus to understand the words.

For example, if the rare book store wanted to extract the first character of a customer's first name, the function call would be written

```
SUBSTRING (first_name FROM 1 FOR 1)
```

The substring being created begins at the first character of the column and is one character long.

You could then incorporate this into a query with

```
SELECT SUBSTRING (first_name FROM 1 FOR 1)
     || '. ' || last_name AS whole_name
FROM customer;
```

The results can be found in Figure 6-9.

Date and Time Manipulation

SQL DBMSs provide column data types for dates and times. When you store data using these data types, you make it possible for SQL to perform chronological operations on those values. You can, for example, subtract two dates to find out the number of days between them or add an interval to a date to advance the date a specified number of days. In this section you will read about the types of date manipulations that SQL provides along with a simple way to get current date and time information from the computer.

The core SQL standard specifies four column data types that relate to dates and times (jointly referred to as *datetime* data types):

◊ DATE: A date only

◊ TIME: A time only

◊ TIMESTAMP: A combination of date and time

◊ INTERVAL: The interval between two of the preceding data types

As you will see in the next two sections, these can be combined in a variety of ways.

Date and Time System Values

To help make date and time manipulations easier, SQL lets you retrieve the current date and/or time with the following three keywords:

◊ CURRENT_DATE: Returns the current system date

◊ CURRENT_TIME: Returns the current system time

◊ CURRENT_TIMESTAMP: Returns a combination of the current system date and time

```
whole_name
- - - - - - - - - - -
 J. Jones
 J. Jones
 J. Doe
 J. Doe
 J. Smith
 J. Smith
 H. Brown
 H. Jerry
 M. Collins
 P. Collins
 E. Hayes
 F. Hayes
 P. Johnson
 P. Johnson
 J. Smith
```

Figure 6-9: Output of a query including the SUBSTRING function

For example, to see all sales made on the current day, someone at the rare book store uses the following query:

```
SELECT first_name, last_name, sale_id
FROM customer JOIN sale
WHERE sale_date = CURRENT_DATE;
```

You can also use these system date and time values when performing data entry, as you will read about beginning in Chapter 8.

Date and Time Interval Operations

SQL dates and times can participate in expressions that support queries such as "how many days/months/years in between?" and operations such as "add 30 days to the invoice date." The types of date and time manipulations available with SQL are summarized in Table 6-3. Unfortunately, expressions involving these operations aren't as straightforward as they might initially appear. When you work with date and time intervals, you must also specify the portions of the date and/or time that you want.

Each datetime column will include a selection of the following fields:

◊ MILLENNIUM

◊ CENTURY

◊ DECADE

◊ YEAR

◊ QUARTER

◊ MONTH

◊ DAY

◊ HOUR

◊ MINUTE

◊ SECOND

◊ MILLISECONDS

◊ MICROSECONDS

Table 6-3: Datetime arithmetic

Expression	Result
DATE ± integer	DATE
DATE ± time_interval	TIMESTAMP
DATE + time	TIMESTAMP
INVERVAL ± INTERVAL	INTERVAL
TIMESTAMP ± INTERVAL	TIMESTAMP
TIME ± time_interval	TIME
DATE - DATE	integer
TIME - TIME	INTERVAL
integer * INTERVAL	INTERVAL

When you write an expression that includes an interval, you can either indicate that you want the interval expressed in one of those fields (for example, DAY for the number of days between two dates) or specify a range of fields (for example, YEAR TO MONTH to give you an interval in years and months). The *start field* (the first field in the range) can be only YEAR, DAY, HOUR, or MINUTE. The second field in the range (the *end field*) must be a chronologically smaller unit than the start field.

Note: There is one exception to the preceding rule. If the start field is YEAR, then the end field must be MONTH.

To see the number of years between a customer's orders and the current date, someone at the rare book store might use

```
SELECT CURRENT_DATE - sale_date YEAR
FROM sale
WHERE customer_numb = 6;
```

To see the same interval expressed in years and months, the query would be rewritten as

```
SELECT CURRENT_DATE - sale_date YEAR TO MONTH
FROM sale
WHERE customer_numb = 6;
```

To add 7 days to an order date to give a customer an approximate delivery date, someone at the rare book store would write a query like

```
SELECT sale_date + INTERVAL '7' DAY
FROM sale
WHERE sale_id = 12;
```

Notice that when you include an interval as a literal, you precede it with the keyword INTERVAL, put the interval's value in single quotes, and follow it with the datetime unit in which the interval is expressed.

The SQL OVERLAPS operator is a special-purpose keyword that returns true or false, depending on whether two date-time intervals overlap. The operator has the following general syntax:

```
SELECT (start_date1, end_date1)
OVERLAPS (start_date2, end_date2)
```

An expression such as

```
SELECT (DATE '16-Aug-2013', DATE '31-Aug-2013')
OVERLAPS
(DATE '18-Aug-2013', DATE '9-Sep-2013');
```

produces the following result:

```
overlaps
----------
t
```

Notice that the dates being compared are preceded by the keyword DATE and surrounded by single quotes. Without the specification of the type of data in the operation, SQL doesn't know how to interpret what is within the quotes.

The two dates and/or times that are used to specify an interval can be either DATE/TIME/TIMESTAMP values or they can be intervals For example, the following query checks to see whether the second range of dates is within 90 days of the first start date and returns false:

```
SELECT (DATE '16-Aug-2013', INTERVAL '90 DAYS')
OVERLAPS
(DATE '12-Feb-2013', DATE '4-Jun-2013');
```

Note: Because the OVERLAPS operator returns a Boolean, it can be used as the logical expression in a CASE statement.

EXTRACT

The EXTRACT operator pulls out a part of a date and/or time. It has the following general format:

```
EXTRACT (datetime_field FROM datetime_value)
```

For example, the query

```
SELECT EXTRACT (YEAR FROM CURRENT_DATE);
```

returns the current year.

In addition to the datetime fields you saw earlier in this section, EXTRACT also can provide the day of the week (DOW) and the day of the year (DOY).

CASE Expressions

The SQL CASE expression, much like a CASE in a general purpose programming language, allows a SQL statement to pick from among a variety of actions based on the truth of logical expressions. Like arithmetic and string operations, the CASE statement generates a value to be displayed and therefore is part of the SELECT clause.

The CASE expression has the following general syntax:

```
CASE
      WHEN logical condition THEN action
      WHEN logical condition THEN action
      :
      :
      ELSE default action
END
```

It fits within a SELECT statement with the structure found in Figure 6-10.

The CASE does not necessarily need to be the last item in the SELECT clause. The END keyword can be followed by a comma and other columns or computed quantities.

```
SELECT column1, column2,
CASE
WHEN logical condition THEN action
        WHEN logical condition THEN action
        :
        :
        ELSE default action
END
FROM table(s)
WHERE predicate;
```

Figure 6-10: Using CASE within a SELECT statement

As an example, assume that the rare book store wants to offer discounts to users based on the price of a book. The more the asking price for the book, the greater the discount. To include the discounted price in the output of a query, you could use

```
SELECT isbn, asking_price,
CASE
        WHEN asking_price < 50
            THEN asking_price * .95
        WHEN asking_price < 75
            THEN asking_price * .9
        WHEN asking_price < 100
            THEN asking_price * .8
        ELSE asking_price * .75
END
FROM volume;
```

The preceding query displays the ISBN and the asking price of a book. It then evaluates the first CASE expression following WHEN. If that condition is true, the query performs the computation, displays the discounted price, and exits the CASE. If the first condition is false, the query proceeds to the second WHEN, and so on. If none of the conditions are true, the query executes the action following ELSE. (The ELSE is optional.)

The first portion of the output of the example query appears in Figure 6-11. Notice that the value returned by the CASE construct appears in a column named *case*. You can, however, rename the computed column just as you would rename any other computed column by adding AS followed by the desired name.

The output of the modified statement—

```
SELECT isbn, asking_price,
CASE
     WHEN asking_price < 50
          THEN asking_price * .95
     WHEN asking_price < 75
          THEN asking_price * .9
     WHEN asking_price < 100
          THEN asking_price * .8
     ELSE asking_price * .75
END AS discounted_price
FROM volume;
```

—can be found in Figure 6-12.

```
      isbn         | asking_price |   case
-------------------+--------------+----------
978-1-11111-111-1  |      175.00  | 131.2500
978-1-11111-131-1  |       50.00  |  45.000
978-1-11111-137-1  |       80.00  |  64.000
978-1-11111-133-1  |      300.00  | 225.0000
978-1-11111-142-1  |       25.95  | 2465.25
978-1-11111-146-1  |       22.95  | 2180.25
978-1-11111-144-1  |       80.00  |  64.000
978-1-11111-137-1  |       50.00  |  45.000
978-1-11111-136-1  |       75.00  |  60.000
978-1-11111-136-1  |       50.00  |  45.000
978-1-11111-143-1  |       25.00  | 2375.00
978-1-11111-132-1  |       15.00  | 1425.00
978-1-11111-133-1  |       18.00  | 1710.00
978-1-11111-121-1  |      110.00  |  82.5000
978-1-11111-121-1  |      110.00  |  82.5000
978-1-11111-121-1  |      110.00  |  82.5000
```

Figure 6-11: Default output of a SELECT statement containing CASE

```
      isbn         | asking_price | discounted_price
-------------------+--------------+------------------
978-1-11111-111-1  |      175.00  |         131.2500
978-1-11111-131-1  |       50.00  |          45.000
978-1-11111-137-1  |       80.00  |          64.000
978-1-11111-133-1  |      300.00  |         225.0000
978-1-11111-142-1  |       25.95  |         2465.25
978-1-11111-146-1  |       22.95  |         2180.25
978-1-11111-144-1  |       80.00  |          64.000
978-1-11111-137-1  |       50.00  |          45.000
978-1-11111-136-1  |       75.00  |          60.000
978-1-11111-136-1  |       50.00  |          45.000
978-1-11111-143-1  |       25.00  |         2375.00
978-1-11111-132-1  |       15.00  |         1425.00
978-1-11111-133-1  |       18.00  |         1710.00
978-1-11111-121-1  |      110.00  |          82.5000
978-1-11111-121-1  |      110.00  |          82.5000
978-1-11111-121-1  |      110.00  |          82.5000
```

Figure 6-12: CASE statement output using a renamed column for the CASE value

Working with Groups of Rows

The queries you have seen so far in this book for the most part operate on one row at a time. However, SQL also includes a variety of keywords and functions that work on groups of rows—either an entire table or a subset of a table. In this chapter you will read about what you can do to and with grouped data.

Note: Many of the functions that you will be reading about in this chapter are often referred to as SQL's OLAP (Online Analytical Processing) functions.

Set Functions

The basic SQL *set*, or *aggregate*, *functions* (summarized in Table 7-1) compute a variety of measures based on values in a column in multiple rows. The result of using one of these set functions is a computed column that appears only in a result table.

The basic syntax for a set function is

```
Function_name (input_argument)
```

You place the function call following SELECT, just as you would an arithmetic calculation. What you use for an input argument depends on which function you are using.

Table 7-1: SQL set functions

Function	Meaning
Functions implemented by most DBMSs	
COUNT	Returns the number of rows
SUM	Returns the total of the values in a column from a group of rows
AVG	Returns the average of the values in a column from a group of rows
MIN	Returns the minimum value in a column from among a group of rows
MAX	Returns the maximum value in a column from among a group of rows
Less widely implemented functions	
COVAR_POP	Returns a population's covariance
COVAR_SAMP	Returns the covariance of a sample
REGR_AVGX	Returns the average of an independent variable
REGR_AVGY	Returns the average of a dependent variable
REGR_COUNT	Returns the number of independent/dependent variable pairs that remain in a population after any rows that have null in either variable have been removed
REGR_INTERCEPT	Returns the Y-intercept of a least-squares-fit linear equation
REGR_R2	Returns the square of the correlation coefficient R
REGR_SLOPE	Returns the slope of a least-squares-fit linear equation
REGR_SXX	Returns the sum of the squares of the values of an independent variable
REGR_SXY	Returns the product of pairs of independent and dependent variable values
REGR_SYY	Returns the sum of the square of the values of a dependent variable
STDDEV_POP	Returns the standard deviation of a population
STDDEV_SAMP	Returns the standard deviation of a sample
VAR_POP	Returns the variance of a population
VAR_SAMP	Returns the variance of a sample

Note: For the most part, you can count on a SQL DBMS support-
ing COUNT, SUM, AVG, MIN, and MAX. In addition, many
DBMSs provide additional aggregate functions for measures such
as standard deviation and variance. Consult the DBMSs docu-
mentation for details.

The COUNT function is somewhat different from other SQL
set functions in that instead of making computations based on
data values, it counts the number of rows in a table. To use it,
you place COUNT (*) in your query. COUNT's input argument is always an asterisk:

COUNT

```
SELECT COUNT (*)
FROM volume;
```

The response appears as

```
count
-------
    71
```

To count a subset of the rows in a table, you can apply a
WHERE predicate:

```
SELECT COUNT (*)
FROM volume
WHERE isbn = '978-1-11111-141-1';
```

The result—

```
Count
-------
    7
```

—tells you that the store has sold or has in stock seven books
with an ISBN of 978-1-11111-141-1. It does not tell you
how many copies of the book are in stock or how many were
purchased during any given sale because the query is simply
counting the number of rows in which the ISBN appears. It
does not take into account data in any other column.

Alternatively, the store could determine the number distinct items contained in a specific order with a query like

```
SELECT COUNT (*)
FROM volume
WHERE sale_id = 6;
```

When you use * as an input parameter to the COUNT function, the DBMS includes all rows. However, if you wish to exclude rows that have nulls in a particular column, you can use the name of the column as an input parameter. To find out how many volumes are currently in stock, the rare book store could use

```
SELECT COUNT (selling_price)
FROM volume;
```

If every row in the table has a value in the *selling_date* column, then COUNT (*selling_date*) is the same as COUNT (*). However, if any rows contain null, then the count will exclude those rows. There are 71 rows in the *volume* table. However, the count returns a value of 43, indicating that 43 volumes have not been sold and therefore are in stock.

You can also use COUNT to determine how many unique values appear in any given column by placing the keyword DISTINCT in front of the column name used as an input parameter. For example, to find out how many different books appear in the *volume* table, the rare book store would use

```
SELECT COUNT (DISTINCT isbn)
FROM volume;
```

The result—27—is the number of unique ISBNs in the table.

SUM

If someone at the rare book store wanted to know the total amount of an order so that value could be inserted into the *sale* table, then the easiest way to obtain this value is to add up the values in the *selling_price* column:

```
SELECT SUM (selling_price)
FROM volume
WHERE sale_id = 6;
```

The result appears as

```
  sum
- - - - - - - -
 505.00
```

In the preceding example, the input argument to the SUM function was a single column. However, it can also be an arithmetic operation. For example, to find the total of a sale if the books are discounted 15 percent, the rare book store could use the following query:

```
SELECT SUM (selling_price * .85)
FROM volume
WHERE sale_id = 6;
```

The result—

```
   sum
- - - - - - - - - -
 429.2500
```

—is the total of the multiplication of the selling price times the selling percentage after the discount.

If we needed to add tax to a sale, a query could then multiply the result of the SUM by the tax rate:

```
SELECT SUM (selling_price * .85) * 1.0725
FROM volume
WEHRE sale_id = 6;
```

producing a final result of 429.2500.

Note: Rows that contain nulls in any column involved in a SUM are excluded from the computation.

AVG

The AVG function computes the average value in a column. For example, to find the average price of a book, someone at the rare book store could use a query like

```
SELECT AVG (selling_price)
FROM volume;
```

The result is 68.2313953488372093 (approximately $68.23).

Note: Rows that contain nulls in any column involved in an AVG are excluded from the computation.

MIN and MAX

The MIN and MAX functions return the minimum and maximum values in a column or expression. For example, to see the maximum price of a book, someone at the rare book store could use a query like

```
SELECT MAX (selling_price)
FROM volume;
```

The result is a single value: $205.00.

The MIN and MAX functions are not restricted to columns or expression that return numeric values. If someone at the rare book store wanted to seethe latest date on which a sale had occurred, then

```
SELECT MAX (sale_date)
FROM volume;
```

returns the chronologically latest date (in our particular sample data, 01-Sep-13).

By the same token, if you use

```
SELECT MIN (last_name)
FROM customer;
```

you will receive the alphabetically first customer last name (Brown).

Set functions can also be used in WHERE predicates to generate values against which stored data can be compared. Assume, for example, that someone at the rare book store wants to see the titles and cost of all books that were sold that cost more than the average cost of a book.

The strategy for preparing this query is to use a subquery that returns the average cost of a sold book and to compare the cost of each book in the *volume* table to that average:

```
SELECT title, selling_price
FROM work, book, volume
WHERE work.work_numb = book.work_numb
AND book.isbn = volume.isbn
AND selling_price > (SELECT AVG (selling_price)
                     FROM volume);
```

Although it would seem logical that the DBMS would calculate the average once and use the result of that single computation to compare to rows in the *volume*, that's not what happens. This is actually an uncorrelated subquery; the DBMS recalculates the average for every row in *volume*. As a result, a query of this type will perform relatively slowly on large amounts of data. You can find the result in Figure 7-1.

One of the problems with the output of the SUM and AVG functions that you saw in the preceding section of this chapter is that they give you no control over the *precision* (number of places to the right of the decimal point) of the output. One way to solve that problem is to change the data type of the result to something that has the number of decimal places you want using the CAST function.

Changing Data Types: CAST

CAST requires that you know a little something about SQL data types. Although we will cover them in depth in Chapter 8, a brief summary can be found in Table 7-2.

```
title                              | selling_price
-----------------------------------+---------------
Jane Eyre                          |        175.00
Giles Goat Boy                     |        285.00
Anthem                             |         76.10
Tom Sawyer                         |        110.00
Tom Sawyer                         |        110.00
Adventures of Huckleberry Finn, The|         75.00
Treasure Island                    |        120.00
Fountainhead, The                  |        110.00
I, Robot                           |        170.00
Fountainhead, The                  |         75.00
Giles Goat Boy                     |        125.00
Fountainhead, The                  |         75.00
Foundation                         |         75.00
Treasure Island                    |        150.00
Lost in the Funhouse               |         75.00
Hound of the Baskervilles          |         75.00
```

Figure 7-1: Output of a query that uses a set function in a subquery

Table 7-2: SQL data types for use with the CAST function

Data Type	Arguments	Explanation
DECIMAL (n, m)	n: Total length of number, including decimal point; m: number of digits to the right of the decimal point	A signed floating point number
INT		A signed integer
VARCHAR (n)	n: Maximum number of characters allowed	A text value that can be as large as the number of characters actually stored, up to the maximum specified
CHAR (n)	n: Maximum number of characters allowed	A fixed-length character value
DATE		A date
TIME		A time
TIMESTAMP		A combination date and time value

CAST has the general syntax

```
CAST (source_data AS new_data_type)
```

To restrict the output of the average price of books to a precision of 2, you could then use

```
CAST (AVG (selling_price) AS DECIMAL (10,2))
```

and incorporate it into a query using

```
SELECT CAST (AVG (selling_price) AS DECIMAL
(10,2))
FROM volume;
```

The preceding specifies that the result should be displayed as a decimal number with a maximum of 10 characters (including the decimal point) with two digits to the right of the decimal point. The result is 68.23, a more meaningful currency value than the original 68.2313953488372093.

CAST also can be used, for example, to convert a string of characters into a date. The expression

```
CAST ('10-Aug-2013' AS DATE)
```

returns a datetime value.

Valid conversions for commonly used data types are represented by the light gray boxes in Table 7-3. Those conversions that may be possible if certain conditions are met are represented by the dark gray boxes. In particular, if you are attempting to convert a character string into a shorter string, the result will be truncated.

Grouping Queries

SQL can group rows based on matching values in specified columns and computer summary measures for each group. When these *grouping queries* are combined with the set functions that you saw earlier in this chapter, SQL can provide simple reports without requiring any special programming.

Table 7-3: Valid data type conversion for commonly used data types (light gray boxes are valid; dark gray boxes may be valid)

Original data type	New Data Type						
	Integer or fixed point	Floating point	Variable length character	Fixed length character	Date	Time	Timestamp
Integer or fixed point	valid	valid	valid	valid			
Floating point	valid	valid	valid	valid			
Character (fixed or variable length)	valid	valid	may be valid	may be valid	valid	valid	valid
Date			valid	valid	valid		valid
Time			valid	valid		valid	valid
Timestamp			valid	valid	valid	valid	valid

Forming Groups

To form a group, you add a GROUP BY clause to a SELECT statement, followed by the columns whose values are to be used to form the groups. All rows whose values match on those columns will be placed in the same group.

For example, if someone at the rare book store wants to see how many copies of each book edition have been sold, he or she can use a query like

```
SELECT isbn, COUNT(*)
FROM volume
GROUP BY isbn
ORDER BY isbn;
```

The query forms groups by matching ISBNs. It displays the ISBN and the number of rows in each group (see Figure 7-2).

There is a major restriction that you must observe with a grouping query: You can display values only from columns that are used to form the groups. As an example, assume that someone at the rare book store wants to see the number of copies of each title that have been sold. A working query could be written

```
        isbn         | count
---------------------+-------
978-1-11111-111-1 |     1
978-1-11111-115-1 |     1
978-1-11111-121-1 |     3
978-1-11111-122-1 |     1
978-1-11111-123-1 |     2
978-1-11111-124-1 |     1
978-1-11111-125-1 |     1
978-1-11111-126-1 |     3
978-1-11111-127-1 |     5
978-1-11111-128-1 |     1
978-1-11111-129-1 |     1
978-1-11111-130-1 |     4
978-1-11111-131-1 |     4
978-1-11111-132-1 |     3
978-1-11111-133-1 |     5
978-1-11111-135-1 |     1
978-1-11111-136-1 |     6
978-1-11111-137-1 |     4
978-1-11111-138-1 |     4
978-1-11111-139-1 |     4
978-1-11111-140-1 |     1
978-1-11111-141-1 |     7
978-1-11111-142-1 |     1
978-1-11111-143-1 |     1
978-1-11111-144-1 |     1
978-1-11111-145-1 |     3
978-1-11111-146-1 |     2
```

Figure 7-2: *Counting the members of a group*

```
SELECT title, COUNT (*)
FROM volume, book, work
WHERE volume.isbn = book.isbn
AND book.work_numb = work.work_numb
GROUP BY title
ORDER BY title;
```

The result appears in Figure 7-3. The problem with this approach is that titles may duplicate. Therefore, it would be better to group by the work number. However, given the restriction as to what can be displayed, you wouldn't be able to display the title.

The solution is to make the DBMS do a bit of extra work: Group by both the work number and the title. The DBMS will

```
                             title            | count
-------------------------------------------------+--------
Adventures of Huckleberry Finn, The          |    1
Anathem                                       |    1
Anthem                                        |    4
Atlas Shrugged                                |    5
Bourne Supremacy, The                         |    1
Cryptonomicon                                 |    2
Foundation                                    |   11
Fountainhead, The                             |    4
Giles Goat Boy                                |    5
Hound of the Baskervilles                     |    1
I, Robot                                      |    4
Inkdeath                                      |    7
Inkheart                                      |    1
Jane Eyre                                     |    1
Kidnapped                                     |    2
Last Foundation                               |    4
Lost in the Funhouse                          |    3
Matarese Circle, The                          |    2
Snow Crash                                    |    1
Sot Weed Factor, The                          |    4
Tom Sawyer                                    |    3
Treasure Island                               |    4
```

Figure 7-3: Grouping rows by book title

then form groups that have the same values in both columns. There is only one title per work number, so the result will be the same as that in Figure 7-3 if there are no duplicated titles. We therefore gain the ability to display the title when grouping by the work number. The query could be written

```
SELECT work.work_numb title, COUNT (*)
FROM volume, book, work
WHERE volume.isbn = book.isbn
AND book.work_numb = work.work_numb
GROUP BY work_numb, title
ORDER BY title;
```

As you can see in Figure 7-4, the major difference between the two results is the appearance of the work number column.

work_numb	title	count
9	Adventures of Huckleberry Finn, The	1
28	Anathem	1
30	Anthem	4
14	Atlas Shrugged	5
12	Bourne Supremacy, The	1
31	Cryptonomicon	2
23	Foundation	11
13	Fountainhead, The	4
20	Giles Goat Boy	5
3	Hound of the Baskervilles	1
25	I, Robot	4
27	Inkdeath	7
26	Inkheart	1
1	Jane Eyre	1
16	Kidnapped	2
24	Last Foundation	4
19	Lost in the Funhouse	3
11	Matarese Circle, The	2
29	Snow Crash	1
18	Sot Weed Factor, The	4
8	Tom Sawyer	3
17	Treasure Island	4

Figure 7-4: *Grouped output using two grouping columns*

You can use any of the set functions in a grouping query. For example, someone at the rare book store could generate the total cost of all sales with

```
SELECT sale_id, SUM (selling_price)
FROM volume
GROUP BY sale_id;
```

The result can be seen in Figure 7-5. Notice that the last line of the result has nulls for both output values. This occurs because those volumes that haven't been sold have null for the sale ID and selling price. If you wanted to clean up the output, removing rows with nulls, you could add a WHERE clause:

```
SELECT sale_id, SUM (selling_price)
FROM volume
WHERE NOT (sale_id IS NULL)
GROUP BY sale_id;
```

```
sale_id |   sum
--------+--------
      1 | 510.00
      2 | 125.00
      3 |  58.00
      4 | 110.00
      5 | 110.00
      6 | 505.00
      7 |  80.00
      8 | 130.00
      9 |  50.00
     10 | 125.00
     11 | 200.00
     12 | 225.00
     13 |  25.95
     14 |  80.00
     15 | 100.00
     16 | 130.00
     17 | 100.00
     18 | 100.00
     19 |  95.00
     20 |  75.00
```

Figure 7-5: The result of using a set function in a grouping query

Including the title as part of the GROUP BY clause was a trick to allow us to display the title in the result. However, more commonly we use multiple columns to created nested groups. For example, if someone at the rare book store wanted to see the total cost of purchases made by each customer per day, the query could be written

```
SELECT customer.customer_numb, sale_date,
      SUM (selling_price)
FROM customer, sale, volume
WHERE customer.customer_numb =
      sale.customer_numb
AND sale.sale_id = volume.sale_id
GROUP BY customer.customer_numb, sale_date;
```

Because the *customer_numb* column is listed first in the GROUP BY clause, its values are used to create the outer groupings. The DBMS then groups orders by date *within* customer numbers. The default output (see Figure 7-6) is somewhat hard to interpret because the outer groupings are not in order. However, if you add an ORDER BY clause to sort the output by customer number, you can see the ordering by date within each customer (see Figure 7-7).

Restricting Groups

The grouping queries you have seen to this point include all the rows in the table. However, you can restrict the rows that are included in grouped output using one of two strategies:

◊ Restrict the rows before groups are formed.

◊ Allow all groups to be formed and then restrict the groups.

The first strategy is performed with the WHERE clause in the same way we have been restricting rows to this point. The second requires a HAVING clause, which contains a predicate that applies to groups after they are formed.

```
customer_numb |      sale_date       |   sum
--------------+----------------------+--------
            1 | 15-JUN-13 00:00:00   |   58.00
            6 | 01-SEP-13 00:00:00   |   95.00
            2 | 01-SEP-13 00:00:00   |   75.00
            5 | 22-AUG-13 00:00:00   |  100.00
            2 | 25-JUL-13 00:00:00   |  130.00
            1 | 25-JUL-13 00:00:00   |  100.00
            8 | 07-JUL-13 00:00:00   |   50.00
            5 | 07-JUL-13 00:00:00   |  130.00
           12 | 05-JUL-13 00:00:00   |  505.00
            8 | 05-JUL-13 00:00:00   |   80.00
            6 | 10-JUL-13 00:00:00   |   80.00
            2 | 10-JUL-13 00:00:00   |   25.95
            6 | 30-JUN-13 00:00:00   |  110.00
            9 | 10-JUL-13 00:00:00   |  200.00
           10 | 10-JUL-13 00:00:00   |  225.00
            4 | 30-JUN-13 00:00:00   |  110.00
           11 | 10-JUL-13 00:00:00   |  125.00
           11 | 12-JUL-13 00:00:00   |  100.00
            1 | 05-JUN-13 00:00:00   |  125.00
            1 | 29-MAY-13 00:00:00   |  510.00
```

Figure 7-6: Group by two columns (default row order)

Assume, for example, that someone at the rare book store wants to see the number of books ordered at each price over $75. One way to write the query is to use a WHERE clause to throw out rows with a selling price less than or equal to $75:

```
SELECT selling_price, count (*)
FROM volume
WHERE selling_price > 75
GROUP BY selling_price;
```

Alternatively, you could let the DBMS form the groups and then throw out the groups that have a cost less than or equal to $75 with a HAVING clause:

```
SELECT selling_price, count (*)
FROM volume
GROUP BY selling_price
HAVING selling_price > 75;
```

```
customer_numb |      sale_date       |   sum
--------------+----------------------+---------
            1 | 29-MAY-13 00:00:00   |  510.00
            1 | 05-JUN-13 00:00:00   |  125.00
            1 | 15-JUN-13 00:00:00   |   58.00
            1 | 25-JUL-13 00:00:00   |  100.00
            2 | 10-JUL-13 00:00:00   |   25.95
            2 | 25-JUL-13 00:00:00   |  130.00
            2 | 01-SEP-13 00:00:00   |   75.00
            4 | 30-JUN-13 00:00:00   |  110.00
            5 | 07-JUL-13 00:00:00   |  130.00
            5 | 22-AUG-13 00:00:00   |  100.00
            6 | 30-JUN-13 00:00:00   |  110.00
            6 | 10-JUL-13 00:00:00   |   80.00
            6 | 01-SEP-13 00:00:00   |   95.00
            8 | 05-JUL-13 00:00:00   |   80.00
            8 | 07-JUL-13 00:00:00   |   50.00
            9 | 10-JUL-13 00:00:00   |  200.00
           10 | 10-JUL-13 00:00:00   |  225.00
           11 | 10-JUL-13 00:00:00   |  125.00
           11 | 12-JUL-13 00:00:00   |  100.00
           12 | 05-JUL-13 00:00:00   |  505.00
```

Figure 7-7: Grouping by two columns (rows sorted by outer grouping column)

The result in both cases is the same (see Figure 7-8). However, the way in which the query is processing is different.

```
selling_price | count
--------------+-------
        76.10 |   1
       110.00 |   3
       120.00 |   1
       125.00 |   1
       150.00 |   1
       170.00 |   1
       175.00 |   1
       285.00 |   1
```

Figure 7-8: Restrict groups to volumes that cost more than $75

Windowing and Window Functions

Grouping queries have two major drawbacks: They can't show you individual rows at the same time they show you computations made on groups of rows and you can't see data from non-grouping columns unless you resort to the group making trick shown earlier. The more recent versions of the SQL standard (from SQL:2003 onward), however, include a new way to compute aggregate functions yet display the individual rows within each group: *windowing*. Each window (or *partition*) is a group of rows that share some criteria, such as a customer number. The window has a *frame* that "slides" to present to the DBMS the rows that share the same value of the partitioning criteria. *Window functions* are a special group of functions that can act only on partitions.

Note: By default, a window frame includes all the rows as its partition. However, as you will see shortly, that can be changed.

Let's start with a simple example. Assume that someone at the rare book store wants to see the volumes that were part of each sale as well as the average cost of books for each sale. A grouping query version wouldn't be able to show the individual volumes in a sale nor would it be able to display the ISBN or sale ID unless those two values were added to the GROUP BY clause. However, what if the query were written using windowing—

```
SELECT sale_id, isbn, CAST (AVG(selling_price)
OVER (PARTITION BY sale_id) as DECIMAL (7.2))
FROM volume
WHERE sale_id IS NOT NULL;
```

—it would produce the result in Figure 7-9. Notice that the individual volumes from each sale are present and that the rightmost column contains the average cost for the specific sale on which a volume was sold. This mean that the *avg* column in the result table is the same for all rows that come from a given sale.

The query itself includes two new keywords: OVER and PAR-TITION BY. (The CAST is present to limit the display of the average to a normal money display format and therefore isn't part of the windowing expression.) OVER indicates that the rows need to be grouped in some way. PARTITION BY indicates the criteria by which the rows are to be grouped. This particular example computes the average for groups of rows that are separated by their sale ID.

To help us explore more of what windowing can do, we're going to need a sample table with some different types of data. Figure 7-10 (a) shows you a table that describes sales representative and the value of product they have sold in specific quarters. The names of the sales reps are stored in the table labeled (b) in Figure 7-10.

Note: Every windowing query must have an ORDER clause, but you can leave out the PARTITION BY clause—using only OVER ()—if you want all the rows in the table to be in the same partition.

Ordering the Partitioning

When SQL processes a windowing query, it scans the rows in the order they appear in the table. However, you control the order in which rows are processed by adding an ORDER BY clause to the PARTITION BY expression. As you will see, doing so can alter the result, producing a "running" average or sum.

Consider first a query similar to the first windowing example:

```
SELECT first_name, last_name, quarter, year,
     sales_amt, CAST (AVG (sales_amt OVER
     (PARTITION BY quarterly_sales.sales_id) AS
     DECIMAL (7,2))
FROM rep_names, quarterly_sales
WHERE rep_names.id = quarterly_sales.id;
```

```
 sale_id |         isbn          |   avg
---------+-----------------------+--------
       1 | 978-1-11111-111-1     | 170.00
       1 | 978-1-11111-131-1     | 170.00
       1 | 978-1-11111-133-1     | 170.00
       2 | 978-1-11111-142-1     |  41.67
       2 | 978-1-11111-146-1     |  41.67
       2 | 978-1-11111-144-1     |  41.67
       3 | 978-1-11111-143-1     |  42.00
       3 | 978-1-11111-132-1     |  42.00
       3 | 978-1-11111-133-1     |  42.00
       3 | 978-1-11111-121-1     |  42.00
       5 | 978-1-11111-121-1     | 110.00
       6 | 978-1-11111-146-1     | 101.00
       6 | 978-1-11111-122-1     | 101.00
       6 | 978-1-11111-130-1     | 101.00
       6 | 978-1-11111-126-1     | 101.00
       6 | 978-1-11111-139-1     | 101.00
       7 | 978-1-11111-125-1     |  40.00
       7 | 978-1-11111-131-1     |  40.00
       8 | 978-1-11111-126-1     |  65.00
       8 | 978-1-11111-133-1     |  65.00
       9 | 978-1-11111-139-1     |  50.00
      10 | 978-1-11111-133-1     | 125.00
      11 | 978-1-11111-126-1     |  66.67
      11 | 978-1-11111-130-1     |  66.67
      11 | 978-1-11111-136-1     |  66.67
      12 | 978-1-11111-130-1     | 112.50
      12 | 978-1-11111-132-1     | 112.50
      13 | 978-1-11111-129-1     |  25.95
      14 | 978-1-11111-141-1     |  40.00
      14 | 978-1-11111-141-1     |  40.00
      15 | 978-1-11111-127-1     |  50.00
      15 | 978-1-11111-141-1     |  50.00
      16 | 978-1-11111-141-1     |  43.33
      16 | 978-1-11111-123-1     |  43.33
      16 | 978-1-11111-127-1     |  43.33
      17 | 978-1-11111-133-1     |  50.00
      17 | 978-1-11111-127-1     |  50.00
      18 | 978-1-11111-135-1     |  33.33
      18 | 978-1-11111-131-1     |  33.33
      18 | 978-1-11111-127-1     |  33.33
      19 | 978-1-11111-128-1     |  47.50
      19 | 978-1-11111-136-1     |  47.50
      20 | 978-1-11111-115-1     |  75.00
```

Figure 7-9: Output of a simple query using windowing

```
(a)

quarterly_sales
id | quarter | year | sales_amt
---+---------+------+-----------
 1 |       1 | 2012 |     518.00
 1 |       2 | 2012 |    1009.00
 1 |       3 | 2012 |    1206.00
 1 |       4 | 2012 |     822.00
 1 |       1 | 2013 |     915.00
 1 |       2 | 2013 |    1100.00
 2 |       1 | 2012 |     789.00
 2 |       2 | 2012 |    1035.00
 2 |       3 | 2012 |    1235.00
 2 |       4 | 2012 |    1355.00
 2 |       1 | 2013 |    1380.00
 2 |       2 | 2013 |    1400.00
 3 |       3 | 2012 |     795.00
 3 |       4 | 2012 |     942.00
 3 |       1 | 2013 |    1012.00
 3 |       2 | 2013 |    1560.00
 4 |       1 | 2012 |    1444.00
 4 |       2 | 2012 |    1244.00
 4 |       3 | 2012 |     987.00
 4 |       4 | 2012 |     502.00
 5 |       1 | 2012 |    1200.00
 5 |       2 | 2012 |    1200.00
 5 |       3 | 2012 |    1200.00
 5 |       4 | 2012 |    1200.00
 5 |       1 | 2013 |    1200.00
 5 |       2 | 2013 |    1200.00
 6 |       1 | 2012 |     925.00
 6 |       2 | 2012 |    1125.00
 6 |       3 | 2012 |    1250.00
 6 |       4 | 2012 |    1387.00
 6 |       1 | 2013 |    1550.00
 6 |       2 | 2013 |    1790.00
 7 |       1 | 2013 |    2201.00
 7 |       2 | 2013 |    2580.00
 8 |       1 | 2013 |    1994.00
 8 |       2 | 2013 |    2121.00
 9 |       1 | 2013 |     502.00
 9 |       2 | 2013 |     387.00
10 |       1 | 2013 |     918.00
10 |       2 | 2013 |    1046.00
```

Figure 7-10:   Quarterly sales tables for use in windowing examples
(continued on next page)

```
(b)

rep_names

 id | first_name | last_name
----+------------+-----------
  1 | John       | Anderson
  2 | Jane       | Anderson
  3 | Mike       | Baker
  4 | Mary       | Carson
  5 | Bill       | Davis
  6 | Betty      | Esteban
  7 | Jack       | Fisher
  8 | Jen        | Grant
  9 | Larry      | Holmes
 10 | Lily       | Imprego
```

Figure 7-10: (continued) Quarterly sales tables for use in windowing

As you can see in Figure 7-11, the output is what you would expect: Each line displays the average sales for the given sales representative. The DBMS adds up the sales for all quarters for the salesperson and divides by the number of quarters. However, if we add an ORDER BY clause to force processing in quarter and year order, the results are quite different.

The query changes only a bit:

```
SELECT first_name, last_name, quarter, year,
    sales_amt, CAST (AVG (sales_amt
    OVER (PARTITION BY quarterly_sales.sales_id
ORDER BY year, quarter) AS DECIMAL (7,2))
FROM rep_names, quarterly_sales
WHERE rep_names.id = quarterly_sales.id;
```

However, in this case the ORDER BY clause forces the DBMS to process the rows in year and quarter order. As you can see in Figure 7-12, the average column is now a moving average. What is actually happening is that the window frame is changing in the partition each time a row is scanned. The first row in a partition is averaged by itself. Then the window frame

first_name	last_name	quarter	year	sales_amt	avg
John	Anderson	1	2012	518.00	928.33
John	Anderson	1	2013	915.00	928.33
John	Anderson	2	2012	1009.00	928.33
John	Anderson	2	2013	1100.00	928.33
John	Anderson	3	2012	1206.00	928.33
John	Anderson	4	2012	822.00	928.33
Jane	Anderson	1	2012	789.00	1199.00
Jane	Anderson	1	2013	1380.00	1199.00
Jane	Anderson	2	2012	1035.00	1199.00
Jane	Anderson	2	2013	1400.00	1199.00
Jane	Anderson	3	2012	1235.00	1199.00
Jane	Anderson	4	2012	1355.00	1199.00
Mike	Baker	1	2013	1012.00	1077.25
Mike	Baker	2	2013	1560.00	1077.25
Mike	Baker	3	2012	795.00	1077.25
Mike	Baker	4	2012	942.00	1077.25
Mary	Carson	1	2012	1444.00	1044.25
Mary	Carson	2	2012	1244.00	1044.25
Mary	Carson	3	2012	987.00	1044.25
Mary	Carson	4	2012	502.00	1044.25
Bill	Davis	1	2012	1200.00	1200.00
Bill	Davis	1	2013	1200.00	1200.00
Bill	Davis	2	2012	1200.00	1200.00
Bill	Davis	2	2013	1200.00	1200.00
Bill	Davis	3	2012	1200.00	1200.00
Bill	Davis	4	2012	1200.00	1200.00
Betty	Esteban	1	2012	925.00	1337.83
Betty	Esteban	1	2013	1550.00	1337.83
Betty	Esteban	2	2012	1125.00	1337.83
Betty	Esteban	2	2013	1790.00	1337.83
Betty	Esteban	3	2012	1250.00	1337.83
Betty	Esteban	4	2012	1387.00	1337.83
Jack	Fisher	1	2013	2201.00	2390.50
Jack	Fisher	2	2013	2580.00	2390.50
Jen	Grant	1	2013	1994.00	2057.50
Jen	Grant	2	2013	2121.00	2057.50
Larry	Holmes	1	2013	502.00	444.50
Larry	Holmes	2	2013	387.00	444.50
Lily	Imprego	1	2013	918.00	982.00
Lily	Imprego	2	2013	1046.00	982.00

Figure 7-11: Computing the windowed average without ordering the rows

expands to include two rows and both are included in the average. This process repeats until all the rows in the partition have been included in the average. Therefore, each line in the output of this version of the query gives you the average at the end of that quarter rather than for all quarters.

Note: If you replace the AVG in the preceding query with the SUM function, you'll get a running total of the sales made by each sales representative.

If you don't want a running sum or average, you can use a *frame clause* to change the size of the window (which rows are included). To suppress the cumulative average in Figure 7-12, you would add ROWS BETWEEN UNBOUNDED PRECEDING AND CURRENT ROW following the columns by which the rows within the partition are to be ordered.

Specific Functions

The window functions built into SQL perform actions that are only meaningful on partitions. Many of them include ways to rank data, something that is difficult to do otherwise. They can also number rows and compute distribution percentages. In this section we'll look at some of the specific functions: what they can do for you and how they work.

Note: Depending on your DBMS, you may find additional window functions available, some of which are not part of the SQL standard.

RANK

The RANK function orders and numbers rows in a partition based on the value in a particular column. It has the general format

```
RANK () OVER (partition_specifications)
```

first_name	last_name	quarter	year	sales_amt	avg
John	Anderson	1	2012	518.00	518.00
John	Anderson	2	2012	1009.00	763.50
John	Anderson	3	2012	1206.00	911.00
John	Anderson	4	2012	822.00	888.75
John	Anderson	1	2013	915.00	894.00
John	Anderson	2	2013	1100.00	928.33
Jane	Anderson	1	2012	789.00	789.00
Jane	Anderson	2	2012	1035.00	912.00
Jane	Anderson	3	2012	1235.00	1019.67
Jane	Anderson	4	2012	1355.00	1103.50
Jane	Anderson	1	2013	1380.00	1158.80
Jane	Anderson	2	2013	1400.00	1199.00
Mike	Baker	3	2012	795.00	795.00
Mike	Baker	4	2012	942.00	868.50
Mike	Baker	1	2013	1012.00	916.33
Mike	Baker	2	2013	1560.00	1077.25
Mary	Carson	1	2012	1444.00	1444.00
Mary	Carson	2	2012	1244.00	1344.00
Mary	Carson	3	2012	987.00	1225.00
Mary	Carson	4	2012	502.00	1044.25
Bill	Davis	1	2012	1200.00	1200.00
Bill	Davis	2	2012	1200.00	1200.00
Bill	Davis	3	2012	1200.00	1200.00
Bill	Davis	4	2012	1200.00	1200.00
Bill	Davis	1	2013	1200.00	1200.00
Bill	Davis	2	2013	1200.00	1200.00
Betty	Esteban	1	2012	925.00	925.00
Betty	Esteban	2	2012	1125.00	1025.00
Betty	Esteban	3	2012	1250.00	1100.00
Betty	Esteban	4	2012	1387.00	1171.75
Betty	Esteban	1	2013	1550.00	1247.40
Betty	Esteban	2	2013	1790.00	1337.83
Jack	Fisher	1	2013	2201.00	2201.00
Jack	Fisher	2	2013	2580.00	2390.50
Jen	Grant	1	2013	1994.00	1994.00
Jen	Grant	2	2013	2121.00	2057.50
Larry	Holmes	1	2013	502.00	502.00
Larry	Holmes	2	2013	387.00	444.50
Lily	Imprego	1	2013	918.00	918.00
Lily	Imprego	2	2013	1046.00	982.00

Figure 7-12: Computing the windowed average with row ordering

Table 7-4: Window frame clauses

Frame Clause	Action
RANGE UNBOUNDED PRECEDING *(default)* RANGE BETWEEN UNBOUNDED PRECEDING AND CURRENT ROW	Include all rows within the current partition through the current row, based on the ordering specified in the ORDER BY clause. If no ORDER BY clause, include all rows. If there are duplicate rows, their values are included only once.

RANGE BETWEEN UNBOUNDED PRECEDING AND
    UNBOUNDED FOLLOWING
ROWS BETWEEN UNBOUNDED PRECEDING AND
    UNBOUNDED FOLLOWING
	Include all rows in the partition.

ROWS UNBOUNDED PRECEDING ROWS BETWEEN UNBOUNDED PRECEDING AND CURRENT ROW	Include all rows within the current partition through the current row, including duplicate rows.

For example, if we wanted to see all the quarterly sales data ranked for all the sales representatives, the query could look like the following:

```
SELECT first_name, last_name quarter, year,
sales_amt, RANK () OVER (order by sales_amt
desc)
FROM rep_names, quarterly_sales
WHERE rep_names.id = quarterly_sales.id;
```

The output appears in Figure 7-13. Notice that because there is no PARTITION BY clause in the query, all of the rows in the table are part of a single ranking.

Alternatively, you could rank each sales representative's sales to identify the quarters in which each representative sold the most. The query would be written

```
SELECT first_name, last_name, quarter, year,
sales_amt, RANK () OVER (PARTITION BY quarter-
ly_sales.id ORDER BY sales_amt DESC)
```

first_name	last_name	quarter	year	sales_amt	rank
Jack	Fisher	2	2013	2580.00	1
Jack	Fisher	1	2013	2201.00	2
Jen	Grant	2	2013	2121.00	3
Jen	Grant	1	2013	1994.00	4
Betty	Esteban	2	2013	1790.00	5
Mike	Baker	2	2013	1560.00	6
Betty	Esteban	1	2013	1550.00	7
Mary	Carson	1	2012	1444.00	8
Jane	Anderson	2	2013	1400.00	9
Betty	Esteban	4	2012	1387.00	10
Jane	Anderson	1	2013	1380.00	11
Jane	Anderson	4	2012	1355.00	12
Betty	Esteban	3	2012	1250.00	13
Mary	Carson	2	2012	1244.00	14
Jane	Anderson	3	2012	1235.00	15
John	Anderson	3	2012	1206.00	16
Bill	Davis	4	2012	1200.00	17
Bill	Davis	3	2012	1200.00	17
Bill	Davis	1	2013	1200.00	17
Bill	Davis	2	2013	1200.00	17
Bill	Davis	1	2012	1200.00	17
Bill	Davis	2	2012	1200.00	17
Betty	Esteban	2	2012	1125.00	23
John	Anderson	2	2013	1100.00	24
Lily	Imprego	2	2013	1046.00	25
Jane	Anderson	2	2012	1035.00	26
Mike	Baker	1	2013	1012.00	27
John	Anderson	2	2012	1009.00	28
Mary	Carson	3	2012	987.00	29
Mike	Baker	4	2012	942.00	30
Betty	Esteban	1	2012	925.00	31
Lily	Imprego	1	2013	918.00	32
John	Anderson	1	2013	915.00	33
John	Anderson	4	2012	822.00	34
Mike	Baker	3	2012	795.00	35
Jane	Anderson	1	2012	789.00	36
John	Anderson	1	2012	518.00	37
Larry	Holmes	1	2013	502.00	38
Mary	Carson	4	2012	502.00	38
Larry	Holmes	2	2013	387.00	40

Figure 7-13: Ranking all quarterly sales

first_name	last_name	quarter	year	sales_amt	rank
John	Anderson	3	2012	1206.00	1
John	Anderson	2	2013	1100.00	2
John	Anderson	2	2012	1009.00	3
John	Anderson	1	2013	915.00	4
John	Anderson	4	2012	822.00	5
John	Anderson	1	2012	518.00	6
Jane	Anderson	2	2013	1400.00	1
Jane	Anderson	1	2013	1380.00	2
Jane	Anderson	4	2012	1355.00	3
Jane	Anderson	3	2012	1235.00	4
Jane	Anderson	2	2012	1035.00	5
Jane	Anderson	1	2012	789.00	6
Mike	Baker	2	2013	1560.00	1
Mike	Baker	1	2013	1012.00	2
Mike	Baker	4	2012	942.00	3
Mike	Baker	3	2012	795.00	4
Mary	Carson	1	2012	1444.00	1
Mary	Carson	2	2012	1244.00	2
Mary	Carson	3	2012	987.00	3
Mary	Carson	4	2012	502.00	4
Bill	Davis	1	2012	1200.00	1
Bill	Davis	2	2012	1200.00	1
Bill	Davis	3	2012	1200.00	1
Bill	Davis	4	2012	1200.00	1
Bill	Davis	1	2013	1200.00	1
Bill	Davis	2	2013	1200.00	1
Betty	Esteban	2	2013	1790.00	1
Betty	Esteban	1	2013	1550.00	2
Betty	Esteban	4	2012	1387.00	3
Betty	Esteban	3	2012	1250.00	4
Betty	Esteban	2	2012	1125.00	5
Betty	Esteban	1	2012	925.00	6
Jack	Fisher	2	2013	2580.00	1
Jack	Fisher	1	2013	2201.00	2
Jen	Grant	2	2013	2121.00	1
Jen	Grant	1	2013	1994.00	2
Larry	Holmes	1	2013	502.00	1
Larry	Holmes	2	2013	387.00	2
Lily	Imprego	2	2013	1046.00	1
Lily	Imprego	1	2013	918.00	2

Figure 7-14: Ranking within partitions

```
FROM rep_names, quarterly_sales
WHERE rep_names.id = quarterly_sales.id;
```

The output can be found in Figure 7-14.

Note: When there are duplicate rows, the RANK function includes only one of the duplicates. However, if you want to include the duplicates, use DENSE_RANK instead of RANK.

PERCENT_RANK

The PERCENT_RANK function calculates the percentage rank of each value in a partition relative to the other rows in the partition. It works in the same way as RANK but rather than returning a rank as an integer, it returns the percentage point at which a given value occurs in the ranking.

Let's repeat the query used to illustrate RANK, using PER-CENT_RANK instead:

```
SELECT first_name, last_name, quarter, year,
sales_amt, PERCENT_RANK () OVER (PARTITION BY
quarterly_sales.id ORDER BY sales_amt DESC)
FROM rep_names, quarterly_sales
WHERE rep_names.id = quarterly_sales.id;
```

The output can be found in Figure 7-15. As you can see, the result is exactly the same as the RANK result in Figure 7-14, with the exception of the rightmost column, where the integer ranks are replaced by percentage ranks.

ROW_NUMBER

The ROW_NUMBER function numbers the rows within a partition. For example, to number the sales representatives in alphabetical name order, the query could be

```
SELECT first_name, last_name ROW_NUMBER () OVER
(ORDER BY last_name, first_name) AS row_numb
FROM rep_names;
```

As you can see from Figure 7-16, the result includes all 10 sales representatives, numbered and sorted by name (last name as the outer sort).

Choosing Windowing or Grouping for Ranking

Given the power and flexibility of SQL's windowing capabilities, is there any time that you should use grouping queries instead? Actually, there just might be. Assume that you want to rank all the sales representatives based on their total sales rather than simply ranking within each person's sales. Probably the easiest way to get that ordered result is to use a query like the following:

```
SELECT id, SUM (sales_amt)
FROM quarterly_sales
GROUP BY id
ORDER BY SUM (sales_amt) DESC;
```

You get the following output:

```
 id |    sum
----+--------
  6 | 8027.00
  5 | 7200.00
  2 | 7194.00
  1 | 5570.00
  7 | 4781.00
  3 | 4309.00
  4 | 4177.00
  8 | 4115.00
 10 | 1964.00
  9 |  889.00
```

The highest ranking total sales are at the top of the listing, the lowest ranking sales at the bottom. The output certainly isn't as informative as the windowed output because you can't include the names of the sales representatives, but it does provide the required information.

Yes, you could use a windowing function to generate the same output, but it still needs to include the aggregate function SUM to generate the totals for each sales representative:

```
SELECT id, SUM (SUM(sales_amt)) OVER (PARTITION
BY quarterly_sales.id)
FROM quarterly_sales
GROUP BY id
ORDER BY SUM (sales_amt) DESC;
```

It works, but it's more code and the presence of the GROUP BY clause still means that you can't include the names unless they are part of the grouping criteria. Using the GROUP BY and the simple SUM function just seems easier.

Note: The SQL standard allows a named ROW_NUMBER result to be placed in a WHERE clause to restrict the number of rows in a query. However, not all DBMSs allows window functions in WHERE clauses.

CUME_DIST

When we typically think of a cumulative distribution, we think of something like that in Table 7-5, where the actual data values are gathered into ranges. SQL, however, can't discern the data grouping that we would like and therefore must consider each value (whether it be an individual data row or a row of an aggregate function result) as a line in the distribution.

The CUME_DIST function returns a value between 0 and 1, which when multiplied by 100, gives you a percentage. Each "range" in the distribution, however, is a single value. In other words, the frequency of each group is always 1. As an example, let's create a cumulative frequency distribution of the total sales made by each sales representative. The SQL can be written

```
SELECT id, SUM (sales_amt), 100 * (CUME_DIST()
OVER (ORDER BY SUM (sales_amt))) AS cume_dist
FROM quarterly_sales
GROUP BY id
ORDER BY cume_dist;
```

As you can see in Figure 7-17, each range is a group of 1.

first_name	last_name	quarter	year	sales_amt	percent_rank
John	Anderson	3	2012	1206.00	0
John	Anderson	2	2013	1100.00	0.2
John	Anderson	2	2012	1009.00	0.4
John	Anderson	1	2013	915.00	0.6
John	Anderson	4	2012	822.00	0.8
John	Anderson	1	2012	518.00	1
Jane	Anderson	2	2013	1400.00	0
Jane	Anderson	1	2013	1380.00	0.2
Jane	Anderson	4	2012	1355.00	0.4
Jane	Anderson	3	2012	1235.00	0.6
Jane	Anderson	2	2012	1035.00	0.8
Jane	Anderson	1	2012	789.00	1
Mike	Baker	2	2013	1560.00	0
Mike	Baker	1	2013	1012.00	0.333333333333333
Mike	Baker	4	2012	942.00	0.666666666666667
Mike	Baker	3	2012	795.00	1
Mary	Carson	1	2012	1444.00	0
Mary	Carson	2	2012	1244.00	0.333333333333333
Mary	Carson	3	2012	987.00	0.666666666666667
Mary	Carson	4	2012	502.00	1
Bill	Davis	1	2012	1200.00	0
Bill	Davis	2	2012	1200.00	0
Bill	Davis	3	2012	1200.00	0
Bill	Davis	4	2012	1200.00	0
Bill	Davis	1	2013	1200.00	0
Bill	Davis	2	2013	1200.00	0
Betty	Esteban	2	2013	1790.00	0
Betty	Esteban	1	2013	1550.00	0.2
Betty	Esteban	4	2012	1387.00	0.4
Betty	Esteban	3	2012	1250.00	0.6
Betty	Esteban	2	2012	1125.00	0.8
Betty	Esteban	1	2012	925.00	1
Jack	Fisher	2	2013	2580.00	0
Jack	Fisher	1	2013	2201.00	1
Jen	Grant	2	2013	2121.00	0
Jen	Grant	1	2013	1994.00	1
Larry	Holmes	1	2013	502.00	0
Larry	Holmes	2	2013	387.00	1
Lily	Imprego	2	2013	1046.00	0
Lily	Imprego	1	2013	918.00	1

Figure 7-15: Percent ranking within partitions

```
first_name | last_name | row_numb
-----------+-----------+----------
  Jane     | Anderson  |         1
  John     | Anderson  |         2
  Mike     | Baker     |         3
  Mary     | Carson    |         4
  Bill     | Davis     |         5
  Betty    | Esteban   |         6
  Jack     | Fisher    |         7
  Jen      | Grant     |         8
  Larry    | Holmes    |         9
  Lily     | Imprego   |        10
```

Figure 7-16: Row numbering

```
id |   sum   | cume_dist
---+---------+-----------
 9 |  889.00 |        10
10 | 1964.00 |        20
 8 | 4115.00 |        30
 4 | 4177.00 |        40
 3 | 4309.00 |        50
 7 | 4781.00 |        60
 1 | 5570.00 |        70
 2 | 7194.00 |        80
 5 | 7200.00 |        90
 6 | 8027.00 |       100
```

Figure 7-17: A SQL-generated cumulative frequency distribution

Table 7-5: A cumulative frequency distribution

Sales amount	Frequency	Cumulative Frequency	Cumulative Percentage
$0–1999	2	2	20
$2000–3999	0	0	20
$4000–5999	5	7	70
$6000–7999	2	9	90
> $8000	1	10	100

NTILE

NTILE breaks a distribution into a specified number of partitions and indicates which rows are part of which group. SQL keeps the numbers of rows in each group as equal as possible. To see how this works, consider the following query:

```
SELECT id, SUM (sales_amt), NTILE(2)
    OVER (ORDER BY SUM (sales_amt) DESC) AS n2,
    NTILE(3) OVER (ORDER BY SUM
        (sales_amt DESC) as n3,
    NTILE(4) OVER (ORDER BY SUM (sales_amt
        DESC) as n4
FROM quarterly_sales
GROUP BY id;
```

For the result, see Figure 7-18. The columns labeled n2, n3, and n4 contain the results of the NTILE calls. The highest number in each of those columns corresponds to the number of groups into which the data have been placed, which is the same value used as an argument to the function call.

Inverse Distributions: PERCENTILE_CONT and PERCENTILE_DISC

The SQL standard includes two inverse distribution functions—PERCENTILE_CONT and PERCENTILE_DISC—that are most commonly used to compute the median of a distribution. PERCENTILE_CONT assumes that the

id	sum	n2	n3	n4
6	8027.00	1	1	1
5	7200.00	1	1	1
2	7194.00	1	1	1
1	5570.00	1	1	2
7	4781.00	1	2	2
3	4309.00	2	2	2
4	4177.00	2	2	3
8	4115.00	2	3	3
10	1964.00	2	3	4
9	889.00	2	3	4

Figure 7-18: Using the NTILE function to divide data into groups

distribution is continuous and interpolates the median as needed. PERCENTILE_DISC, which assumes a discontinuous distribution, chooses the median from existing data values. Depending on the data themselves, the two functions may return different answers.

The functions have the following general format:

```
PERCENTILE_cont/disc (0.5)
        WITHIN GROUP (optional ordering
            clause)
        OVER (optional partition and ordering
            clauses)
```

If you replace the 0.5 following the name of the function with another probability between 0 and 1, you will get the nth percentile. For example, 0.9 returns the 90th percentile. Each function examines the percent rank of the values in a partition until it finds the one that is equal to or greater than whatever fraction you've placed in parentheses.

When used without partitions, each function returns a single value. For example,

```
SELECT PERCENTILE_CONT (0.5)
    WITHIN GROUP (ORDER BY SUM (sales_amt)
        DESC) AS continuous,
    PERCENTILE_DISC (0.5)
        WITHIN GROUP (ORDER BY SUM (sales_amt
        DESC) AS discontinuous
FROM quarterly_sales
GROUP BY id;
```

Given the sales data, both functions return the same value: 1200. (There are 40 values, and the two middle values are 1200. Even with interpolation the continuous median computes to the same answer.)

If we partition the data by sales representative, then we can compute the median for each sales representative:

```
SELECT first_name, last_name,
    PERCENTILE_CONT (0.5) WITHIN GROUP
        (ORDER BY SUM (sales_amt) DESC) OVER
        (PARTITION BY id) AS continuous,
    PERCENTILE_DISC (0.5) WITHIN GROUP
        (ORDER BY SUM (sales_amt DESC) OVER
        (PARTITION BY id) as discontinuous
FROM quarterly_sales JOIN rep_names
GROUP BY id
ORDER BY last_name, first_name;
```

As you can see in Figure 7-19, the result contains one row for each sales representative, including both medians.

```
first_name | last_name | continuous | discontinuous
-----------+-----------+------------+---------------
John       | Anderson  |     962.0  |        915.0
Jane       | Anderson  |    1295.0  |       1235.0
Mike       | Baker     |     977.0  |        942.0
Mary       | Carson    |    1115.5  |        987.0
Bill       | Davis     |    1200.0  |       1200.0
Betty      | Esteban   |    1318.5  |       1250.0
Jack       | Fisher    |    2350.5  |       2201.0
Jen        | Grant     |    2057.5  |       1994.0
Larry      | Holmes    |     484.5  |        387.0
Lily       | Imprego   |     982.0  |        918.0
```

Figure 7-19: Continuous and discontinuous medians for partitioned data

8

Data Modification

SQL includes three statements for modifying the data in tables INSERT, UPDATE, and DELETE. Most of the time, application programs provide forms-driven data modification, removing the need for end users to issue SQL data modification statements directly to the DBMS. (As you will see, this is a good thing because using SQL data modification statements is rather clumsy.) Nonetheless, if you are developing and testing database elements and need to populate tables and modify data, you will probably be working at the command line with the SQL syntax.

Note: This chapter is where it will make sense that we covered retrieval before data modification.

Inserting Rows

The SQL INSERT statement has two variations: one that inserts a single row into a table and a second that copies one or more rows from another table.

Inserting One Row

To add one row to a table, you use the general syntax

```
INSERT INTO table_name VALUES (value_list)
```

In the preceding form, the value list contains one value for every column in the table, in the order in which the columns were created. For example, to insert a new row into the *customer* table someone at the rare book store might use

```
INSERT INTO customer VALUES
    (8,'Helen','Jerry','16 Main Street',
    'Newtown','NJ','18886','209-555-8888');
```

There are two things to keep in mind when inserting data in this way:

◊ The format of the values in the value list must match the data types of the columns into which the data will be placed. In the current example, the first column requires an integer. The remaining columns all require characters and therefore the values have been surrounded by single quotes.

◊ When you insert a row of data, the DBMS checks any integrity constraints that you have placed on the table. For the preceding example, it will verify that the customer number is unique and not null. If the constraints are not met, you will receive an error message and the row will not be added to the table.

If you do not want to insert data into every column of a table, you can specify the columns into which data should be placed:

```
INSERT INTO table_name (column_list)
    VALUES (value_list)
```

There must be a one-to-one correspondence between the columns in the column list and the values in the value list because the DBMS matches them by their relative positions in the lists.

As an example, assume that someone at the rare book store wants to insert a row into the *book* table but doesn't know the binding type. The SQL would then be written

```
INSERT INTO book (isbn, work_numb, publisher_id,
        edition, copyright_year)
    VALUES ('978-1-11111-199-1',16,2,12,1960);
```

There are five columns in the column list and therefore five values in the value list. The first value in the list will be inserted into the *isbn* column, the second value into the *work_numb* column, and so on. The column omitted from the lists—*binding*—will remain null. You therefore must be sure to place values at least in primary key columns. Otherwise, the DBMS will not permit the insertion to occur.

Although it is not necessary to list column names when inserting values for every column in a table, there is one good reason to do so, especially when embedding the INSERT statement in an application program. If the structure of the table changes—if columns are added, deleted, or rearranged—then an INSERT without column names will no longer work properly. By always specifying column names, you can avoid unnecessary program modifications as your database changes to meet your changing needs.

The SQL INSERT statement can also be used to copy one or more rows from one table to another. The rows that will be copied are specified with a SELECT, giving the statement the following general syntax:

Copying Existing Rows

```
INSERT INTO table_name
    SELECT complete_SELECT_statement
```

The columns in the SELECT must match the columns of the table. For the purposes of this example, we will add a simple table to the rare book store database:

```
summary (isbn, how_many)
```

This table will contain summary information gathered from the *volume* table. To add rows to the new table, the INSERT statement can be written:

```
INSERT INTO summary
    SELECT isbn, COUNT (*)
    FROM volume
    GROUP BY isbn;
```

The result is 27 rows copied into the *summary* table, one for each unique ISBN in the *volume* table.

Note: Should you store summary data like that placed in the table created in the preceding example? The answer is "it depends." If it takes a long time to generate the summary data and you use the data frequently, then storing it probably makes sense. But if you can generate the summary data easily and quickly, then it is just as easy not to store it and to create the data whenever it is needed for output.

Placement of New Rows

Where do new rows go when you add them? That depends on your DBMS. Typically, a DBMS maintains unique internal identifiers for each row that is not accessible to users (something akin to the combination of a row number and a table identifier) to provide information about the row's physical storage location. These identifiers continue to increase in value.

If you were to use the SELECT * syntax on a table, you would see the rows in internal identifier order. At the beginning of a table's life, this order corresponds to the order in which rows were added to the table. New rows appear to go at the "bottom" of the table, after all existing rows. As rows are deleted from the table, there will be gaps in the sequence of row identifiers. However, the DBMS does not reuse them (to "fill in the holes") until it has used up all available identifiers. If a database is very old, very large, and/or very active, the DBMS will run out of new identifier and will then start to reuse those made available by deleted rows. In that case, new rows may appear anywhere in the table. Give that you can view rows in any order by using the ORDER BY clause, it should make absolutely no difference to an end user or an application program where a new row is added.

Updating Data

Although most of today's end users modify existing data using an on-screen form, the SQL statements to modify the data must nonetheless be issued by the program providing the form. For example, as someone at the rare book store adds volumes to a sale, the *volume* table is updated with the selling price and the sale ID. The selling_price is also added to the total amount of the sale in the *sale* table.

The SQL UPDATE statement affects one or more rows in a table, based on row selection criteria in a WHERE predicate. UPDATE as the following general syntax:

```
UPDATE table_name
SET column1 = new_value, column2 = new_value, …
WHERE row_selection_predicate
```

If the WHERE predicate contains a primary key expression, then the UPDATE will affect only one row. For example, to change a customer's address, the rare book store could use

```
UPDATE customer
SET street = '195 Main Street'
    city = 'New Town'
    zip = '11111'
WHERE customer_numb = 5;
```

However, if the WHERE predicate identifies multiple rows, each row that meets the criteria in the predicate will be modified. To raise all $50 prices to $55, someone at the rare book store might write a query as

```
UPDATE books
SET asking_price = 55
WHERE asking_price = 50;
```

Notice that it is possible to modify the value in a column being used to identify rows. The DBMS will select the rows to be modified before making any changes to them.

If you leave the WHERE clause off an UPDATE, the same modification will be applied to every row in the table. For example, assume that we add a column for sales tax to the *sale* table. Someone at the rare book store could use the following statement to compute the tax for every sale:

```
UPDATE sale
SET sales_tax = sale_total_amt * 0.075;
```

The expression in the SET clause takes the current value in the *sale_total_amt* column, multiplies it by the tax rate, and puts it in the *sales_tax* column.

Deleting Rows

Like the UPDATE statement, the DELETE statement affects one or more rows in a table based on row selection criteria in a WHERE predicate. The general syntax for DELETE is

```
DELETE FROM table_name
WHERE row_selection_predicate
```

For example, if a customer decided to cancel an entire purchase, then someone at the rare book store would use something like

```
DELETE FROM sale
WHERE customer_numb = 12 AND sale_date = '05-
Jul-2013';
```

Assuming that all purchases on the same date are considered a single sale, the WHERE predicate identifies only one row. Therefore, only one row is deleted.

When the criteria in a WHERE predicate identify multiple rows, all those matching rows are removed. If someone at the rare book store wanted to delete all sales for a specific customer, then the SQL would be written

```
DELETE FROM sale
WHERE customer_numb = 6;
```

In this case, there are multiple rows for customer number 6, all of which will be deleted.

DELETE is a potentially dangerous operation. If you leave off the WHERE clause—DELETE FROM sale—you will delete every row in the table! (The table remains in the database without any rows.)

The preceding examples of DELETE involve a table that has a foreign key in another table (*sale_id* in *volume*) referencing it. It also has a foreign key of its own (*customer_numb* referencing the primary key of *customer*). You can delete rows containing foreign keys without any effect on the rest of the database, but what happens when you attempt to delete rows that *do* have foreign keys referencing them?

Note: The statement in the preceding paragraph refers to database integrity issues and clearly misses the logical issue of the need to decrement the total sale amount in the sale table whenever a volume is removed from the sale.

Assume, for example, that a customer cancels a purchase. Your first thought might be to delete the row for that sale from the *sale* table. There are, however, rows in the *volume* table that reference that sale and if the row for the sale is removed from *sale*, there will be no primary key for the rows in *volume* to reference and referential integrity will be violated.

What actually happens in such a situation depends on what was specified when the table containing the primary key being referenced was created. There are four options for handling the deletion of primary key rows that have foreign key rows that reference them:

◊ SET NULL: The values of all foreign keys that reference the deleted primary key row are set to null. This is the option we want for our particular example. However,

Deletes and Referential Integrity

nulls cannot be used when the foreign key is part of the primary key of its own table.

◊ SET DEFAULT: The values of all foreign keys that reference the deleted primary key row are set to a default value. This would not be a reasonable solution for our example because we don't want to set a generic sale ID.

◊ CASCADE: When the primary key row is deleted, all foreign key rows that reference it are deleted as well. This is something we definitely don't want to do in our example. Volumes need to stay in the database, sold or unsold.

◊ NO ACTION: Disallow the deletion of a primary key row if there are foreign key rows that reference it. This alternative makes sense for the *customer* table because we do not want to delete any customers who have purchases in the *sale* table. By the same token, we would probably use this option for the *book* table so that we do not delete data about books that we may be likely to purchase for the store.

MERGE

The SQL:2003 standard introduced a very powerful and flexible way to insert, update, or delete data using the MERGE statement. MERGE includes a condition to be tested and alternative sets of actions that are performed when the condition is or is not met. The model behind this statement is the merging of a table of transactions into a master table.

MERGE has the following general syntax:

```
MERGE INTO target_table_name USING source_ta-
ble_name ON merge_condition
WHEN MATCHED THEN
      update/delete_specification
WHEN NOT MATCHED THEN
      insert specification
```

Deleting All Rows: TRUNCATE TABLE

The 2008 SQL standard introduces a new command—TRUNCATE TABLE—that removes all rows from a table more quickly than a DELETE without a WHERE clause. The command's general syntax is

```
TRUNCATE TABLE table_name
```

Like the DELETE without a WHERE clause, the table structure remains intact and in the data dictionary.

There are some limits to using the command:

◊ It cannot be used on a table that has foreign keys referencing it.

◊ It cannot be used on a table on which indexed views are based.

◊ It cannot activate a trigger.

Although DELETE and TRUNCATE TABLE seem to have the same effect, they do work differently. DELETE removes the rows one at a time and writes an entry into the database log file for each row. In contrast, TRUNCATE TABLE deallocates space in the database files, making the space formerly occupied by the truncated table's rows available for other use.

Note: Some DBMSs call MERGE functionality UPSERT.

Notice that when the merge condition is matched (in other words, evaluates as true for a given row) an update and/or delete is performed. When the condition is not matched, an insert is performed. Either the MATCHED or NOT MATCHED clause is optional.

The target table is the table that will be affected by the changes made by the statement. The source table—which can be a base table or a virtual table generated by a SELECT—provides the source of the table. To help you understand how MERGE works, let's use the classic model of applying transactions to a master table. First, we need a transaction table:

```
transactions (sale_id, inventory_id,
        selling_price, sale_date, customer_numb)
```

The *transactions* table contains information about the sale of a single volume. (It really doesn't contain all the necessary rows for the *sale* table, but it will do for this example.) If a row for the sale exists in the *sale* table, then the selling price of the volume should be added to existing sale total. However, if the sale is not in the *sale* table, then a new row should be created and the sale total set to the selling price of the volume. A MERGE statement that will do the trick might be written as

```
MERGE INTO sale S USING transactions T
        ON (S.sale_id = T.sale_id)
WHEN MATCHED THEN
    UPDATE SET sale_total_amt =
        sale_total_amt + selling_price
WHEN NOT MATCHED
    INSERT (sale_id, customer_numb,
        sale_date, sale_total_amt)
    VALUES (T.sale_id, T.customer_numb,
        T.sale_date, T.selling_price);
```

The target table is *sale*; the source table is *transactions*. The merge condition looks for a match between sale IDs. If a match is found, then the UPDATE portion of the command performs the modification of the *sale_total_amt* column. If no match is found, then the insert occurs. Notice that the IN-SERT portion of the command does not need a table name because the table affected by the INSERT has already been specified as the target table.

As we said earlier, the source table for a merge operation doesn't need to be a base table; it can be a virtual table created on the fly using a SELECT. For example, assume that someone at the rare book store needs to keep a table of total purchases made by each customer. The following table can be used to hold that data:

```
summary_stats (customer_numb, year,
     total_purchases)
```

You can find the MERGE statement below. The statement assembles the summary data using a SELECT that extracts the year from the sale date and sums the sale amounts. Then, if a summary row for a year already exists in *summary_stats*, the MERGE adds the amount from the source table to what is stored already in the target table. Otherwise, it adds a row to the target table.

```
MERGE INTO summary_stats AS S USING
     (SELECT customer_numb,
          EXTRACT (YEAR FROM sale_date) AS Y,
               SUM (sale_total_amt AS M) AS T
     FROM sale
     GROUP BY customer_numb, Y)
ON (CAST(S.customer_numb AS CHAR (4)) ||
     CAST (S.year AS CHAR(4)) =
               CAST(T.customer_numb AS CHAR (4)) ||
               CAST (T.year AS CHAR(4)))
WHEN MATCHED
     UPDATE SET total_purchases = T.M
WHEN NOT MATCHED
     INSERT VALUES (customer_numb, Y, M);
```

As powerful as MERGE seems to be, the restriction of UPDATE/DELETE to the matched condition and INSERT to the unmatched prevents it from being able to handle some situations. For example, if someone at the rare book store wanted to archive all orders more than two years old, the process would involve creating a row for each sale that didn't exist in the archive table and then deleting the row from the *sale* table. (We're assuming that the delete cascades, removing all rows from *volume* as well.) The problem is that the delete needs to occur on the unmatched condition, which isn't allowed with the MERGE syntax.

Part III
Managing
Database
Structure

Schemas and Tables

As a complete data manipulation language, SQL contains statements that let you create, modify, and delete structural elements in a database. In this chapter we will begin the discussion of a database's structural elements by looking at schemas and the permanent base tables that you create within them. This discussion will be concluded in Chapter 10, which covers additional structural elements such as views, temporary tables, and indexes.

The actual file structure of a database is implementation dependent, as is the procedure needed to create database files. Therefore, the discussion in this chapter assumes that the necessary database files are already in place.

Database Object Hierarchy

The objects in a database maintained using SQL are arranged in a hierarchy diagrammed in Figure 9-1.[1] The smallest units with which a database works—the columns and rows—appear in the center. These in turn are grouped into tables and views.

The tables and views that constitute a single logical database are collected into a *schema*. Multiple schemas are grouped into *catalogs*, which can then be grouped into *clusters*. A catalog

---

1   Some DBMSs support a "create database" capabiity, which provides an overall named unit for all the elements in a database. However, a "database" isn't a structural element in the SQL standard.

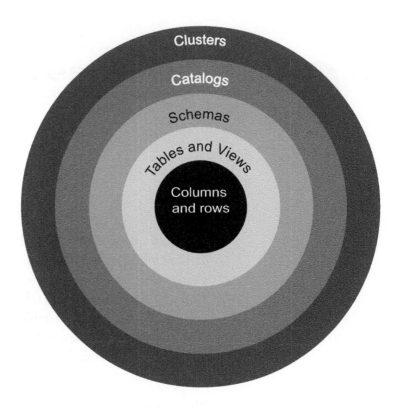

Figure 9-1: The SQL database object hierarchy

usually contains information describing all the schemas handled by one DBMS. Catalog creation is implementation dependent and therefore not part of the SQL standard.

Prior to SQL-92, clusters often represented database files, and the clustering of objects into files was a way to increase database performance. The current concept of a cluster, however, is a group of catalogs that are accessible using the same connection to a database server. None of the groupings of database objects in the SQL standard are related to physical storage structures. If you are working with a centralized mainframe DBMS, you may find multiple catalogs stored in the same database file. However, on smaller or distributed systems, you are just as likely to find one catalog or schema per database file or to find a catalog or schema split between multiple files.

Clusters, catalogs, and schemas are not required elements of a database environment. In a small installation where there is one collection of tables serving a single purpose, for example, it may not even be necessary to create a schema to hold them.

The way in which you name and identify database objects is in some measure dictated by the object hierarchy:

◊ Column names must be unique within the table.

◊ Table names must be unique within the schema.

◊ Schema names must be unique within their catalog.

◊ Catalog names must be unique within their cluster.

As you saw when you were reading about data retrieval, when a column name appears in more than one table in a query, you must specify the table from which a column should be taken (even if it makes no difference which table is used). The general form for specifying duplicate names is

table_name.column_name

If an installation has more than one schema, then you must also indicate the schema in which a table resides:

schema_name.table_name.column_name

This naming convention means that two different schemas can include tables with the same name.

By the same token, if an installation has multiple catalogs, you will need to indicate the catalog from which an object comes

catalog_name.schema_name.table_name.column_name

Naming and Identifying Objects

Note: The SQL standard refers to element names that use the dot notation as "identifier chains."

The names that you assign to database elements can include the following:

◊ Letters

◊ Numbers

◊ Underscores (_)

Names can be up to 128 characters long. They are not case sensitive. (In fact, many SQL command processors convert names to all upper- or lowercase characters before submitting a SQL statement to a DBMS for processing.)

Note: Some DBMSs also allow pound signs (#) and dollar signs ($) in element names, but neither is recognized by SQL queries so their use should be avoided.

Schemas

To a database designer, a schema represents the overall, logical design of a complete database. As far as SQL is concerned, however, a schema is nothing more than a container for tables, views, and other structural elements. It is up to the database designer to place a meaningful group of elements within each schema.

A schema is not required to create tables and views. In fact, if you are installing a database for an environment in which there is likely to be only one logical database, then you can just as easily do without one. However, if more than one database will be sharing the same DBMS and the same server, organizing database elements into schemas can greatly simplify the maintenance of the individual databases.

To create a schema, you use the CREATE SCHEMA statement. In its simplest form, it has the syntax

```
CREATE SCHEMA schema_name
```

as in

```
CREATE SCHEMA rare_books;
```

By default, a schema belongs to the user who created it (the user ID under which the schema was created). The owner of the schema is the only user ID that can modify the schema unless the owner grants that ability to other users.

To assign a different owner to a schema, you add an AUTHORIZATION clause

```
CREATE SCHEMA schema_name AUTHORIZATION owner_
user_ID
```

For example, to assign the rare book store schema to the user ID DBA, someone could use

```
CREATE SCHEMA rare_books AUTHORIZATION dba;
```

When creating a schema, you can also create additional database elements at the same time. To do so, you use braces to group the CREATE statements for the other elements, as in

```
CREATE SCHEMA schema_name AUTHORIZATION owner_
user_ID
{
     other CREATE statements go here
}
```

This automatically assigns the elements within the braces to the schema.

One of the nicest things about a relational database is that you can add or delete database structure elements at any time. There must therefore be a way to specify a current schema for

Identifying the Schema You Want to Use

new database elements after the schema has been created initially with the CREATE SCHEMA statement.

```
SET SCHEMA schema_name
```

To use SET SCHEMA, the user ID under which you are working must have authorization to work with that schema.

Alternatively, you can qualify the name of a database element with the name of the schema. For example, if you are creating a table, then you would use something like:

```
CREATE TABLE schema_name.table_name
```

For DBMSs that do not support SET SCHEMA, this is the only way to attach new database elements to a schema after the schema has been created.

Domains

A *domain* is an expression of the permitted values for a column in a relation. When you define a table, you assign each column a data type (for example, character or integer) that provides a broad domain. A DBMS will not store data that violate that constraint.

The SQL-92 standard introduced the concept of user-defined domains, which can be viewed as user-defined data types that can be applied to columns in tables. (This means that you have to create a domain before you can assign it to a column!)

Domains can be created as part of a CREATE SCHEMA statement or, if your DBMS supports SET SCHEMA, at any time after a schema has been defined.

To create a domain, you use the CREATE DOMAIN statement, which has the following general syntax:

```
CREATE DOMAIN domain_name data_type
    CHECK constraint_name
        (expression_to_validate_values)
```

The CHECK clause is actually a generic way to express a condition that data must meet. It can include a SELECT to validate data against other data stored in the database or it can include a logical expression. In that expression, the keyword VALUE represents the data being checked. Naming the constraint is optional, but doing so makes it possible to access the constraint if you want to remove it at some time in the future.

For example, if the rare book store database should validate the price of a book, someone might create the following domain:

```
CREATE DOMAIN price NUMERIC (7,2)
CHECK price_check (VALUE >= 15);
```

After creating this domain, a column in a table can be given the data type of PRICE. The DBMS will then check to be certain that the value in that column is always greater than or equal to 15. (We will leave a discussion of the data type used in the preceding SQL statement until we cover creating tables in the next section of this chapter.)

The domain mechanism is very flexible. Assume, for example, that you want to ensure that telephone numbers are always stored in the format XXX-XXX-XXXX. A domain to validate that format might be created as

```
CREATE DOMAIN telephone CHAR (12)
    CHECK phone_format
        (SUBSTRING FROM 4 FOR 1 = '-') AND
        SUBSTRING (VALUE FROM 8 FOR 1 = ' ');
```

You can also use the CREATE DOMAIN statement to give a column a default value. For example, the following statement sets up a domain that holds either Y or N and defaults to Y.

```
CREATE DOMAIN char_boolean CHAR (1)
DEFAULT 'Y'
    CHECK (UPPER(VALUE) = 'Y'
    OR UPPER(VALUE) = 'N');
```

Tables

The most important structure within a relational database is the table. Tables contain just about everything, including business data and the data dictionary.

SQL divides its tables into three categories:

◊ Permanent base tables: Permanent base tables are tables whose contents are stored in the database and remain permanently in the database unless they are explicitly deleted.

◊ Global temporary base tables: Global temporary base tables are tables used for working storage that are destroyed at the end of a SQL session. The definitions of the tables are stored in the data dictionary, but their data are not. The tables must be loaded with data each time they are going to be used. Global temporary tables can be used only by the current user, but they are visible to an entire SQL session (either an application program or a user working with an interactive facility.)

◊ Local temporary base tables: Local temporary base tables are similar to global temporary tables. However, they are visible only to the specific program module in which they are created.

Note: Temporary base tables are subtly different from views, which assemble their data by executing a SQL query. You will read more about this difference and how temporary tables are created and used in Chapter 10.

Most of the tables you will use will be permanent base tables. You create them with the CREATE TABLE statement:

```
CREATE TABLE table_name
    (column1_name column1_data_type,
        column1_constraints,
    column2_name column2_data_type,
        column2_constraints, …
    table_constraints)
```

The constraints on a table include declarations of primary and foreign keys. The constraints on a column include whether values in are mandatory as well as other constraints you may decide to include in a CHECK clause.

Each column in a table must be given a data type. Although data types are somewhat implementation dependent, you can expect to find most of the following:

Column Data Types

◊ INTEGER (abbreviated INT): A positive or negative whole number. The number of bits occupied by the value is implementation dependent. On today's desktop computers, an integer is either 32 or 64 bits. Large computers may use up to 128 bits for integers.

◊ SMALLINT: A positive or negative whole number. A small integer is usually half the size of a standard integer. Using small integers when you know you will need to store only small values can save space in the database.

◊ NUMERIC (or occasionally, NUMBER): A fixed-point positive or negative number. A numeric value has a whole number portion and a fractional portion. When you create it, you must specify the total length of the number (including the decimal point) and how many of those digits will be to the right of the decimal point (its *precision*). For example,

```
NUMERIC (6,2)
```

creates a number in the format XXX.XX. The DBMS will store exactly two digits to the right of the decimal point.

◊ DECIMAL: A fixed-point positive or negative number. A decimal is similar to a numeric value. However, the DBMS may store more digits to the right of the decimal than you specify. Although there is no guarantee that you will get the extra precision, its presence can provide more accurate results in computations.

◊ REAL: A "single precision" floating point value. A floating point number is expressed in the format

```
±X.XXXXX * 10ʸʸ
```

where YY is the power to which 10 is raised. Because of the way in which computers store floating point numbers, a real number will never be an exact representation of a value, but only a close approximation. The range of values that can be stored is implementation dependent, although a common range is $\pm10^{38}$. You therefore cannot specify a size for a real number column.

◊ DOUBLE PRECISION (abbreviated DOUBLE): A "double precision" floating point number. The range and precision of double precision values are implementation dependent, but generally will be greater than with single precision real numbers. For example, if the single precision range is $\pm10^{38}$, then a typical double precision range is $\pm10^{308}$.

◊ FLOAT: A floating point number for which you can specify the precision. The DBMS will maintain at least the precision that you specify. (It may be more.)

◊ BOOLEAN: A logical value that can take only the values true and false.

◊ BIT: Storage for a fixed number of individual bits. You must indicate the number of bits, as in

```
BIT (n)
```

where n is the number of bits. (If you do not include

the number of bits, you will have room for only one bit.)

◊ DATE: A date.

◊ TIME: A time.

◊ TIMESTAMP: The combination of a date and a time.

◊ CHARACTER (abbreviated CHAR): A fixed-length space to hold a string of characters. When declaring a CHAR column, you need to indicate the width of the column:

```
CHAR (n)
```

where n is the amount of space that will be allocated for the column in every row. Even if you store less than n characters, the column will always take up n bytes and the column will be padded with blanks to fill up empty space. The maximum number of characters allowed is implementation dependent.

◊ CHARACTER VARYING (abbreviated VARCHAR): A variable length space to hold a string of characters. You must indicate the maximum width of the column—

```
VARCHAR (n)
```

—but the DBMS stores only as many characters as you insert, up to the maximum n. The overall maximum number of characters allowed is implementation dependent.

◊ INTERVAL: A date or time interval. An interval data type is followed by a qualifier that specifies the unit of the interval and optionally the number of digits. For example,

```
INTERVAL YEAR
INTERVAL YEAR (n)
INTERVAL MONTH
INTERVAL MONTH (n)
INTERVAL YEAR TO MONTH
INTERVAL YEAR (n) TO MONTH
INTERVAL DAY
INTERVAL DAY (n)
INTERVAL DAY TO HOUR
INTERVAL DAY (n) TO HOUR
INTERVAL DAY TO MINUTE
INTERVAL DAY (n) TO MINUTE
INTERVAL MINUTE
INTERVAL MINUTE (n)
```

In the preceding examples, n specifies the number of digits. When the interval covers more than one date/time unit, such as YEAR TO MONTH, you can specify a size for only the first unit. Year/month intervals can include years, months, or both. Time intervals can include days, hours, minutes, and/or seconds.

◊ BLOB (Binary Large Object): Although not universal, the BLOB data type is supported by many current DBMSs. It can be used to store elements such as graphics. Unlike other data types, however, BLOB columns cannot be searched because the contents are an undifferentiated group of binary data.

In Figure 9-2 you will find the bare bones CREATE TABLE statements for the rare book store database. These statements include only column names and data types. SQL will create tables from statements in this format, but because the tables have no primary keys, some DBMSs will not let you enter data.

As you are defining columns, you can designate a default value for individual columns. To indicate a default value, you add a DEFAULT keyword to the column definition, followed by the default value. For example, in the *sale* relation, it makes sense to assign the current date to the *sale_date* column as a default. The column declaration is therefore written

Default Values

```
sale_date DATE DEFAULT CURRENT_DATE
```

Notice that this particular declaration is using the SQL value CURRENT_DATE. However, you can place any value after DEFAULT that is a valid instance of the column's domain.

The values in primary key columns must be unique and not null. In addition, there may be columns for which you want to require a value. You can specify such columns by adding NOT NULL after the column declaration. Since the staff of the rare book store wants to ensure that an order date is always entered, the complete declaration for the column in the *sale* table is

NOT NULL Constraints

```
sale_date DATE NOT NULL DEFAULT CURRENT_DATE
```

To specify a table's primary key, you add a PRIMARY KEY clause to a CREATE TABLE statement. The keywords PRIMARY KEY are followed by the names of the primary key column or columns, surrounded by parentheses. In the case of a concatenated primary key, place all columns that are part of the primary key within the parentheses.

Primary Keys

In Figure 9-3 you will find the CREATE TABLE statements for the rare book store database including primary key declarations.

As you know, a foreign key is a column (or concatenation of columns) that is exactly the same as the primary key of another table. When a foreign key value matches a primary key value, we know that there is a logical relationship between the database objects represented by the matching rows.

Foreign Keys

```
CREATE TABLE publisher
(
  publisher_id int,
  publisher_name char (50),
);

CREATE TABLE sale
(
  sale_id int,
  customer_numb int,
  sale_date date,
  sale_total_amt decimal (8,2),
  credit_card_numb char (20),
  exp_month int,
  exp_year int,
);

CREATE TABLE customer
(
  customer_numb int,
  first_name varchar (30),
  last_name varchar (30),
  street varchar (50),
  city varchar (30),
  state_province char (2),
  zip_postcode char (10),
  contact_phone char (12),
);


CREATE TABLE condition_codes
(
  condition_code int,
  condition_description varchar (128),
);
```

Figure 9-2: Initial CREATE TABLE statements for the rare book store database (continued on next page)

One of the major constraints on a relation is referential integrity, which states that every nonnull foreign key must reference an existing primary key value. Early implementations of SQL and early versions of the SQL standard did not include support for foreign keys. Validation of referential integrity was

```
CREATE TABLE volume
(
   inventory_id int,
   isbn char (17),
   condition_code int,
   date_acquired date,
   asking_price decimal (7,2),
   selling_price decimal (7,2),
   sale_id int,
);

CREATE TABLE work
(
   work_numb int,
   author_numb int,
   title char (50),
);

CREATE TABLE author
(
    author_numb int,
    author_last_first char (128),
);

CREATE TABLE book
(
   isbn char (17),
   work_numb int,
   publisher_id int,
   edition int,
   binding char (20),
   copyright_year char (4),
);
```

Figure 9-2 (continued): Initial CREATE TABLE statements for the rare book store database

left up to application programmers. However, it is far better to have foreign keys identified in the data dictionary and referential integrity enforced directly by a DBMS. Referential integrity was therefore added to the SQL-89 standard.

Listing Table Structure

Although not part of the SQL standard, many DBMSs support a DESCRIBE command that displays the structure of a table. (The standard SQL DESCRIBE returns information about a prepared embedded SQL statement.) To use it, follow the keyword DESCRIBE with the name of the table, as in

```
DESCRIBE customer
```

The result is a table showing the structure of the named table in a format similar to the following:

```
            Table "enterprisedb.customer"
    Column       |          Type          | Modifiers
-----------------+------------------------+-----------
 customer_numb   | integer                | not null
 first_name      | character varying(30)  |
 last_name       | character varying(30)  |
 street          | character varying(50)  |
 city            | character varying(30)  |
 state_province  | character(2)           |
 zip_postcode    | character(10)          |
 contact_phone   | character(12)          |
Indexes:
    "pk_customer" PRIMARY KEY, btree (customer_numb)
```

To specify a foreign key for a table, you add a FOREIGN KEY clause:

```
FOREIGN KEY foreign_key_name (foreign_key_col-
umns)
REFERENCES primary_key_table (primary_key_col-
umns)
ON UPDATE update_action
ON DELETE delete_action
```

The names of the foreign key columns follow the keywords FOREIGN KEY. The REFERENCES clause contains the name of the primary key table being referenced. If the primary key columns are named in the PRIMARY KEY clause of their

```
CREATE TABLE publisher
(
  publisher_id int,
  publisher_name char (50),
  PRIMARY KEY (publisher_id)
);

CREATE TABLE condition_codes
(
  condition_code int,
  condition_description varchar (128),
  PRIMARY KEY (condition_code)
);

CREATE TABLE sale
(
  sale_id int,
  customer_numb int,
  sale_date date NOT NULL DEFAULT CURRENT_DATE,
  sale_total_amt decimal (8,2),
  credit_card_numb char (20),
  exp_month int,
  exp_year int,
  PRIMARY KEY (sale_id)
);

CREATE TABLE book
(
  isbn char (17),
  work_numb int,
  publisher_id int,
  edition int,
  binding char (20),
  copyright_year char (4),
  PRIMARY KEY (isbn)
);

CREATE TABLE work
(
  work_numb int,
  author_numb int,
  title char (50),
  PRIMARY KEY (work_numb)
);
```

Figure 9-3: CREATE TABLE statements for the rare book store database including primary key declarations (continued on next page)

```
CREATE TABLE customer
(
  customer_numb int,
  first_name varchar (30),
  last_name varchar (30),
  street varchar (50),
  city varchar (30),
  state_province char (2),
  zip_postcode char (10),
  contact_phone char (12),
  PRIMARY KEY (customer_numb)
);


CREATE TABLE volume
(
  inventory_id int,
  isbn char (17),
  condition_code int,
  date_acquired date,
  asking_price decimal (7,2),
  selling_price decimal (7,2),
  sale_id int,
  PRIMARY KEY (inventory_id)
);



CREATE TABLE author
(
    author_numb int,
    author_last_first char (128),
    PRIMARY KEY (author_numb)
);
```

Figure 9-3 (continued): CREATE TABLE statements for the rare book store database including primary key declarations

table, then you don't need to list the column names. However, if the columns aren't part of a PRIMARY KEY clause, you must list the primary key columns in the REFERENCES clause.

The final part of the FOREIGN KEY specification indicates what should happen when a primary key value being referenced by the foreign key is deleted or updated. There are three options that apply to both updates and deletions and one additional option for each:

◊ SET NULL: Replace the foreign key value with null. This isn't possible when the foreign key is part of the primary key of its table.

◊ SET DEFAULT: Replace the foreign key value with the column's default value.

◊ CASCADE: Delete or update all foreign key rows.

◊ NO ACTION: On update, make no modification of foreign key values.

◊ RESTRICT: Do not allow deletion of the primary key value.

The complete declarations for the rare book store database tables, which include foreign key constraints, can be found in Figure 9-4. Notice that although there are no restrictions on how to name foreign keys, the foreign keys in this database have been named to indicate the tables involved. This makes them easier to identify if you need to delete or modify a foreign key at a later date.

Note: The precise syntax allowed for foreign key declarations is somewhat implementation dependent. For example, some DBMSs do not support named foreign keys. You will need to check your DBMS's documentation to verify the exact syntax required.

The SQL Core standard provides some additional flexibility in the definition of foreign keys, including the following:

Additional Foreign Key Options

◊ Rules for determining what occurs when all or part of a foreign key is null. By default, if any part of a foreign key is null, then the DBMS will accept it. If you add a

```
CREATE TABLE publisher
(
  publisher_id int,
  publisher_name char (50),
  PRIMARY KEY (publisher_id)
);

CREATE TABLE sale
(
  sale_id int,
  customer_numb int,
  sale_date date NOT NULL DEFAULT CURRENT_DATE,
  sale_total_amt decimal (8,2),
  credit_card_numb char (20),
  exp_month int,
  exp_year int,
  PRIMARY KEY (sale_id),
  FOREIGN KEY fk_sale2customer (customer_numb)
    REFERENCES customer
    ON UPDATE CASCADE
    ON DELETE RESTRICT
);

CREATE TABLE customer
(
  customer_numb int,
  first_name varchar (30),
  last_name varchar (30),
  street varchar (50),
  city varchar (30),
  state_province char (2),
  zip_postcode char (10),
  contact_phone char (12),
  PRIMARY KEY (customer_numb)
);

CREATE TABLE condition_codes
(
  condition_code int,
  condition_description varchar (128),
  PRIMARY KEY (condition_code0
);
```

Figure 9-4: Complete CREATE TABLE statements for the rare book store database including primary and foreign key declarations (continued on next page)

```
CREATE TABLE book
(
   isbn char (17),
   work_numb int,
   publisher_id int,
   edition int,
   binding char (20),
   copyright_year char (4),
   PRIMARY KEY (isbn),
   FOREIGN KEY fk_book2work (work_numb)
      REFERENCES work
      ON UPDATE CASCADE
      ON DELETE RESTICT
);

CREATE TABLE volume
(
   inventory_id int,
   isbn char (17),
   condition_code int,
   date_acquired date,
   asking_price decimal (7,2),
   selling_price decimal (7,2),
   sale_id int,
   PRIMARY KEY (inventory_id),
   FOREIGN KEY fk_volume2book (isbn)
      REFERENCES book
      ON UPDATE CASCADE
      ON DELETE RESTRICT,
    FOREIGN KEY fk_volume2condition (condition_code)
      REFERENCES condition_codes
      ON UPDATE CASCADE
      ON DELETE SET NULL
);

CREATE TABLE author
(
   author_numb int,
   author_last_first char (128),
   PRIMARY KEY (author_numb)
);
```

Figure 9-4 (continued): Complete CREATE TABLE statements for the rare book store database including primary and foreign key declarations (continued on next page)

```
CREATE TABLE work
(
    work_numb int,
    author_numb int,
    title char (50),
    PRIMARY KEY (work_numb),
    FOREIGN KEY fk_work2author (author_numb)
        REFERENCES author
        ON UPDATE CASCADE
        ON DELETE RESTRICT
);
```

Figure 9-4 (continued): Complete CREATE TABLE statements for the rare book store database including primary and foreign key declarations

MATCH PARTIAL to the foreign key definition and part of a foreign key is null, then the nonnull portions of the foreign key must match parts of an existing foreign key. If you add MATCH FULL, a foreign key must either be completely null or match an existing primary key completely.

◊ Rules for determining the action to take when a primary key referenced by the foreign key is updated. If you specify ON UPDATE CASCADE, then the DBMS will automatically update the foreign key values when the primary key values they reference are modified. (In most cases, this will be the desired option because it maintains the consistency of cross-references throughout the database.) In addition, you can choose to ON UPDATE SET NULL (set the foreign key values to null), ON UPDATE SET DEFAULT (set the foreign key values to their columns' default value), or ON UPDATE NO ACTION (do nothing).

Note: In a well-designed relational DBMS, primary key values should never be modified. However, given that people persist in

using meaningful primary keys, you may want to be certain that cross-references are maintained.

Additional Column Constraints

There are additional constraints that you can place on columns in a table beyond primary and foreign key constraints. These include requiring unique values and predicates in CHECK clauses.

Requiring Unique Values

If you want to ensure that the values in a non-primary key column are unique, you can use the UNIQUE keyword. UNIQUE verifies that all nonnull values are unique. For example, if you were storing social security numbers in an employees table that used an employee ID as the primary key, you could also enforce unique social security numbers with

```
ssn CHAR (11) UNIQUE
```

The UNIQUE clause can also be placed at the end of a CREATE TABLE statement, along with the primary key and foreign key specifications. In that case, it takes the form

```
UNIQUE (column_names)
```

Check Clauses

The CHECK clause to which you were introduced earlier in this chapter in the Domains section can also be used with individual columns to declare column-specific constraints. To add a constraint, you place a CHECK clause after the column declaration, using the keyword VALUE in a predicate to indicate the value being checked. For example, to verify that a column used to hold T-shirt sizes should be limited to S, M, L, XL, XXL, and XXXL, you could write a CHECK clause as

```
CHECK (UPPER(VALUE) IN ('S','M','L','XL','XXL',
    'XXXL'))
```

Assertions

An *assertion* is a constraint that is applied to any or all tables in a schema, rather than to a specific table. It can therefore be based on more than one table or be used to verify that a table is not empty. Assertions exist as independent database objects that can be created and dropped as needed.

To create an assertion you use the CREATE ASSERTION command:

```
CREATE ASSERTION assertion_name
CHECK (logical_expression_for_validation)
```

For example, to ensure that the *author* table has at least one row, someone at the rare book store could define the following assertion:

```
CREATE ASSERTION validate_author
CHECK (SELECT COUNT(*) FROM author > 0);
```

Because an assertion is a database object, you remove one from a schema just as you would any other database object:

```
DROP ASSERTION assertion_name
```

Determining When Constraints Are Checked

Most of today's DBMSs check constraints whenever any modification is made to the contents of a table. The SQL standard, however, gives users the ability to determine when constraints are checked. Constraints may be *not deferrable* (the default), in which case they are checked after each SQL statement. If constraints are *deferrable*, they are checked at the end of a transaction.

Note: If you are working in an interactive environment where each statement is a distinct transaction, then deferring constraints essentially has no effect.

There are several places where you can specify when constraints are to be checked:

◊ When constraints are defined within a table definition. In this case you can set constraints to INITIALLY DE-

FERRED or INITIALLY IMMEDIATE to determine the initial setting for constraint checking. If you want to prevent anyone from deferring constraints at a later time, you can also specify that the constraints are NOT DEFERRABLE. To allow constraints to be deferred at a later time, you can specify them as DEFERRABLE.

◊ When you create a domain using CREATE DOMAIN, you can indicate that domain checking should be INITIALLY IMMEDIATE or INITIALLY DEFERRED. In addition, you can prevent domain checking from ever being deferred by adding NOT DEFERRABLE. To allow deferring of domain checking at a later time, specify DEFERRABLE.

◊ When you create an assertion using CREATE ASSERTION, you can indicate that the assertion checking should be INITIALLY IMMEDIATE or INITIALLY DEFERRED. In addition, you can prevent assertion checking from ever being deferred by adding NOT DEFERRABLE. To allow deferring of assertion check at a later time, specify DEFERRABLE.

Changing the Constraint Mode

The point at which constraints defined as database objects are checked can be altered with the SET CONSTRAINTS MODE statement:

```
SET CONSTRAINTS MODE constraint_name DEFERRED
```

or

```
SET CONSTRAINTS MODE constraint_name IMMEDIATE
```

Of course, the preceding assume that the named constraint is deferrable.

Note: If you want to affect all the named constraints in the current schema, use the keyword ALL instead of one or more constraint names.

Because the SET CONSTRAINT MODE statement requires a named constraint, it cannot be applied to constraints created within a CREATE TABLE statement unless those constraints have been named. This means that if you want to have control over when the checking of such constraints occurs, you need to add a CONSTRAINT clause to the table declaration so you have somewhere to name a constraint.

As an example, consider the table declaration in Figure 9-5. The addition of the CONSTRAINT clause allows both the primary and foreign keys to be named, making them accessible to a SET CONSTRAINTS MODE statement (although the primary key has been specified as not deferrable.)

```
CREATE TABLE employee
(
    id_numb int,
    first vchar (20),
    last vchar (20),
    department_name vchar (20),
    CONSTRAINT pk_employee
        PRIMARY KEY (id_numb)
        INITIALLY IMMEDIATE NOT DEFERRABLE,
    CONSTRAINT fk_employee2dept
        FOREIGN KEY (department_name)
        REFERENCES departments (department_name)
        INITIALLY IMMEDIATE DEFERRABLE
);
```

Figure 9-5: A table declaration including constraints accessible to a SET CONSTRAINTS MODE statement

10 Views, Temporary Tables, CTEs, and Indexes

A database is made up of more than just a schema and permanent base tables. It can contain views, temporary tables, and *common table expressions* (CTEs). It may also contain indexes, which although no longer part of the SQL standard, are supported by most DBMSs for enforcing primary key constraints and speeding retrieval performance.

Views

A view is a virtual table that is produced by executing a SQL-query. It is stored in the data dictionary as a named SELECT. Whenever a SQL query contains the name of a view, the DBMS executes the query associated with the view's definition to create its virtual result table. That table can the be used as a source table by the remainder of the query in which its name appears.

Why Use Views?

There are several important reasons for using views in a database environment:

◊ Views provide a way to store commonly used complex queries in the database. Users can use a simple query such as

```
SELECT column1, column2, column3
FROM view_name
```

instead of typing a complex SQL statement.

◊ Views can help you tailor the database environment to individual users, groups of users, or uses. You create

237

views that package the data needed by specific people or for specific purposes, making it easier for those users to access their data.

◊ Views can help maintain database security. Rather than giving users access to entire base tables, you can create views that provide users with exactly the data they need to see. You then grant users access to the views but not to the base tables. (A complete discussion of granting and revoking access rights can be found later in this chapter.)

Creating Views

To create a view whose columns have the same name as the columns in the base table(s) from which it is derived, you give the view and name and include the SQL query that defines its contents:

```
CREATE VIEW view_name AS
     SELECT …
```

For example, if someone at the rare book store wanted to create a view that would contain data about only leather bound books, the SQL is written

```
CREATE VIEW leather_bound AS
     SELECT author, title
     FROM author JOIN work JOIN book
         JOIN volume
     WHERE UPPER (binding) = 'LEATHER';
```

If you want to rename the columns in the view, you include the new column names in the CREATE VIEW statement:

```
CREATE VIEW leather_bound
         (leather_author, leather_title) AS
     SELECT author, title
     FROM author JOIN work JOIN book
         JOIN volume
     WHERE UPPER (binding) = 'LEATHER';
```

The preceding statement will produce a view with two columns named *leather_author* and *leather_title*. Notice if you want to change even one column name, you must include *all* column names in the parentheses following the name of the view. The DBMS will match the columns following SELECT with the view column names by their position in the list.

Views can be created from nearly any SQL query, including those that perform joins, unions, and grouping. For example, to simplify looking at sales figures, someone at the rare book store might create a view like the following:

```
CREATE VIEW sales_summary AS
    SELECT customer_numb,
        SUM (sale_total_amt)
        AS total_purchases
    FROM sale
    GROUP BY customer_numb;
```

The view table will then contain grouped data along with a computed column. The beauty of this view is that each time its name is used, the sum will be computed again, ensuring that the data remain up to date.

Note: Views cannot be created from queries that include local temporary tables.

Querying Views

You use a view in a SQL SELECT just as you would a base table. For example, to see the entire contents of the *sales_summary* view created in the preceding section, someone at the rare book store could use the simple query

```
SELECT *
FROM sales_summary;
```

which produces the result table in Figure 10-1.

```
customer_numb | total_purchases
--------------+----------------
            8 |          130.00
            4 |          110.00
            1 |          793.00
            5 |          190.00
           11 |          200.00
           12 |          505.00
           10 |          200.00
            9 |          200.00
            6 |          285.00
            2 |          230.95
```

Figure 10-1: *The output of querying a view that includes grouping and a calculated column*

You can apply additional predicates to a view, as in the following example that restricts rows by date:

```
SELECT *
FROM sales_summary
WHERE total_purchases >= 500;
```

This time, the result contains only two rows:

```
customer_numb | total_purchases
--------------+----------------
            1 |          793.00
           12 |          505.00
```

View Updatability Issues

Theoretically, you should be able to perform INSERT, UPDATE, and DELETE on views as well as SELECT. However, not all views are *updatable* (capable of being used for updating). Keep in mind that a view's table exists only in main memory. If it is to be used for updates, then the DBMS must be able to propagate the update back to the view's base table(s).

The SQL:2006 places the following restrictions on updatability:

◊ The view must obtain its source data from tables and/ or views. The data cannot come from a virtual table defined by a SELECT that is part of the view's query (no table constructors).

◊ The view must not use UNION DISTINCT, EXCEPT ALL, EXCEPT DISTINCT, or INTERSECT.

◊ Each updatable column in the view must correspond to an updatable column in a source table; each non-updatable column in the view must correspond to a non-updatable column in a source table.

If you have created a view based on another view, then the underlying view must also be updatable. In addition, you will be unable to insert rows into views that do not contain the primary key columns of their base tables. (Doing so will violate the base table's primary key constraint.) Although updates and deletes are possible when the primary key columns aren't present in a view, performing such modifications may have unexpected results because you can't be certain which rows will be affected.[1]

A temporary table is a base table that is not stored in the database, but instead exists only while the database session in which it was created is active. At first glance, this may sound like a view, but views and temporary tables are rather different:

Temporary Tables

◊ A view exists only for a single query. Each time you use the name of a view, its table is recreated from existing data.

◊ A temporary table exists for the entire database session in which it was created.

---

1   Some current DBMSs support an INSTEAD OF trigger that lets you create a procedure that updates the underlying table(s) of a view when the view itself isn't updatable. For example, such a procedure might generate values where needed to complete a primary key. However, INSTEAD OF triggers are not part of the SQL standard,

◊ A view is automatically populated with the data retrieve by the query that defines it.

◊ You must add data to a temporary table with SQL INSERT commands.

◊ Only views that meet the criteria for view updatability can be used for data modification. When you use a view for updating, the updates are permanently propagated to the underlying base tables.

◊ Because temporary tables are base tables, all of them can be updated. However, the updates are as temporary as the table.

◊ Because the contents of a view are generated each time the view's name is used, a view's data are almost always current.

◊ The data in a temporary table reflect the state of the database at the time the table was loaded with data. If the data in table(s) from which the temporary table was loaded are modified after the temporary table has received its data, then the contents of the temporary table may be out of sync with other parts of the database.

If the contents of a temporary table become outdated when source data change, why use a temporary table at all? Wouldn't it be better simply to use a view whose contents are continually regenerated? The answer lies in performance. It takes processing time to create a view table. If you are going to use the data only once during a database session, then a view will actually perform better than a temporary table because you don't need to create a structure for it. However, if you are going to be using the data repeatedly during a session, then a temporary table provides better performance because it needs to be created only once. The decision therefore results in a trade-off. Using a view repeatedly takes more time but provides continually updated data; using a temporary table repeatedly saves time, but you run the risk that the table's contents may be out of date.

Creating a temporary table is very similar to creating a permanent base table. You do, however, need to decide on the *scope* of the table. A temporary table can be *global*, in which case it is accessible to the entire application program that created it. Alternatively, it can be *local*, in which case it is accessible only to the program module in which it was created.

To create a global temporary table, you add the keyword GLOBAL TEMPORARY to the CREATE TABLE statement:

```
CREATE GLOBAL TEMPORARY TABLE
    (remainder of CREATE statement)
```

For example, if someone at the rare book store was going to use the sales summary information repeatedly, then he or she might create the following temporary table instead of using a view:

```
CREATE GLOBAL TEMPORARY TABLE sales_summary
    (customer_numb INT,
    total_purchases NUMERIC (7,2),
    PRIMARY KEY (customer_numb));
```

To create a local temporary table, you replace GLOBAL with LOCAL:

```
CREATE LOCAL TEMPORARY TABLE sales_summary
    (customer_numb INT,
    total_purchases NUMERIC (7,2),
    PRIMARY KEY (customer_numb));
```

To place data in a temporary table, you use one or more SQL INSERT statements. For example, to load the *sales_summary* table created in the preceding section, you could use

Creating Temporary Tables

Loading Temporary Tables with Data

```
INSERT INTO sales_summary
     SELECT customer_numb,
            sum (total_sale_amt)
     FROM sale
     GROUP BY customer numb;
```

You can now query and manipulate the *sales_summary* table just as you would a permanent base table.

Disposition of Temporary Table Rows

When you write embedded SQL you have control over the amount of work that the DBMS considers to be a unit (a *transaction*). We will discuss transactions in depth in Chapter 13. However, to understand what happens to the rows in a temporary table, you do need to know that a transaction can end in one of two ways: It can be *committed* (its changes made permanent) or it can be *rolled back* (its changes undone).

By default, the rows in a temporary table are purged whenever a transaction is committed. You can, however, instruct the DBMS to retain the rows by including ON COMMIT PRESERVE ROWS to the end of the table creation statement:

```
INSERT INTO sales_summary
     SELECT customer_numb,
            sum (total_sale_amt)
     FROM sale
     GROUP BY customer numb
ON COMMIT PRESERVE ROWS;
```

Because a rollback returns the database to the state it was in before the transaction began, a temporary table will also be restored to its previous state (with or without rows).

Common Table Expressions (CTEs)

A *common table expression* (CTE) is yet another way of extracting a subset of a database for use in another query. CTEs are like views in that they generate virtual tables. However, the definitions of a CTE is not stored in the database and it must be used immediately after it is defined.

To get started, let's look at a very simple example. The general format of a simple CTE is

```
WITH CTE_name (columns) AS
      (SELECT_statement_defining_table)
CTE_query
```

For example, a CTE and its query to view all of the rare book store's customers could be written

```
WITH customer_names (first, last) AS
      (SELECT first_name, last_name
        FROM customer)
SELECT *
FROM customer_names;
```

The result is a listing of the first and last names of the customers. This type of structure for a simple query really doesn't buy you much except that the CTE isn't stored in the database like a view and doesn't require INSERT statements to populate it like a temporary table. However, the major use of CTEs is for *recursive queries*, queries that query themselves. (That may sound a bit circular, and it is, intentionally.) The typical application of a recursive query using a CTE is to process hierarchical data, data arranged in a tree structure. It will allow a single query to access every element in the tree or to access subtrees that begin somewhere other than the top of the tree.

As an example, let's create a table that handles the descendants of a single person (in this case, John). As you can see in Figure 10-2, each node in the tree has at most one parent and any number of children. The numbers in the illustration represent the ID of each person.

Relational databases are notoriously bad at handling this type of hierarchically structured data. The typical way to handle it is to create a relation something like this:

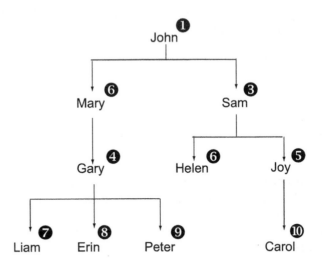

Figure 10-2: A tree structure that can be represented in a relational database and traversed with a recursive query

```
genealogy (person_id, parent_id, person_name)
```

Each row in the table represents one node in the tree. For this example, the table is populated with the 10 rows in Figure 10-3. John, the node at the top of the tree, has no parent ID. The *parent_ID* column in the other rows is filled with the person ID of the node above in the tree. (The order of the rows in the table is irrelevant.)

We can access every node in the tree by simply accessing every row in the table. However, what can we do if we want to process just the people who are Sam's descendants? There is no easy way with a typical SELECT to do that. However, a CTE used recursively will identify just the rows we want.

The syntax of a recursive query is similar to the simple CTE query with addition of the keyword RECURSIVE following WITH. For our particular example, the query will be written:

```
person_id | parent_id |          person_name
----------+-----------+--------------------------------
        1 |           | John
        2 |         1 | Mary
        3 |         1 | Sam
        4 |         2 | Gary
        5 |         3 | Joy
        6 |         3 | Helen
        7 |         4 | Liam
        8 |         4 | Erin
        9 |         4 | Peter
       10 |         5 | Carol
```

Figure 10-3: Sample data for use with a recursive query

```
WITH RECURSIVE show_tree AS
      (SELECT
      FROM genealogy
      WHERE person_name = 'Sam'
      UNION ALL
      SELECT g.*
      FROM genealogy as g, show_tree as st
      WHERE g.parent_id = st.person_id)
SELECT *
FROM show_tree
ORDER BY person_name;
```

The result is

```
person_id | parent_id |     person_name
----------+-----------+------------------------
       10 |         5 | Carol
        6 |         3 | Helen
        5 |         3 | Joy
        3 |         1 | Sam
```

The query that defines the CTE called *show_tree* has two parts. The first is a simple SELECT that retrieves Sam's row and places it in the result table and in an intermediate table that represents the current state of *show_tree*. The second SELECT (below UNION ALL) is the recursive part. It will use the intermediate table in place of *show_tree* each time it executes and add the results of each iteration to the result table. The recursive portion will execute repeatedly until it returns no rows.

Here's how the recursion will work in our example:

1. Join the intermediate result table to *genealogy*. Because the intermediate result table contains just Sam's row, the join will match Helen and Joy.

2. Remove Sam from the intermediate table and insert Helen and Joy.

3. Append Helen and Joy to the result table.

4. Join the intermediate table to *genealogy*. The only match from the join will be Carol. (Helen has no children and Joy has only one.)

5. Remove Helen and Joy from the intermediate table and insert Carol.

6. Append Carol to the result table.

7. Join the intermediate table to *genealogy*. The result will be no rows and the recursion stops.

CTEs cannot be reused; the declaration of the CTE isn't saved. Therefore they don't buy you much for most queries. However, they are enormously useful if you are working with tree-structured data. CTEs and recursion can also be helpful when working with bill of materials data.

Indexes

An *index* is a data structure that provides a fast access path to rows in a table based on the values in one or more columns (the index key). Because the DBMS can use a fast search technique to find the values rather than being forced to search each row in an unordered table sequentially, data retrieval is often much faster.

The conceptual operation of an index is diagrammed in Figure 10-4. (The different weights of the lines have no significance other than to make it easier for you to follow the crossed lines.) In this illustration, you are looking at the *work* relation and an index that provides fast access to the rows in the table based on a book's title.

The index itself contains an ordered list of keys (the book titles) along with the locations of the associated rows in the *book* table. The rows in the *book* table are in relatively random order. However, because the index is in alphabetical order by title, it can be searched quickly to locate a specific title. Then the DBMS can use the information in the index to go directly to the correct row or rows in the *book* table, thus avoiding a slow sequential scan of the base table's rows.

Once you have created an index, the DBMS's query optimizer will use the index whenever it determines that using the index will speed up data retrieval. You never need to access the index again yourself unless you want to delete it.

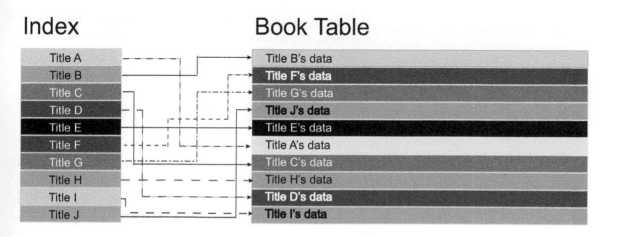

Figure 10-4: The operation of an index to a relation

When you create a primary key for a table, the DBMS either automatically creates an index for that table using the primary key column or columns as the index key or requires you to create a unique index for the primary key. The first step in inserting a new row into a table is therefore verification that the index key (the primary key of the table) is unique to the index. In fact, uniqueness is enforced by requiring the index entries to be unique, rather than by actually searching the base table. This is much faster than attempting to verify uniqueness directly on the base table because the ordered index can be searched much more rapidly than the unordered base tab

Deciding Which Indexes to Create

You have no choice as to whether the DBMS creates indexes for your primary keys; you get them whether you want them or not. In addition, you can create indexes to provide fast access to any column or combination of columns you want. However, before you jump head first into creating indexes on every column in every table, there are some trade-offs to consider:

◊ Indexes take up space in the database. Given that disk space is relatively inexpensive today, this is usually not a major drawback.

◊ When you insert, modify, or delete data in indexed columns, the DBMS must update the index as well as the base table. This may slow down data modification operations, especially if the tables have a lot of rows.

◊ Indexes definitely speed up access to data.

The trade-off therefore is generally between update speed and retrieval speed. A good rule of thumb is to create indexes for foreign keys and for other columns that are used frequently in WHERE clause predicates. If you find that update speed is severely affected, you may choose at a later time to delete some of the indexes you created.

How Much Faster?

How much faster can an index actually make searching? Some simple examples will give you an idea. Assume that you have a list of 10,000 names that are in random order. To search for a specific name, the only technique available is to start with the first name and read the names sequentially. On average, you will need to check 5,000 names to find the one you want, and if the name isn't in the list or there are duplicates in the list, you will need to look at all 10,000 names.

One way to speed things up would be to sort the list in alphabetical order. We could then use a technique known as a *binary search*. The search starts by looking at the name in the middle of the list. It will either be the middle name, or above or below the middle name. Because the list is ordered, we can determine which half of the list contains the name we're trying to find, which means that we can continue by searching just that half. We repeat the process until we either find the name we want or the portion of the list we are searching shrinks to nothing (in which case, the name isn't in the list). In the worst case scenario—the name isn't in the list—you will need to look at only 15 or 16 names. When the name is in the list, the number of names you will need to look at will be less. This is significantly fewer comparisons than with the sequential search!

DBMSs no longer use lists as the data structure for indexes. Most use some type of hierarchical (tree) structure, similar to the tree we used for the CTE example. The specifics of such tree structures are very implementation dependent, but in general they provide even better search performance than an ordered list.

Creating Indexes

You create indexes with the CREATE INDEX statement:

```
CREATE INDEX index_name ON
    table_name (index_key_columns)
```

For example, to create an index on the *author_last_first* column in the *author* table, someone at the rare book store could use

```
CREATE INDEX author_name
    ON author (author_first_last);
```

By default the index will allow duplicate entries and sort the entries in ascending order. To require unique index entries, add the keyword UNIQUE after CREATE:

```
CREATE UNIQUE INDEX author_name
    ON (author_first_last);
```

To sort in descending order, insert DESC after the column whose sort order you to want to change. For example, someone at the rare book store might want to create an index on *sale_date* in the *sale* relation in descending order so that the most recent sales are first:

```
CREATE INDEX sale_date
    ON sale (sale_date DESC);
```

If you want to create an index on a concatenated key, you include all the columns that should be part of the index key in the column list. For example, the following creates an index organized by title and author number:

```
CREATE INDEX book_order ON book (title, author_
numb);
```

Although you do not need to access an index directly unless you want to delete it from the database, it helps to give indexes names that tell you something about their keys. This makes it easier to remember them should you need to get rid of the indexes.

11

Keeping the Design Up to Date

One of the benefits that relational DBMSs have over DBMSs based on older data models is that the schema is easy to change. As long as a table isn't being used at the time you want to modify it, its design can be changed without affecting other tables in the database. (This is said with the caveat that the presence of foreign key constraints may prevent some deletions and modifications or cause other modifications to occur.) The SQL statements that modify database structures are therefore an important part of a database administrator's arsenal. In this chapter, we'll look at the types of changes that can be made and how to make them.

Modifying Tables

With the exception of tables, structural database elements are largely unchangeable. When you want to modify them, you must delete them from the database and create them from scratch. In contrast, just about every characteristic of a table can be modified without deleting the table using the ALTER TABLE statement.

Note: DBMS support for the parts of ALTER TABLE varies considerably. It is not unusual to find that all you can do is add a column or increase the size of a character column, for example. As always, you will need to consult the documentation for your particular DBMS to see exactly what is available.

Adding New Columns

To add a new column to a table, you use the ALTER TABLE statement with the following syntax:

```
ALTER TABLE table_name
ADD column_name column_data_type
    column_constraints
```

For example, if someone at the rare book store wanted to add a telephone number to the *publisher* table, he or she would use

```
ALTER TABLE publisher
ADD publisher_phone CHAR (11);
```

To add more than one column at the same time, simply separate the clauses for the new columns with commas:

```
ALTER TABLE publisher
ADD publisher_phone CHAR (11),
ADD publisher_street CHAR (30),
ADD publisher_city CHAR (30),
ADD publisher_state_prov CHAR (2),
ADD publisher_zip_postcode CHAR (12),
ADD publisher_country CHAR (10);
```

There is one caveat that goes along with adding columns: If you have any application programs that use the SELECT * syntax, then any new columns that you add to a table will be included in the output of that query. The result may be either the disclosure of data you wanted to keep secret or application programs that no longer work properly. Because SQL allows you to add columns to tables without restriction, you should avoid using the SELECT * syntax in application programs.

Adding Table Constraints

You can add table constraints such as foreign keys at any time. To do so, include the new constraint in the ADD clause of an ALTER TABLE statement:

```
ALTER TABLE table_name
    ADD table_constraint
```

Assume, for example, that someone at the rare book store created a new table named *regions* and included all the two-character U.S. state and Canadian province abbreviations. The table would then need to add a reference from the *customer* table:

```
ALTER TABLE customer
     ADD FOREIGN KEY customer2regions (state_
province)
     REFERENCES regions (region_name);
```

When you add a foreign key constraint to a table, the DBMS verifies that all existing data in the table meet that constraint. If they do not, the ALTER TABLE will fail.

If you have created a table without a primary key, you can add one with

```
ALTER TABLE some_table
     ADD PRIMARY KEY (key_columns);
```

You modify columns by changing any characteristic of the column, including its type, size, and constraints:

◊ To replace a complete column definition, use an ALTER clause with the current column and the new column characteristics:

```
ALTER TABLE table_name
     ALTER COLUMN column_name
          TYPE new_data_type
```

◊ To add or change a default value only (without changing the data type or size of the column), include the DEFAULT keyword:

```
ALTER TABLE table_name
     ALTER column_name
          SET DEFAULT new_default_value
```

Modifying Columns

◊ To switch between allowing nulls and not allowing nulls without changing any other column characteristics, add SET or DROP NOT NULL as appropriate:

```
ALTER TABLE table_name
    ALTER column_name SET NOT NULL
```

or

```
ALTER TABLE table_name
    MODIFY column_name DROP NOT NULL
```

When you change the data type of a column, the DBMS will attempt to convert any existing values to the new data type. If the current values cannot be converted, then the table modification will not be performed. In general, most columns can be converted to characters. However, conversions from a character data type to numbers or datetimes require that existing data represent legal values in the new data type.

Deleting Table Elements

You can delete parts of a table as needed:

◊ To delete a column, use a DROP clause in an ALTER TABLE statement, followed by the name of the column to be deleted:

```
ALTER TABLE table_name
    DROP COLUMN column_name;
```

◊ To delete a table constraint such as a primary or foreign key, use DROP CONSTRAINT:

```
ALTER TABLE table_name
    DROP CONSTRAINT constraint_name;
```

Although you can delete a table's primary key, keep in mind that if you do not add a new one, you may not be able to modify the contents of the table.

◊ To remove a default value from a column use:

```
ALTER TABLE table_name
    DROP column_name DEFAULT;
```

You can rename both tables and columns:

Renaming Table Elements

◊ To rename a table, place the new table name after the RENAME keyword:

```
ALTER TABLE current_table_name
    RENAME TO new_table_name
```

◊ To rename a column, include both the old and new column names separated by the keyword TO:

```
ALTER TABLE table_name
    RENAME current_column_name
        TO new_column_name
```

Modifying Domains

If you have created custom domains, those domains can be modified as needed. Keep in mind, however, that if the data currently in the column don't meet the criteria of the modified domain, the modification may not be allowed. (Such behavior is implementation dependent)

Domain modifications use the ALTER statement, much like modifying tables:

◊ To change a domain's default value, use

```
ALTER DOMAIN domain_name
    SET DEFAULT default_value
```

◊ To remove a domain's default value, use

```
ALTER DOMAIN domain_name
    DROP DEFAULT
```

◊ To change a domain's NULL or NOT NULL status, use

```
ALTER DOMAIN domain_name
    SET NOT NULL
```

or

```
ALTER DOMAIN domain_name
    DROP NOT NULL
```

◊ To add a new constraint to the domain, use

```
ALTER DOMAIN domain_name
    ADD constraint_name
        domain_constraint_expression
```

◊ To remove a constraint from the domain, use

```
ALTER DOMAIN domain_name
    DROP constraint_name
```

Deleting Database Elements

To delete a structural element from a database, you *drop* the element. For example, to delete a table, you would type

```
DROP TABLE table_name
```

Dropping a table is irreversible. In most cases, the DBMS will not bother to ask "Are you sure?" but will immediately delete the structure of the table and all of its data.

You can remove the following structural elements from a database with the DROP statement:

◊ Tables

◊ Views

```
DROP VIEW view_name
```

◊ Indexes

```
DROP INDEX index_name
```

◊ Domains

```
DROP DOMAIN domain_name
```

A DROP of a table or view will fail if the element being dropped is currently in use by another user.

The action of a DBMS when you attempt to DROP a table depends to some extent on whether the table contains primary keys with foreign key references and what action was specified when the table was created. If the action is RESTRICT, then the DROP will fail. In contrast, for example, if the action is CASCADE, related foreign key rows will be deleted from their table(s) when the primary key table is dropped.

12

Users and Access Rights

For many network and database administrators, security has become an almost overwhelming concern. Relational DBMSs have always had some measure of security separate from that provided by networks. In this chapter we will look at some examples of managing database user accounts as well as SQL's support for granting and revoking access rights.

Managing User Accounts

Many multiuser DBMSs maintain user names and passwords that are distinct from any authentication that may be imposed by a network. A user must supply the DBMS's authentication information before being allowed to connect to the database.

Most DBMSs are shipped with only one or two authorized users (often DBA, SYSTEM, and/or ADMIN) that have access to the entire database. All other users must be created by one of these accounts or another account that has been given the appropriate rights.

Although the specific syntax for creating and maintaining user names and passwords is not a part of the SQL standard and therefore implementation dependent, the syntax used by many products is very similar.

Oracle and the two major open source DBMSs (mySQL and Postgres) use some type of CREATE USER syntax. mySQL has the simplest version:

```
CREATE USER user_name IDENTIFIED BY 'password'
```

Oracle's version uses the following pattern:

```
CREATE USER user_name
     IDENTIFIED BY password
     DEFAULT TABLESPACE tablespace_name
     QUOTA storage_space_allocation
```

The DEFAULT TABLESPACE and QUOTA clauses set the area of the database the user will use for temporary storage and the amount of temporary storage the user can fill.

Postgres varies the syntax slightly:

```
CREATE USER user_name
     PASSWORD 'password'
```

Postgres also supports clauses to allow/disallow the creation of databases and the creation of other users.

SQL Server uses yet another similar syntax:

```
CREATE LOGIN user_name
     WITH PASSWORD = 'password'
```

In contrast, DB2 does not provide its own user names and passwords. Instead, it uses a person's account with the operating system. In other words, once a user is authenticated by the operating system, DB2 requires no further account authorization. Access rights to database elements are therefore linked to OS accounts rather than to special DB2 accounts.[1]

Having a user ID does not necessarily give a user the right to access the database. Although the details are implementation dependent, you typically will find that the DBMS has extended the

---

1   For more information on DB2 security, see http://www.databasesecurity.com/db2/db2cert2v8-a4.pdf.

GRANT command—which we will discuss shortly—to support user-level access. For example,

```
GRANT CONNECT TO user_id
```

grants the user the right to connect to the database. Connect rights, however, do not give the user the right to create database elements or access existing database elements. The right to create database elements usually must be granted by someone with DBA rights, using a syntax similar to

```
GRANT RESOURCE TO user_id
```

Rights to database elements such as tables and views are given using the SQL GRANT command (discussed in the next section of this chapter).

DBA rights permit a user to grant connect and resource rights to others, to create accounts, and access all database elements. Any user ID with DBA rights also can assign them to another user ID:

```
GRANT DBA TO user_name
```

Because DBA rights have such broad access, in most cases they will be restricted to only one or two user IDs.

When you create an element of database structure, the user name under which you are working becomes that element's owner. The owner has the right to do anything to that element; all other users have no rights at all. This means that if tables and views are going to accessible to other users, you must grant them access rights.[2]

Granting and Revoking Access Rights

---

2   Some major DBMSs (for example, Oracle and DB2) also provide support for *multilevel security* (MLS). An MLS scheme classifies data into levels, such as top secret, secret, classified, and unclassified. Users are then given clearance levels. A user can view data at or below his or her clearance level and cannot change a classification level to anything less

Types of Access Rights

There are six types of access rights that you can grant:

◊ SELECT: Allows a user to retrieve data from a table or view.

◊ INSERT: Allows a user to insert new rows into a table or updatable view. Permission may be granted to specific columns rather than the entire database element.

◊ UPDATE: Allows a user to modify rows in a table or updatable view. Permission may be granted to specific columns rather than the entire database element.

◊ DELETE: Allows a user to delete rows from a table or updatable view.

◊ REFERENCES: Allows a user to reference a table as a foreign key in a table he or she creates. Permission may be granted to specific columns rather than the entire table.

◊ EXECUTE: Allows the user to execute stored procedures. (You will read about stored procedures in Chapter 14.)

◊ ALL PRIVILEGES: Gives a user all of the preceding rights to a table or view.

By default, granting access rights to another user does not give that user the ability to pass on those rights to others. If, however, you add a WITH GRANT OPTION clause, you give the user the ability to grant the right that he or she has to another user.

---

than the data's current level. MLS is used in many government databases and to satisfy government regulations surrounding data access.

Access rights to tables and views are stored in the data dictionary. Although the details of the data dictionary tables vary from one DBMS to another, you will usually find access rights split between two system tables named something like SYSTABLEPERM and SYSCOLPERM.[3]

Storing Access Rights

The first table is used when access rights are granted to entire tables or views; the second is used when rights are granted to specific columns within a table or view.

A SYSTABLEPERM table has a structure similar to the following:

```
Systableperm (table_id, grantee, grantor,
    selectauth, insertauth, deleteauth,
    updateauth, updatecols, referenceauth)
```

The columns represent

◊ TABLE_ID: An identifier for the table or view.

◊ GRANTEE: The user ID to which rights have been granted.

◊ GRANTOR: The user ID granting the rights.

◊ SELECTAUTH: The grantee's SELECT rights.

◊ INSERTAUTH: The grantee's INSERT rights.

◊ DELETEAUTH: The grantee's DELETE rights.

◊ UPDATEAUTH: The grantee's UPDATE rights.

◊ UPDATECOLS; Indicates whether rights have been granted to specific columns within the table or view. When this value is Y (yes), the DBMS must also look

---

3   DB2, for example, uses AUTH (authorization) in its system authorization tables rather than PERM.

in SYSCOLPERM to determine whether a user has the rights to perform a specific action against the database.

◊ REFERENCEAUTH: The grantee's REFERENCE rights.

The columns that hold the access rights take one of three values: Y (yes), N (no), or G (yes with grant option).

Whenever a user makes a request to the DBMS to manipulate data, the DBMS first consults the data dictionary to determine whether the user has the rights to perform the requested action. (SQL-based DBMSs are therefore said to be *data dictionary driven*.) If the DBMS cannot find a row with a matching user ID and table identifier, then the user has no rights at all to the table or view. If a row with a matching user ID and table identifier exists, then the DBMS checks for the specific rights that the user has to the table or view and—based on the presence of Y, N, or G in the appropriate column—either permits or disallows the requested database access.

Granting Rights

To grant rights to another user, a user who either created the database element (and therefore has all rights to it) or who has GRANT rights issues a GRANT statement:

```
GRANT type_of_rights
ON table_or_view_name TO user_ID
```

For example, if the DBA of the rare book store wanted to allow the accounting manager (who has a user ID of *acctg_mgr*) to access the *sales_summary* view, the DBA would type:

```
GRANT SELECT
ON sales_summary TO acctg_mgr;
```

To allow the accounting manager to pass those rights on to other users, the DBMS would need to add one line to the SQL:

```
GRANT SELECT
ON sales_summary TO acctg_mgr
WITH GRANT OPTION;
```

If the DBA wanted to give some student interns limited rights to some of the base tables, the GRANT might be written

```
GRANT SELECT, UPDATE (selling_price, sale_date)
ON volume TO intern1, intern2, intern3;
```

The preceding example grants SELECT rights to the entire table but gives UPDATE rights only on two specific columns. Notice also that you can grant multiple rights in the same command as well as give the same group of rights to more than one user. However, a single GRANT statement applies to only one table or view.

In most cases, rights are granted to specific user IDs. You can, however, make database elements accessible to anyone by granting rights to the special user ID PUBLIC. For example, the following statement gives every authorized user the rights to see the *sales_summary* view:

```
GRANT SELECT
ON sales_summary TO PUBLIC;
```

Revoking Rights

To remove previously granted rights, you use the REVOKE statement, whose syntax is almost opposite to that of GRANT:

```
REVOKE access_rights
ON table_or_view_name FROM user_ID
```

For example, if the rare book store's summer interns have finished their work for the year, the DBA might want to remove their access from the database:

```
REVOKE SELECT, UPDATE (selling_price, sale_
date)
ON volume FROM intern1, intern2, intern3;
```

If the user from which you are revoking rights has the GRANT option for those rights, then you also need to make a decision about what to do if the user has passed on those rights. In the following case, the REVOKE will be disallowed if the accounting manager has passed on his or her rights:

```
REVOKE SELECT
ON sales_summary FROM acctg_mgr
RESTRICT;
```

In contrast, the syntax

```
REVOKE SELECT
ON sales_summary FROM acctg_mgr
CASCADE;
```

will remove the rights from the *acctg_mgr* ID along with any user IDs to which the *acctg_mgr* granted rights.

Note: Some DBMSs also support a DENY command, which explicitly prohibits a user from performing a given action. It is not a part of the SQL standard, however,

Roles

As the number of people working with a database grows, it becomes difficult to keep track of which rights have been assigned to each individual user. SQL therefore lets you group rights together and assign them as a unit called a *role*.

You create a role with the CREATE ROLE statement:

```
CREATE ROLE role_name
```

The DBA at the rare book store, for example, might create a role for the summer interns:

```
CREATE ROLE interns;
```

Then the DBA assigns rights to the role:

```
GRANT SELECT, UPDATE (selling_price, sale_date)
ON volume TO interns;
```

Finally, the role is then assigned to the users that should have
the rights that are grouped into the role:

```
GRANT interns TO intern1, intern2, intern3;
```

To revoke privileges that are part of a role, use

```
REMOVE role_name FROM user_ID
```

as in

```
REVOKE interns FROM intern1, intern2, intern;
```

A role is removed from the database with

```
DROP ROLE role_name
```

13 Users, Sessions, and Transaction Control

An end user can interact with a database either by issuing SQL statements directly by typing them or by running an application program in which SQL has been embedded. In either case, the database must recognize the user as an authorized database user, the user must connect to the database to establish a database session, and there must be control of the user's transactions. As an introduction, this chapter begins with a discussion of the environment in which multiple users operate and what a DBMS has to do to preserve data integrity when multiple users attempt to modify the same data. The chapter then turns to SQL specifics as a prelude to the discussion of embedded SQL in Chapter 15.

The Concurrent Use Data Environment

A *transaction* is a unit of work submitted as a whole to a database for processing. (A database session consists of one or more transactions.) When more than one user of an application program is interacting with the database at one time, we say that their transactions are running *concurrently*. Concurrent transactions can run in one of two ways:

◊ They may run *serially*, in which case one transaction completes its work before the second begins.

◊ They may run *interleaved*, in which case the actions of both transactions alternate.

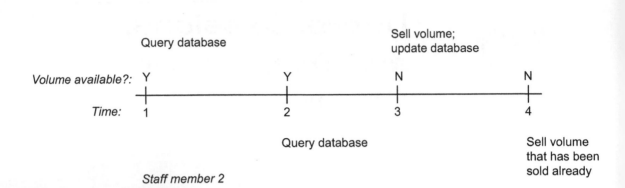

Figure 13-1: A lost update

Ideally, the results of interleaved transaction execution should be the same as that of serial execution (regardless of which transaction went first). If interleaved transaction execution produces such a result, the transactions are said to be *serializable*.

Unfortunately, some very nasty thing can happen if no controls are placed on interleaved execution. As an example, consider what might happen at the rare book store when two customers call at the same time and attempt to order the same volume (see Figure 13-1).

The staff member handling the first customer retrieves data about the volume and notes that it has not been sold. A short time later, a second customer calls and is handled by a second staff member, who also queries the database and sees that the volume is available. After the second staff member's query, the first customer decides to purchase the volume and the first staff member updates the database to indicate that the volume has been sold.

Moments later, the second customer also decides to purchase the volume. As far as the second staff member and the second customer are concerned, the volume is available. The second staff member updates the database with the second customer's purchase, erasing the first customer's purchase. It is likely that the book will be sent to the second customer because no record of the first customer's purchase remains in the database.

This problem, known as a *lost update*, occurred because the second staff member's update was based on old data; the second staff member did not see the first customer's purchase and therefore could not know that the book had already been sold.

The most common solution is to use *locking*, where transaction receive control over database elements they are using to prevent other transactions from updating and/or viewing the same data. Transactions that modify data usually obtain *exclusive*, or *write*, locks that prevent both viewing and modification of data by other transactions while the locks are in place.

To see how locking solves the book purchasing problem, take a look at Figure 13-2. This time, when the first staff member retrieves data about the volume, the transaction receives a lock on the book's data that prevents the second staff member from viewing the data. The second staff member's transaction is placed in a *wait state* by the DBMS until the transaction holding the lock finishes and releases the lock. At this point, the second staff member's transaction can proceed, but when it retrieves the data about the volume, the second staff member sees that the volume has been sold and does not attempt to sell it again.

The second customer is unhappy, but this is a far better situation than what might occur when the first customer discovers that the book that he or she thought was purchased was actually sold to someone else (especially if the first customer's credit card was charged for the book!).

For locking to be effective, a transaction must hold all its locks for the entire length of the transaction. Part of the process that ends a transaction is therefore to release all of the locks,

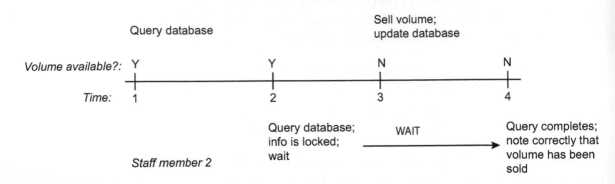

Figure 13-2: Solving a lost update problem with locking

making the data held by the transaction available for other transactions.

In the preceding example, you saw an exclusive lock used to prevent both viewing and updating a part of the database. DBMSs also place *shared*, or *read*, locks that allow many transactions to view a part of the database but allow none to modify it while a shared lock is in place. A DBMS will use a shared lock instead of an exclusive lock whenever it can because a shared lock allows more concurrent use of database resources.

In many cases, the DBMS will place a shared lock on data when a transaction retrieves data and then upgrade that lock to an exclusive lock only when the transaction issue a data modification command. This scheme, known as *two-phase locking*, helps ensure that exclusive locks are held for as short a time as possible and thus promotes the highest level of concurrent use.

The size of the database element on which a lock is placed (the *granularity* of the lock) varies from one DBMS to another and with the type of actions you are performing. It may be as large as an entire disk page (as in early versions of DB2) or an entire table, or it may be as small as a single row in a single table. The smaller the granularity, the more "pieces" there are to lock and the more concurrent use a database can support. However, the DBMS must spent time maintaining locks and keeping track of which transactions are waiting for locks. Therefore, the smaller the granularity and the more locks in place, the more processing time the DBMS must devote to locks rather than data manipulation.

At first glance, it may seem that concurrency control is straight-forward: Either you have serializable transactions or you don't. However, the SQL standard muddies the water a bit by allowing you to specify that a transaction can read data modified by another, uncommitted transaction. The degree to which a transaction has access to such data is known as its *isolation level*.

There are four isolation levels:

◊ SERIALIZABLE: A serializable transaction—the default isolation level—is fully isolated from other transactions. It acts exactly as described in the preceding section of this chapter.

◊ REPEATABLE READ: A repeatable read transaction can read the same data more than once, retrieving rows that satisfy a WHERE predicate. If another transaction has inserted or updated rows and been committed between the first transaction's reads, then the repeated read of the data may return different rows than the first. Depending on the nature of the transaction, such behavior may be desirable. This effect is known as a *phantom read*.

◊ READ COMMITTED: A read committed transaction can also read the same data more than once, but in this case the read returns the same rows. However, the sec-

Muddying the Waters: Isolation Levels

ond read may produce different values if the data have been updated by another transaction that committed between the first and second reads by the transaction in question. Again, depending on the nature of the transaction, this may be something that you want. This effect is known as a *nonrepeatable read*. Such transactions also permit phantom reads.

◊ READ UNCOMMITTED: A read uncommitted transaction can read the same data more than once and read updates made to data by other uncommitted transactions. The danger here is that the uncommitted transaction may be rolled back, voiding their updates. This effect is known as a *dirty read*. Such transactions also permit nonrepeatable reads and phantom reads.

As mentioned earlier, the default isolation level is SERIALIZABLE. To set a lower level, you use the SET TRANSACTION command:

```
SET TRANSACTION
    ISOLATION LEVEL isolation_level
```

Choose the isolation level from one of the four just discussed, as in

```
SET TRANSACTION
    ISOLATION LEVEL REPEATABLE READ;
```

Database Sessions and Connections
SQL for Connecting and Disconnecting

To interact with a database, a user *connects* to it. When the user is finished, he or she *disconnects*. The time between the connection and disconnection is a database *session*.

To establish a connection to a database, you use the keyword CONNECT. For example, to connect under a specific user ID, a user or application would enter

```
CONNECT TO USER user_id
```

The SQL standard includes considerable flexibility in the CONNECT command syntax. If the DBMS has its own way of naming connections, then CONNECT may be enough. If the DBMS requires you to name connections, then you might use

`CONNECT AS connection_identifier`

You should consult your DBMS's documentation for the specific syntax required for a database connection.

Note: The CONNECT command assumes that there is some implementation-specific way to identify the database with which a user will interact once connected and that the database specification occurs before the user attempts to make a connection.

To terminate a connection you use the DISCONNECT command. If you specified a connection name, then the command is written

`DISCONNECT connection_identifier`

If you took the default connection with a user name, then DISCONNECT by itself is usually enough.

There are two possible strategies governing the length of a database connection that come with their own set of trade-offs:

Session Length Considerations

◊ An end user working with a SQL command processor or an application program can connect to the database at the beginning of work and stay connected until work is completed. This eliminates the overhead of repeated connections and disconnections but prevents another user from taking advantage of the connection when the connected user is idle. This strategy is therefore a problem if the number of concurrent users authorized for your DBMS is considerably smaller than the number of people who need to access the database.

◊ An end user working with a SQL command processor or an application program can connect to the database just before a database interaction occurs and disconnect immediately after completing the interaction. (Don't forget that temporary tables exist only during a single database session.) This creates additional overhead for processing the connection and disconnection. However, it ties up the connection for the smallest amount of time necessary and allows more people to access the database.

The bottom line is this: If your DBMS is authorized for the same number of users as people who need to use the database, then you can connect and stay connected. There's no reason not to. However, if you have more people than your software will allow at any one time, you will get less variance in your response times by connecting and disconnecting for each group of database actions.

Transaction Control

Most interactive SQL command processors consider each individual SQL command as a distinct transaction or give the end user a way to "Save changes" after entering a series of commands. However, when you are writing an embedded SQL program, the length of a transaction is totally under your direct control. You also have control over whether the transaction can read and write data, or read only.

Transaction Read/ Write Permissions

By default, transactions can both read and write data. However, read-only transactions never require exclusive (write) locks and therefore in most cases permit higher concurrent use of a database. It therefore can be beneficial to indicate that a retrieval transaction is read only.

If you want a transaction that is read only, you can set that property with the SET TRANSACTION command:

```
SET TRANSACTION READ ONLY;
```

If you are also setting the transaction's isolation level, you can do so with the same command by separating the options with commas, as in

```
SET TRANSACTION ISOLATION LEVEL READ COMMITTED,
READ ONLY;
```

Transactions end in one of two ways:

◊ If a transaction is *committed*, then any changes the transaction made to the database become permanent.

◊ If a transaction is *rolled back*, then any changes the transaction made are undone, restoring the database to the state it was in before the transaction began.

By definition, a committed transaction is never rolled back. To be able to roll back a transaction, a DBMS needs a log of every action taken by a transaction. This log, known more formally as a *before-image file*, contains information about all database transactions currently in progress. When a transaction is committed, its records are purged from the log and the vacated space is used for data about subsequent transactions. When a transaction is rolled back, the DBMS starts at the transaction's last record in the log file and replaces each current value with its old value from the log file. The process repeats, moving forward in the log file, until the DBMS reaches the log record that indicates the start of the transaction. At this point, the log records can be purged.

Although early versions of the SQL standard did not include any statement to start a transaction, the current Core specifications include a START TRANSACTION statement:

```
START TRANSACTION mode
```

The mode of a transaction can include its isolation level and whether it is read only or read/write.

Transaction Termination

Starting Transactions

Note: For those DBMSs that don't support the START TRANS-ACTION statement, a new transaction begins automatically whenever there is no current transaction and a user or application program issues a command that requires database action.

Ending Transactions

If you are using interactive SQL, you may request the end of a transaction in any of the following ways:

◊ Using a GUI, clicking a "Save Changes" or "Execute Command" button executes the command and, if the command executes without error (in other words, violates no constraints), automatically commits the transaction.

◊ Working from the command line, adding a colon to terminate the command and pressing Enter submits the command for processing. The transaction is committed automatically when it executes successfully.

◊ An application program makes its own decision whether to commit or roll back a transaction based on an error code returned by the DBMS. (You will read more about these error codes in Chapter 15.) Once the decision has been made, a program issues COMMIT or COMMIT WORK to commit the transaction. To undo everything done by a transaction, the program issues either ROLLBACK or ROLLBACK WORK.

Transaction Length Considerations

One of the questions that always arises in a discussion of transactions is how long they should be. In general, they should be short, and there are two important reasons why:

◊ A transaction is the *unit of recovery*. When you perform a rollback, you must undo the entire transaction, not just part of it. You stand to lose a lot of processing if you must roll back a long transaction.

◊ As you read earlier in this chapter, for locking to be effective a transaction must hold all its locks until the transaction ends. Long transactions therefore tie up large portions of the database, cutting down on the amount of concurrent use the database can provide. Because all locks are released when a transaction terminates, shorter transactions maximize the number of users that can share the same database elements.

Note: Locking is essential for data consistency and integrity when multiple transactions are running concurrently. It is therefore not an option to remove the locking mechanism.

Programmers often wonder if it is necessary to end a transaction quickly if all the transaction is doing is retrieving data. The answer is "yes," because retrieval transactions lock database elements. Although they typically allow other transactions to view the locked data, they prevent update of the data. Therefore, you should always commit a retrieval transaction immediately after bringing the data from the database into a query result table, freeing up the tables or views used for other users to modify.

Note: There is rarely any reason to roll back a retrieval transaction. The undo process just takes up processing time without affecting the contents of the database.

Part IV
SQL
Programming

14

Writing and Executing SQL Routines and Modules—Triggers and Stored Procedures

Although SQL is not a complete programming language—it lacks I/O statements—the standard does contain statements that perform typical programming language functions such as assignment, selection, and iteration for writing *persistent stored modules* (PSMs). This chapter looks at creating program routines and modules using those language elements and how they are executed as either triggers or stored procedures.

Note: This chapter does not attempt to teach programming concepts. To get the most out of it you should be familiar with a general-purpose programming or scripting language such as COBOL, C, C++, Java, JavaScript, or Perl.

Triggers are SQL program modules that are executed when a specific data modification activity occurs. For example, a trigger may be configured to execute whenever a row is inserted into a table. *Stored procedures* are SQL program modules that are invoked by an application program using the SQL CALL command. Both triggers and stored procedures are stored as part of a database.

Note: Support for SQL programming varies considerably from one DBMS to another. This chapter presents what is documented in the SQL standard, but it is highly likely that what is available with your DBMS will be different from what you see here, at least to some degree. You should therefore use what is in this chapter as a starting point for your DBMS's SQL programming support and verify the specifics with your software's documentation.

SQL Programming Elements

The smallest unit of a SQL PSM is a *routine*. Typically a routine will perform a single action, such as updating a total or inserting a row in a table. Routines are then gathered into *modules*.

There are three types of routines:

◊ Procedures: Procedures are executed with the SQL CALL statement. They do not return a value.

◊ Functions: Functions return a typed value and are used within other SQL statements (in particular, SELECT).

◊ Methods: Methods are used by SQL's object-relational extensions. They are written using the same programming elements as procedures and functions. Therefore, their structure will be discussed in Chapter 19, but the techniques for creating method bodies can be found in this chapter.

To create a procedure, use the CREATE PROCEDURE statement:

```
CREATE PROCEDURE
    procedure_name (input_parameters)
LANGUAGE SQL
MODIFIES SQL DATA
BEGIN
    procedure_body
END
```

Function creation must include the type of data being returned and a RETURN statement:

```
CREATE FUNCTION
      function_name (input_parameters)
RETURNS return_data_type
LANGUAGE SQL
CONTAINS SQL
      function_body
RETURN return_value
```

Note: Functions that you write yourself are often called user-defined functions (UDFs) to distinguish them from functions such as SUM (sometimes called BIFs, for Built-In Functions) that are part of the SQL language.

Notice that the two preceding structures include statements that refer to the language and type of statements in the routine:

◊ LANGUAGE *language_name*: Indicates the programming language used in the routine. In our examples, the language is SQL. If the LANGUAGE clause is not present, then the language defaults to SQL.

◊ Type of SQL statements contained in routine (one of the following):

  o CONTAINS SQL: Indicates that the routine includes SQL statements that do not retrieve or modify data.

  o READS SQL DATA: Indicates that the routine includes SQL statements that read data from a database but that do not modify data.

  o MODIFIES SQL DATA: Indicates that the routine modifies data using SQL commands. This also implies that the routine may be retrieving data.

The routine's contents may include SQL data modification statements (INSERT, UPDATE, and DELETE) along with SQL control structures.

SQL modules are created with the CREATE MODULE statement:

```
CREATE MODULE module_name
      module_contents
END MODULE
```

Like other SQL structural elements, routines, modules, and the contents are stored in the current schema. To remove a module or routine, you must therefore use

```
DROP ROUTINE routine_name
```

or

```
DROP MODULE module_name
```

Note: The interactive SELECT, which typically returns multiple rows, is useful only for display of a result table. To manipulate the data in a result table, you will need to use embedded SQL, which retrieves data into a virtual table and then lets you process the rows in that table one at a time. (Embedded SQL is discussed in Chapter 15.) Dynamic SQL (Chapter 16) further extends programming with SQL by letting the user enter search values at run time.

Within a module, SQL recognizes compound statements using BEGIN and END:

```
BEGIN
      one_or_more_executable_statements
END
```

As you might expect, compound statements can be nested as needed.

Variables and Assignment

SQL modules can maintain their own internal variables and perform assignment. Variables must be declared before they are used:

```
DECLARE variable_name data_type
```

Once a variable has been declared, you assign values to it across the assignment operator:

```
variable_name = value
```

For example, if you need to store a sales tax percentage, the routine could contain

```
DECLARE tax_rate NUMBER (5,2);
tax_rate = 0.075;
```

Important note: Depending on the DBMS, the assignment operator may be = or :-. Check your documentation to be sure.

Important note: Some DBMSs require a special character at the beginning of a variable name. For example, SQL Server requires @. Once again, the only way to be certain is to consult your DBMS's documentation.

Both functions and procedures can accept input parameters. A parameter list contains the names by which the parameters are to be referenced within the body of the routine and a declaration of their data types:

Passing Parameters

```
CREATE routine_type routine_name (
    parameter_1 parameter_1_data_type,
    parameter_2 parameter_2_data_type, … )
```

For example, to pass in a tax rate and a selling price to a function that computes sales tax, the function might be written

```
CREATE FUNCTION compute_tax
    (tax_rate NUMBER (6,3),
     selling_price NUMBER (7,2))
LANGUAGE SQL
RETURNS NUMBER
   RETURN selling_price * tax_rate;
```

Note: Procedures can also use a parameter for output or for both input and output.

Note: Some DBMSs require/allow you to specify whether a parameter is for input, output, or both. If you are working with one of those implementations, each parameter in the parameter list must/ can be labeled with IN, OUT, or INOUT.

Scope of Variables

Variables declared within SQL functions and procedures are local to the routine. Values passed in through a parameter list are declared in the parameter list and therefore become local variables. However, there are circumstances in which you may want to use variables declared outside the function or procedure (*host language variables*). In that case, there are two things you need to do:

◊ Redeclare the host language variables using a SQL declare section.

```
BEGIN SQL DECLARE SECTION;
    redeclaration of host language
            variables;
END SQL DECLARE SECTION;
```

◊ Place a colon in front of the name of each host language variable whenever it is used in the body of the SQL routine.

You will see examples of these techniques in use with embedded SQL in Chapter 15.

Selection

The SQL standard provides two selection structures: IF and CASE. Both function essentially like the analogous elements in general-purpose programming languages.

IF

In its simplest form, the SQL IF construct has the following structure:

```
IF boolean_expression THEN
    body_of_IF
END IF
```

Assume, for example, that the owner of the rare book store wants to give a discount on a total purchase to customers who order more than $100 on a single order. The code to do so could be written

```
IF sale_total_amt >= 100 THEN
     sale_total_amt = sale_total_amt * .9;
END IF;
```

As you would expect, the IF statement can be extended with ELSEIF and ELSE clauses:

```
IF boolean_expression THEN
     body_of_IF
ELSEIF boolean_expression THEN
     body_of_ELSEIF
:
ELSE
     body_of_ELSE
END OF
```

The ELSEIF clause is shorthand for the following:

```
IF boolean_expression THEN
     body_of_IF
ELSE
     IF boolean_expression THEN
          body_of_nested_IF
     END IF
END IF
```

A purchase from the rare book store that must be shipped is assessed shipping charges based on the number of volumes in the purchase. Assuming the number of volumes in the purchase is stored in *how_many*, an IF construct to assign those shipping charges might be written as

```
IF how_many <= 5 THEN
     shipping_charges = how_many * 2;
ELSEIF how_many <= 10 THEN
     shipping_charges = how_many * 1.5;
ELSE
     shipping_charges = how_many;
END IF
```

Note: Obtaining the count of the number of volumes in a single purchase requires embedded SQL, which is discussed in Chapter 15.

CASE

The SQL CASE expression comes in two forms, one with a single condition and one with multiple conditions. (The syntaxes are essentially the same as the CASE statement that can be used in a SELECT clause.) In its simplest form, it has the general format:

```
CASE logical_expression
    WHEN value1 THEN executable_statement(s)
    WHEN value2 THEN executable_statement(s)
    WHEN value3 THEN executable_statement(s)
    :
    ELSE default
END CASE
```

For example, suppose T-shirt sizes are stored as integer codes and you want to translate those sizes to words. The code could be written

```
DECLARE text_size CHAR (10)
CASE size
    WHEN 1 THEN text_size = 'Small'
    WHEN 2 THEN text_size = 'Medium'
    WHEN 3 THEN text_size = 'Large'
    WHEN 4 THEN text_size = 'Extra Large'
END CASE
```

The multiple condition version is a bit more flexible:

```
CASE
    WHEN logical_expression1 THEN executable_
statement(s)
    WHEN logical_expression1 THEN executable_
statement(s)
    WHEN logical_expression1 THEN executable_
statement(s)
    :
    ELSE default
END CASE;
```

Someone could use this second version to compute a book discount based on selling price:

```
CASE
     WHEN asking_price < 50 THEN selling_price
= asking_price * .9
     WHEN asking_price < 100 THEN selling_price
= asking_price * .85
     WHEN asking_price < 150 THEN selling_price
= asking_price * .75
     ELSE selling_price = asking_price * .5
END CASE;
```

Iteration

SQL has four statements that perform iteration—LOOP, WHILE, REPEAT, and FOR—that work somewhat differently from similar statements in general-purpose programming languages.

Note: The SQL FOR statement is not a general-purpose looping construct. Instead, it is designed to work with embedded SQL code that processes each row in a virtual table that has been created as the result of a SELECT. We will therefore defer a discussion of FOR until Chapter 15.

LOOP

The LOOP statement is a simple construct that sets up an infinite loop:

```
loop_name: LOOP
     body_of_loop
END LOOP
```

The condition that terminates the loop and a command to exit the loop must therefore be contained in the body of the loop. A typical structure therefore would be

```
loop_name: LOOP
     body_of_loop
     IF termination_condition
          LEAVE loop_name
END LOOP
```

Assume (for some unknown reason) that we want to total the numbers from 1 through 100. We could do it with a LOOP statement as follows:

```
DECLARE sum INT;
DECLARE count INT;
sum = 0;
count = 1;
sum_loop: LOOP
    sum = sum + count;
    count = count + 1;
    IF count > 100
        LEAVE sum_loop;
END LOOP;
```

Note: LEAVE can be used with any named looping construct. However, it is essential only for a LOOP structure because there is no other way to stop the iteration.

WHILE

The SQL WHILE is very similar to what you will find as part of a general-purpose programming language:

```
loop_name: WHILE boolean_expression DO
        body_of_loop
END WHILE
```

The loop name is optional.

As an example, assume that you wanted to continue to purchase items until all of your funds were exhausted, but that each time you purchased an item the price went up ten percent. Each purchase is stored as a row in a table. Code to handle that could be written as in Figure 14-1.

Note: Whenever a host language (in this case SQL) variable is used in a SQL statement, it must be preceded by a colon, as in :price.

REPEAT

The SQL REPEAT statement is similar to the WHILE DO statement in high-level languages where the test for termination/continuation of the loop is at the bottom of the loop. It has the general format:

```
DECLARE funds NUMBER (7,2);
funds = 1000.00;
DECLARE price NUMBER (5,2);
price = 29.95;

WHILE :funds > :price = DO
     INSERT INTO items_purchased
          VALUES (6, CURRENT_DATE, :price);
     funds = funds - price;
     price = price * 1.1;
END WHILE;
```

Figure 14-1: Using a WHILE loop to make repeated purchases

```
loop_name: REPEAT
     body_of_loop
UNTIL boolean_expression
END REPEAT
```

We could rewrite the example from the preceding section using a REPEAT in the following way:

```
DECLARE funds NUMBER (7,2);
funds = 1000.00;
DECLARE price NUMBER (5,2);
price = 29.95;

REPEAT
     INSERT INTO items_purchased
          VALUES (6, CURRENT_DATE, :price);
     funds = funds - price;
     price = price * 1.1;
UNTIL price > funds
END REPEAT;
```

One of the things you might decide to do with a stored procedure is simplify issuing a query or series of queries. For example, suppose that the owner of the rare book store wants to see the sales that were made each day along with the total sales. A single interactive SQL command won't produce both a

Example #1: Interactive Retrievals

```
CREATE PROCEDURE daily_sales
LANGUAGE SQL
READS SQL DATA
BEGIN
     SELECT first_name, last_name, sale_total_amt
     FROM sale JOIN customer
     WHERE sale_date = CURRENT_DATE;
     SELECT SUM (sale_total_amt)
     FROM sale
     WHERE sale_date = CURRENT_DATE;
END
```

Figure 14-2 A SQL procedure that contains multiple SELECT statements for display

listing of individual sales and a total. However, the two queries in Figure 14-2 will do the trick. The user only needs to run the procedure to see the needed data.

Note: Without embedded-SQL, we can only display data retrieved by a SELECT. We can't process the individual rows.

Example #2: Nested Modules

Procedures and functions can call other procedures and functions. For this example, let's assume that a column for the sales tax has been added to the *sale* table and prepare a procedure that populates the *sale* table and updates the *volume* table when a purchase is made (Figure 14-3). The *sell_it* procedures uses the *compute_tax* function you saw earlier in this chapter.

Executing Modules as Triggers

A trigger is a module that is attached to a single table and executed in response to one of the following events:

◊ INSERT (either before or after an insert occurs)

◊ UPDATE (either before or after a modify occurs)

◊ DELETE (either before or after a delete occurs)

"Before" triggers are run prior to checking constraints on the table and prior to running INSERT, UPDATE, or DELETE

```
CREATE PROCEDURE sell_it (sale_numb INT, customer_id INT, book_id CHAR (17),
price_paid NUMBER (7,2), tax_rate NUMBER (6,3))
LANGUAGE SQL
MODIFIES SQL DATA
BEGIN
     DECLARE tax;
     tax = compute_tax (tax_rate, price_paid);
     IF (SELECT COUNT(*) FROM volume WHERE sale_id = sale_numb) < 1 THEN
          INSERT INTO sale (:sale_id, :customer_numb, :sale_date, :sale_total_
amt, :sales_tax) VALUES (sale_numb, customer_id, CURRENT_DATE, :price_paid,
tax);
     END IF
     UPDATE volume
          SET selling_price = :price_paid,
          SET sale_id = :sale_numb;
END

CREATE FUNCTION compute_tax (tax_rate NUMBER (6,3), selling_price NUMBER (7,2))
LANGUAGE SQL
RETURNS NUMBER
   RETURN selling_price * tax_rate;
```

Figure 14-3: A SQL procedure that calls a user-defined function

command. "After" triggers work on the table after the IN-SERT, UPDATE, or DELETE has been performed, using the table as it has been changed by the command. A trigger can be configured to run once for every row in the table or just once for the entire table.

Note: It is possible to attach multiple triggers for the same event to the same table. The order in which they execute is implementation dependent. Some DBMSs execute them in alphabetical order by name; others execute them chronologically, with the first created being the first executed.

Before creating a trigger, you must create the function or procedure that is to be run. Once that is in place, you use the CREATE TRIGGER statement to attach the trigger to its table and specify when it should be run:

```
CREATE TRIGGER trigger_name when_to_execute
type_of_event
ON table_name row_or_table_specifier
EXECUTE PROCEDURE procedure_or_function_name
```

The *when_to_execute* value is either BEFORE or AFTER, the type of event is INSERT, MODIFY, or DELETE, and the *row_or_table_specifier* is either FOR EACH ROW or FOR EACH STATEMENT.

For example, to trigger the procedure that updates the *sale_total_amt* in the *sale* table whenever a volume is sold, someone at the rare book store could use

```
CREATE TRIGGER t_update_total AFTER UPDATE
ON volume FOR EACH STATEMENT
EXECUTE PROCEDURE p_update_total;
```

The trigger will then execute automatically whenever an update is performed on the *volume* table.

You remove a trigger with the DROP TRIGGER statement:

```
DROP TRIGGER trigger_name
```

However, it can be a bit tedious to continually drop a trigger when what you want to do is replace an existing trigger with a new version. To simply replace an existing trigger, use

```
CREATE OR MODIFY TRIGGER trigger_name …
```

instead of simply CREATE TRIGGER.

Executing Modules as Stored Procedures

Stored procedures are invoked with either the EXECUTE or CALL statement:

```
EXECUTE procedure_name (parameter_list)
```

or

```
CALL procedure_name (parameter_list)
```

Embedded SQL

Although a knowledgeable SQL user can accomplish a great deal with an interactive command processor, much interaction with a database is through application programs that provide a predictable interface for nontechnologically sophisticated users. In this chapter you will read about the preparation of programs that contain SQL statements and the special things you must do to fit SQL within a host programming language.

The Embedded SQL Environment

SQL statements can be embedded in a wide variety of host languages. Some are general-purpose programming languages such as COBOL, C++, or Java. Others are special-purpose database programming languages such as the PowerScript language used by PowerBuilder or Oracle's SQL/Plus, which contains the SQL language elements discussed in Chapter 14 as well as Oracle-specific extensions.

The way in which you handle source code depends on the type of host language you are using: Special-purpose database languages such as PowerScript or extensions of the SQL language (for example, SQL/Plus) need no special processing. Their language translators recognize embedded SQL statements and know what to do with them. However, general-purpose language compilers are not written to recognize syntax that isn't part of the original language. When a COBOL[1] or C++ compiler encounters a SQL statement, it generates an error.

The solution to the problem has several aspects:

◊ Support for SQL statements is provided by a set of program library modules. The input parameters to the modules represent the portions of a SQL statement that are set by the programmer.

◊ SQL statements embedded in a host language program are translated by a *precompiler* into calls to routines in the SQL library.

◊ The host language compiler can access the calls to library routines and therefore can compile the output produced by the precompiler.

◊ During the linking phase of program preparation, the library routines used to support SQL are linked to the executable file along with any other library used by the program.

To make it easier for the precompiler to recognize SQL statements, each one is preceded by EXEC SQL. The way in which you terminate the statement varies from one language to another. The typical terminators are summarized in Table 15-1. For the examples in this book, we will use a semicolon as an embedded SQL statement terminator.

---

1   Many people think COBOL is a dead language. While few new programs are being written, there are literally billions of lines of code for business applications written in COBOL that are still in use. Maintaining these applications is becoming a major issue for many organizations because COBOL programmers are starting to retire in large numbers and young programmers haven't learned the language.

Java and JDBC

Java is an unusual language, in that it is pseudo-compiled. (Language tokens are converted to machine code at runtime by the Java virtual machine.) It also accesses databases in its own way: using a library of routines (an API) known as *Java Database Connectivity*, or JDBC. A JDBC driver provides the interface between the JDBC library and the specific DBMS being used.

JDBC does not require that Java programs be precompiled. Instead, SQL commands are created as strings that are passed as parameters to functions in the JDBC library. The process for interacting with a database using JDBC goes something like this:

1. Create a connection to the database.

2. Use the object returned in Step 1 to create an object for a SQL statement.

3. Store each SQL command that will be used in a string variable.

4. Use the object returned in Step 2 to execute one or more SQL statements.

5. Close the statement object.

6. Close the database connection object.

If you will be using Java to write database applications, then you will probably want to investigate JDBC. Many books have been written about using it with a variety of DBMSs.

Table 15-1: Embedded SQL statement terminators

Language	Terminator
Ada	Semicolon
C, C++	Semicolon
COBOL	END-EXEC
Fortran	None
MUMPS	Close parenthesis
Pascal	Semicolon
PL/1	Semicolon

Using Host Language Variables

General purpose programming languages require that you re-declare any host language variables used in embedded SQL statements.[2] The declarations are bracketed between two SQL statements, using the following format:

```
EXEC SQL BEGIN DECLARE SECTION;
    declarations go here
EXEC SQL END DECLARE SECTION;
```

The specifics of the variable declarations depend on the host language being used. The syntax typically conforms to the host language's syntax for variable declarations.

As mentioned in Chapter 14, when you use a host language variable in a SQL statement, you precede it by a colon so that it is distinct from table, view, and column names. For example, the following statement updates one row in the *customer* table with a value stored in the variable *da_new_phone*, using a value

---

2   Some major DBMSs make the programmer's life easier by providing tools that generate host variables for each column in a table automatically (for example, DB2's DCLGEN).

stored in the variable *da_which_customer* to identify the row to be modified[3]:

```
EXEC SQL UPDATE customer
    SET contact_phone = :da_new_phone
    WHERE customer_numb = :da_which_customer;
```

This use of a colon applies both to general purpose programming languages and to database application languages (even those that don't require a precompiler).

Note: The requirement for the colon in front of host language variables means that theoretically columns and host language variables could have the same names. In practice, however, using the same names can be confusing.

The host language variables that contain data for use in SQL statements are known as *dynamic parameters*. The values that are sent to the DBMS, for example, as part of a WHERE predicate, are known as *input parameters*. The values that accept data being returned by the DBMS, such as the data returned by a SELECT, are known as *output parameters*.

When you are working with interactive SQL, error messages appear on your screen. For example, if an INSERT command violates a table constraint, the SQL command processor tells you immediately. You then read the message and make any necessary changes to your SQL to correct the problem. However, when SQL is embedded in a program, the end user has no access to the SQL and therefore can't make any corrections. Technologically unsophisticated users also may become upset when they see the usually cryptic DBMS errors appearing on the screen. Programs in which SQL is embedded need to be able to intercept the error codes returned by the DBMS and to handle them before the errors reach the end user.

DBMS Return Codes

---

3   Keep in mind that this will work only if the value on which we are searching is a primary key and thus uniquely identifies the row.

The SQL standard defines a status variable named SQL-STATE, a five-character string. The first two characters represent the class of the error. The rightmost three characters are the subclass, which provides further detail about the state of the database. For example, 00000 means that the SQL statement executed successfully. Other codes include a class of 22, which indicates a data exception. The subclasses of class 22 include 003 (numeric value out of range) and 007 (invalid datetime format). A complete listing of the SQLSTATE return codes can be found in Appendix B.

In most cases, an application should check the contents of SQLSTATE each time it executes a SQL statement. For example, after performing the update example you saw in the preceding section, a C++ program might do the following:

```
If (strcmp(SQLSTATE,'00000') == 0)
    EXEC SQL COMMIT;
else
{
    // some error handling code goes here
}
```

Retrieving a Single Row

When the WHERE predicate in a SELECT statement contains a primary key expression, the result table will contain at most one row. For such a query, all you need to do is specify host language variables into which the SQL command processor can place the data it retrieves. You do this by adding an INTO clause to the SELECT.

For example, if someone at the rare book store needed the phone number of a specific customer, a program might include

```
EXEC SQL SELECT contact_phone
INTO :da_phone_numb
FROM customers
WHERE customer_numb = 12;
```

The INTO clause contains the keyword INTO followed by the names of the host language variables in which data will be placed. In the preceding example, data are being retrieved from only one column and the INTO clause therefore contains just a single variable name.

Note: Many programmers have naming conventions that make working with host variables a bit easier. In this book, the names of host language variables that hold data begin with da_; indicator variables, to which you will be introduced in the next section, begin with in_.

If you want to retrieve data from multiple columns, you must provide one host language variable for each column, as in the following:

```
EXEC SQL SELECT first_name, last_name,
     contact_phone
INTO :da_first, :da_last, :da_phone
FROM customer
WHERE customer_numb = 12;
```

The names of the host language variables are irrelevant. The SQL command processor places data into them by position. In other words, data from the first column following SELECT is placed in the first variable following INTO, data from the second column following SELECT is placed in the second variable following INTO, and so on. Keep in mind that all host language variables are preceded by colons to distinguish them from the names of database elements.

After executing a SELECT that contains a primary key expression in its WHERE predicate, an embedded SQL program should check to determine whether a row was retrieved. Assuming we are using C or C++, the code might be written

```
if (strcmp(SQLSTATE,'00000') == )
{
    EXEC SQL COMMIT;
    // display or process data retrieved
)
```

```
else
{
    EXEC SQL COMMIT;
    // display error message
}
// continue processing
```

There are three things to note about the COMMIT statement in this code:

◊ The COMMIT must be issued *after* checking the SQL-STATE. Otherwise, the COMMIT will change the value in SQLSTATE.

◊ There is no need to roll back a retrieval transaction, so the code commits the transaction even if the retrieval fails.

◊ The COMMIT could be placed after the IF construct. However, depending on the length of the code that follows error checking, the transaction may stay open longer than necessary. Therefore, the repeated COMMIT statement is an efficient choice in this situation.

Indicator Variables

The SQLSTATE variable is not the only way in which a DBMS can communicate the results of a retrieval to an application program. Each host variable into which you place data can be associated with an *indicator variable*. When indicator variables are present, the DBMS stores a 0 to indicate that a data variable has valid data of a −1 to indicate that the row contained a null in the specified column and that the contents of the data variable are unchanged.

To use indicator variables, first declare host language variables of an integer data type to hold the indicators. Then, follow each data variable in the INTO clause with the keyword INDICATOR and the name of the indicator variable. For example, to use indicator variables with the customer data retrieval query:

```
EXEC SQL SELECT first_name, last_name,
     contact_phone
INTO :da_first INDICATOR :in_first,
     :da_last INDICATOR :in_last,
     :da_phone INDICATOR :in_phone
FROM customer
WHERE customer_numb = 12;
```

You can then use host language syntax to check the contents of each indicator variable to determine whether you have valid data to process in each data variable.

Note: The INDICATOR keyword is optional. Therefore, the syntax INTO :first :ifirst, :last :ilast, and so on is acceptable.

Indicator variables can also be useful for telling you when character values have been truncated. For example, assume that the host language variable *first* has been declared to accept a 10-character string but that the database column *first_name* is 15 characters long. If the database column contains a full 15 characters, only the first 10 will be placed in the host language variable. The indicator variable will contain 15, indicating the size of the column (and the size to which the host language variable should have been set).

SELECT statements that may return more than one row present a bit of a problem when you embed them in a program. Host language variables can hold only one value at a time and the SQL command processor cannot work with host language arrays. The solution provides you with a pointer (a *cursor*) to a SQL result table that allows you to extract one row at a time for processing.

The procedure for creating and working with a cursor is as follows:

1. *Declare* the cursor by specifying the SQL SELECT to be executed. This does not perform the retrieval.

Retrieving Multiple Rows: Cursors

2. *Open* the cursor. This step actually executes the SELECT and creates the result table in main memory. It positions the cursor just above the first row in the result table.

3. *Fetch* the next row in the result table and process the data in some way.

4. Repeat step 3 until all rows in the result table have been accessed and processed.

5. *Close* the cursor. This deletes the result table from main memory but does not destroy the declaration. You can therefore reopen an existing cursor, recreating the result table, and work with the data without redeclaring the SELECT.

If you do not explicitly close a cursor, it will be closed automatically when the transaction terminates. (This is the default.) If, however, you want the cursor to remain open after a COMMIT, then you add a WITH HOLD option to the declaration.

Even if a cursor is held from one transaction to another, its result table will still be deleted at the end of the database session in which it was created. To return that result table to the calling routine, add a WITH RETURN option to the declaration.

Note: There is no way to "undeclare" a cursor. A cursor's declaration disappears when the program module in which it was created terminates.

By default, a cursor fetches the "next" row in the result table. However, you may also use a *scrollable cursor* to fetch the "next," "prior," "first," or "last" row. In addition, you can fetch by specifying a row number in the result table or by giving an offset from the current row. This in large measure eliminates the need to close and reopen the cursor to reposition the cursor above its current location.

Declaring a Cursor

Declaring a cursor is similar to creating a view in that you include a SQL statement that defines a virtual table. The DECLARE statement has the following general format in its simplest form:

```
DECLARE cursor_name CURSOR FOR
SELECT remainder_of_query
```

For example, assume that someone at the rare book store wanted to prepare labels for a mailing to all its customers. The program that prints mailing labels needs each customer's name and address from the database, which it can then format for labels. A cursor to hold the data might be declared as

```
EXEC SQL DECLARE address_data CURSOR FOR
SELECT first_name, last_name, street, city,
state_province, zip_postcode
FROM customer;
```

The name of a cursor must be unique within the program module in which it is created. A program can therefore manipulate an unlimited number of cursors at the same time.

Scrolling Cursors

One of the options available with a cursor is the ability to retrieve rows in other than the default "next" order. To enable a scrolling cursor, you must indicate that you want scrolling when you declare the cursor by adding the keyword SCROLL after the cursor name:

```
EXEC SQL DECLARE address_data SCROLL CURSOR FOR
SELECT first_name, last_name, street,
      city, state_province, zip_postcode
FROM customer;
```

You will find more about using scrolling cursors a bit later in this chapter when we talk about fetching rows.

Enabling Updates

The data in a cursor are by default read only. However, if the result table meets all updatability criteria, you can use the cursor for data modification. (You will find more about the updatability criteria in the *Modification Using Cursors* section later in this chapter.)

To enable modification for a customer, add the keywords FOR UPDATE at the end of the cursor's declaration:

```
EXEC SQL DECLARE address_data SCROLL CURSOR FOR
SELECT first_name, last_name, street, city,
    state_province, zip_postcode
FROM customer
FOR UPDATE;
```

To restrict updates to specific columns, add the names of columns following UPDATE:

```
EXEC SQL DECLARE address_data SCROLL CURSOR FOR
SELECT first_name, last_name, street, city,
    state_province, zip_postcode
FROM customer
FOR UPDATE street, city, state_province,
    zip_postcode;
```

Sensitivity

Assume, for example, that a program for the rare book store contains a module that computes the average price of books and changes prices based on that average: If a book's price is more than 20 percent higher than the average, the price is discounted 10 percent; if the price is only 10 percent higher, it is discounted 5 percent.

A programmer codes the logic of the program in the following way:

1. Declare and open a cursor that contains the inventory IDs and asking prices for all volumes whose price is greater than the average. The SELECT that generates the result table is

```
SELECT inventory_id, asking_price
FROM volume
WHERE asking_price >
     (SELECT AVG (asking_price)
      FROM volume);
```

2. Fetch each row and modify its price.

The question at this point is: What happens in the result table as data are modified? As prices are lowered, some rows will no longer meet the criteria for inclusion in the table. More important, the average retail price will drop. If this program is to execute correctly, however, the contents of the result table must remain fixed once the cursor has been opened.

The SQL standard therefore defines three types of cursors:

◊ *Insensitive*: The contents of the result table are fixed.

◊ *Sensitive*: The contents of the result table are updated each time the table is modified.

◊ *Indeterminate (asensitive)*: The effects of updates made by the same transaction on the result table are left up to each individual DBMS.

The default is indeterminate, which means that you cannot be certain that the DBMS will not alter your result table before you are through with it.

The solution is to request specifically that the cursor be insensitive:

```
EXEC SQL DECLARE address_data SCROLL
     INSENSITIVE CURSOR FOR
SELECT first_name, last_name, street, city,
     state_province, zip_postcode
FROM customer
FOR UPDATE street, city, state_province,
     zip_postcode;
```

Opening a Cursor

To open a cursor, place the cursor's name following the keyword OPEN:

```
EXEC SQL OPEN address_data;
```

Fetching Rows

To retrieve the data from the next row in a result table, placing data into host language variables, you use the FETCH statement:

```
FETCH FROM cursor_name
INTO host_language_variables
```

For example, to obtain a row of data from the list of customer names and addresses, the rare book store's program could use

```
EXEC SQL FETCH FROM address_data
INTO :da_first, :da_last, :da_street, :da_city,
     :da_state_province, :da_zip_postcode;
```

Notice that as always the host language variables are preceded by colons to distinguish them from table, view, or column names. In addition, the host language variables must match the database columns as to data type. The FETCH will fail if, for example, you attempt to place a string value into a numeric variable.

If you want to fetch something other than the next row, you can declare a scrolling cursor and specify the row by adding the direction in which you want the cursor to move after the keyword FETCH:

◊ To fetch the first row

```
EXEC SQL FETCH FIRST FROM
    address_data
INTO :da_first, :da_last, :da_street,
    :da_city, :da_state_province,
    :da_zip_postcode;
```

◊ To fetch the last row

```
EXEC SQL FETCH LAST FROM address_data
INTO :da_first, :da_last, :da_street,
     :da_city, :da_state_province,
     :da_zip_postcode;
```

◊ To fetch the prior row

```
EXEC SQL FETCH PRIOR FROM address_data
INTO :da_first, :da_last, :da_street,
     :da_city, :da_state_province,
     :da_zip_postcode;
```

◊ To fetch a row specified by its position (row number) in the result table

```
EXEC SQL FETCH ABSOLUTE 12
FROM address_data
INTO :da_first, :da_last, :da_street,
     :da_city, :da_state_province,
     :da_zip_postcode;
```

The preceding fetches the twelfth row in the result table.

◊ To fetch a row relative to and below the current position of the cursor

```
EXEC SQL FETCH RELATIVE 5
FROM address_data
INTO :da_first, :da_last, :da_street,
     :da_city, :da_state_province,
     :da_zip_postcode;
```

The preceding fetches the row five rows below the current position of the cursor (current position + 5).

◊ To fetch a row relative to and above the current position of the cursor

```
EXEC SQL FETCH RELATIVE -5
FROM address_data
INTO :da_first, :da_last, :da_street,
     :da_city, :da_state_province,
     :da_zip_postcode;
```

The preceding fetches the row five rows above the current position of the cursor (current row – 5).

Note: If you use FETCH without an INTO clause, you will move the cursor without retrieving any data.

If there is no row containing data at the position of the cursor, the DBMS returns a "no data" error (SQLSTATE = '02000'). The general strategy for processing a table of data is therefore to create a loop that continues to fetch rows until a SQLSTATE of something other than '00000' occurs. Then you can test to see whether you've simply finished processing or whether some other problem has arisen. In C/C++, the code would look something like Figure 15-1.

```
EXEC SQL FETCH FROM address data
INTO :da_first, :da_last, :da_street, :da_city, :da_state_province,
     :da_zip_postscode;
while (strcmp (SQLSTATE, "00000") == 0)
{
    // Process one row's data in appropriate way
    EXEC SQL FETCH FROM address data
    INTO :da_first, :da_last, :da_street, :da_city, :da_state_province,
         :da_zip_postscode;
)
if (strcmp (SQLSTATE, "0200000") != 0
{
    // Display error message and/or do additional error checking
}
EXEC SQL COMMIT;
```

Figure 15-1: Using a host language loop to process all rows in an embedded SQL result table

Note: One common error that beginning programmers make is to write loops that use a specific error code as a terminating value. This can result in an infinite loop if some other error condition arises. We therefore typically write loops to stop on any error condition and then check to determine exactly which condition occurred.

Note: You can use indicator variables in the INTO clause of a FETCH statement, just as you do when executing a SELECT that retrieves a single row.

Closing a Cursor

To close a cursor, removing its result table from main memory, use

```
CLOSE cursor_name
```

as in

```
EXEC SQL CLOSE address_data;
```

Embedded SQL Data Modification

Although many of today's database development environments make it easy to create forms for data entry and modification, all those forms do is collect data. There must be a program of some type underlying the form to actually interact with the database. For example, whenever a salesperson at the rare book store makes a sale, a program must create the row in *sale* and modify appropriate rows in *volume*.

Direct Modification

Data modification can be performed using the SQL UPDATE command to change one or more rows. In some cases, you can use a cursor to identify which rows should be updated in the underlying base tables.

To perform direct data modification using the SQL UPDATE command, you simply include the command in your program. For example, if the selling price of a purchased volume is stored in the host language variable *da_selling_price*, the sale ID in *da_sale_id*, and the volume's inventory ID in *da_inventory_id*, you could update *volume* with

```
EXEC SQL UPDATE volume
SET selling_price = :da_selling_price,
    sale_id = :da_sale_id
WHERE inventory_id = :da_inventory_id;
```

The preceding statement will update one row in the table because its WHERE predicate contains a primary key expression. To modify multiple rows, you use an UPDATE with a WHERE predicate that identifies multiple rows, such as the following, which increases the prices by two percent for volumes with leather bindings:

```
EXEC SQL UPDATE volume
SET asking_price = asking_price * 1.02
WHERE isbn IN (SELECT isbn
        FROM book
        WHERE binding = "Leather');
```

Indicator Variables and Data Modification

Indicator variables, which hold information about the result of embedded SQL retrievals, can also be used when performing embedded SQL modification. Their purpose is to indicate that you want to store a null in a column. For example, assume that the rare book store has a program that stores new rows in the *volume* table. At the time a new row is inserted, there are no values for the selling price or the sale ID; these columns should be left null.

To do this, the program declares an indicator variable for each column in the table. If the data variable hold a value to be stored, the program sets the indicator variable to 0; if the column is to be left null, the program sets the indicator variable to −1.

Sample pseudocode for performing this embedded INSERT can be found in Figure 15-2.

```
// Data variables
// Initialize all strings to null, all numeric variables to 0
string da_isbn, da_date_acquired;
int da_inventory_id, da_condition_code;
float da_asking_price, da_selling_price, da_sale_id;


// Indicator variables
// Initialize all to 0 except selling price and sale ID
    int in_isbn = 0,
    in_date_acquired = 0,
    in_inventory_id = 0,
    in_condition_code = 0,
    in_asking_price = 0,
    in_selling_price = -1,
    in_sale_id = -1;


// Collect data from user, possibly using on-screen form
// Store data in data variables
// Check to see if anything other that selling price and sale ID
// have no value

if (da_inventory_id == 0 or da_isbn = 0)
{
    // Error handling goes here
    return;
}

if (strcmp(da_date_acquired),"") == 0) in_date_acquired = -1
if (da_condition_code == 0) in_condition_code = -1;
// ... continue checking each data variable and setting
// indcator variable if necessary

EXEC SQL INSERT INTO volume
    VALUES (:da_inventory_id INDICATOR :in_inventory_id,
        :da_isbn INDICATOR :in_isbn,
        :da_condition_code INDICATOR :in_condition_code,
        :da_date_acquired INDICATOR :in_date_acquired,
        :da_asking_price INDICATOR in_asking_price,
        :da_selling_price INDICATOR :in_selling_price,
        :da_sale_id INDICATOR :in_sale_id;

// Finish by checking SQLSTATE to see if insert worked to decide
// whether to commit or rollback
```

Figure 15-2: Using indicator variables to send nulls to a table

Integrity Validation with the MATCH Predicate

The MATCH predicate is designed to be used with embedded SQL modification to let you test referential integrity before actually inserting data into tables. When included in an application program, it can help identify potential data modification errors.

For example, assume that a program written for the rare book store has a function that inserts new books into the database. The program wants to ensure that a work for the book exists in the database before attempting to store the book. The application program might therefore include the following query:

```
EXEC SQL SELECT work_numb
FROM work JOIN author
WHERE (:entered_author, :entered_title)
     MATCH (SELECT author_first_last, title
             FROM work JOIN author);
```

The subquery selects all the rows in the join of the *work* and *author* tables and then matches the author and title columns against the values entered by the user, both of which are stored in host language variables. If the preceding query returns one or more rows, then the author and title pair entered by the customer exist in the *author* and *work* relations. However, if the result table has no rows, then inserting the book into *book* would produce a referential integrity violation and the insert should not be performed.

If a program written for the rare book store wanted to verify a primary key constraint, it could use a variation of the MATCH predicate that requires unique values in the result table. For example, to determine whether a work is already in the database, the program could use

```
EXEC SQL SELECT work_numb
FROM work JOIN author
WHERE UNIQUE (:entered_author, :entered_title)
MATCH (SELECT author_first_last, title
        FROM work JOIN author);
```

By default, MATCH returns true if *any* value being tested is null or, when there are no nulls in the value being tested, a row exists in the result table that matches the values being tested. You can, however, change the behavior of MATCH when nulls are present:

◊ MATCH FULL is true if *every* value being tested is null or, when there are no nulls in the values being tested, a row exists in the result table that matches the values being tested.

◊ MATCH PARTIAL is true if *every* value being tested is null or a row exists in the result table that matches the values being tested.

Note that you can combine UNIQUE with MATCH FULL and MATCH PARTIAL.

Modification Using Cursors

Updates using cursors are a bit different from updating a view. When you update a view, the UPDATE command acts directly on the view by using the view's name. The update is then passed back to the underlying base table(s) by the DBMS. In contrast, using a cursor for updating means you update a base table directly, but identify the row that you want to modify by referring to the row to which the cursor currently is pointing.

To do the modification, you use FETCH without an INTO clause to move the cursor to the row you want to update. Then you can use an UPDATE command with a WHERE predicate that specifies the row pointed to by the cursor. For example, to change the address of the customer in row 15 of the *address_data* cursor's result table, a program for the rare book store could include

```
EXEC SQL FETCH ABSOLUTE 15 FROM address_data;
EXEC SQL UPDATE cutomer
    SET street = '123 Main Street',
    city = 'New Home'
    state_province = 'MA',
    zip_postcode = '02111'
    WHERE CURRENT OF address data;
```

Deletion Using Cursors

The clause CURRENT OF *cursor_name* instructs SQL to work with the row in *customer* currently being pointed to by the name cursor. If there is no valid corresponding row in the *customer* table, the update will fail.

You can apply the technique of modifying the row pointed to by a cursor to deletions as well as updates. To delete the current row, you use

```
DELETE FROM table_name
     WHERE CURRENT OF cursor_name
```

The deletion will fail if the current row indicated by the cursor isn't a row in the table named in the DELETE. For example,

```
EXEC SQL DELETE FROM customers WHERE CURRENT OF
address_data;
```

will probably succeed, but

```
EXEC SQL DELETE FROM volume
     WHERE CURRENT OF address_data;
```

will certainly fail because the *volume* table isn't part of the *address_data* cursor (as declared in the preceding section of this chapter).

Dynamic SQL

The embedded SQL that you have seen to this point is "static," in that entire SQL commands have been specified within the source code. However, there are often times when you don't know exactly what a command should look like until a program is running.

Consider, for example, the screen in Figure 16-1. The user fills in the fields on which he or she wishes to base a search of the rare book store's holdings. When the user clicks a Search button, the application program managing the window checks the contents of the fields on the window and uses the data it finds to create a SQL query.

The query's WHERE predicate will differ depending on which of the fields have values in them. It is therefore impossible to specify the query completely within a program. This is where dynamic SQL comes in.

Immediate Execution

The easiest way to work with dynamic SQL is the EXECUTE IMMEDIATE statement. To use it, you store a SQL command in a host language string variable and then submit that command for process:

```
EXEC SQL EXECUTE IMMEDIATE
    variable_containing_command
```

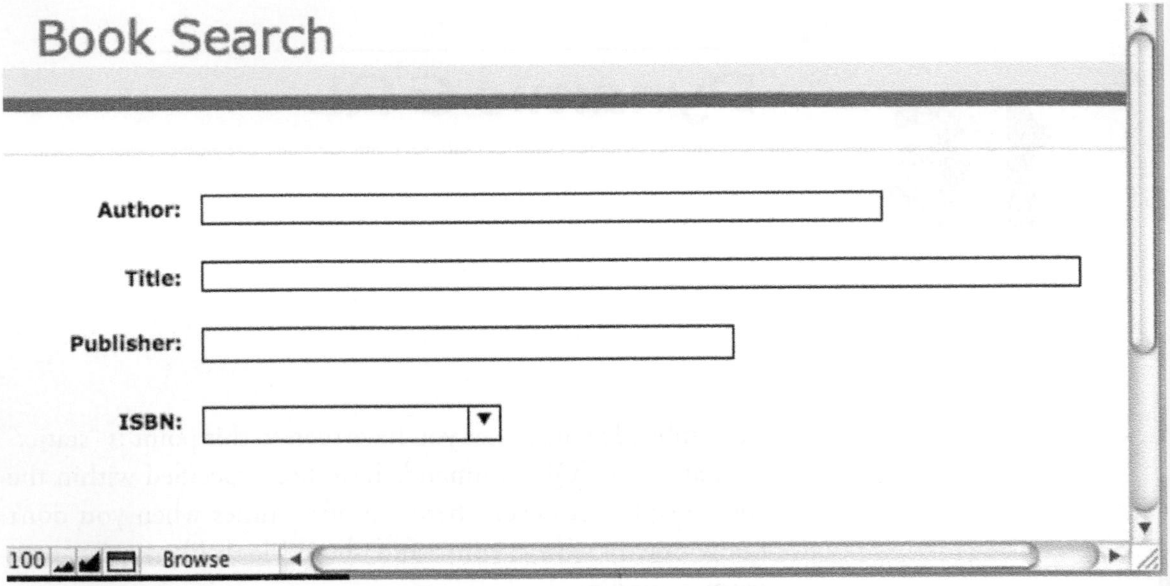

Book Search

Author: [   ]

Title: [   ]

Publisher: [   ]

ISBN: [▼]

100 ▲▲☐ Browse   ◄ ⬤   ►

Figure 16-1: A typical window for gathering information for a dynamic SQL query

For example, assume that a user fills in a data entry form with a customer number and the customer's new address. A program could process the update with code written something like the pseudocode in Figure 16-2. Notice the painstaking way in which the logic of the code examines the values the user entered and builds a syntactically correct SQL UPDATE statement. By using the dynamic SQL, the program can update just those columns for which the user has supplied new data. (Columns whose fields on the data entry are left empty aren't added to the SQL statement.)

There are two major limitations to EXECUTE IMMEDIATE:

◊ The SQL command cannot contain input parameters or output parameters. This means that you can't use SELECT or FETCH statements.

◊ To repeat the SQL statement, the DBMS has to perform the entire immediate execution process again. You can't save the SQL statement, except as a string in a host language

```
String theSQL;
theSQL = "UPDATE customer SET ";
Boolean needsComma = false;

If (valid_contents_in_street_field)
{
    theSQL = theSQL + "street = " + contents_of_street_field;
    needsComma = true;
}
if (valid_contents_in_city_field)
{
    if (needsComma)
        theSQL = theSQL + ", ";
    theSQL = theSQL + "city = " + contents_of_city_field;
    needsComma = true;
}
if (valid_contents_in_state_field)
{
    if (needsComma)
        theSQL = theSQL + ", ";
    the SQL = theSQL + "state_province = " + contents_of_state_field;
    needsComma = true;
}
if (valid_contents_in_zip_field)
{
    if (needsComma)
        theSQL = theSQL + ", ";
    theSQL = theSQL + "zip_postcode = " + contents_of_zip_filed;
}
EXEC SQL EXECUTE IMMEDIATE :theSQL;
If (strcmp (SQLCODE, "00000")
    EXEC SQL COMMIT;
else
{
    EXEC SQL ROLLBACK;
    // Display appropriate error message
}
```

Figure 16-2: Pseudocode to process a dynamic SQL update

variable. This means that such statements execute more slowly than static embedded SQL statements because the SQL command processor must examine them for syntax errors at runtime rather than during preprocessing by a precompiler.

Dynamic SQL with Dynamic Parameters

Each time you EXECUTE IMMEDIATE the same statement, it must be scanned for syntax errors again. Therefore, if you need to execute a dynamic SQL statement repeatedly, you will get better performance if you can have the syntax checked once and save the statement in some way.[1]

If you want to repeat a dynamic SQL statement or if you need to use dynamic parameters (as you would to process the form in Figure 16-1), you need to use a more involved technique for preparing and executing your commands.

The processing for creating and using a repeatable dynamic SQL statement is as follows:

1. Store the SQL statement in a host language string variable using host language variables for the dynamic parameters.

2. *Allocate* SQL *descriptor areas.*

3. *Prepare* the SQL statement. This process checks the statement for syntax and assigns it a name by which it can be referenced.

4. *Describe* one of the descriptor areas as input.

5. *Set* input parameters, associating each input parameter with the input parameter descriptor.

6. (Required only when using a cursor) *Declare* the cursor.

7. (Required only when using a cursor) *Open* the cursor.

8. *Describe* another descriptor area as output.

---

1   A few DBMSs (for example, DB2 for Z/OS) get around this problem by performing dynamic statement caching (DSC), where the DBMS saves the syntax-scanned/prepared statement and retrieves it from the cache if used again.

9. *Set* output parameters, associating each output parameter with the output parameter descriptor.

10. (Required when not using a cursor) *Execute* the query.

11. (Required only when using a cursor) *Fetch* values into the output descriptor area.

12. (Required only when using a cursor) *Get* the output values from the descriptor area and process them in some way.

13. Repeat steps 11 and 12 until the entire result table has been processed.

14. Close the cursor.

15. If through with the statement, deallocate the descriptor areas.

There are a few limitations to the use of dynamic parameters in a statement of which you should be aware:

◊ You cannot use a dynamic parameter in a SELECT clause.

◊ You cannot place a dynamic parameter on both sides of a relationship operator such as <, >, or =.

◊ You cannot use a dynamic parameter as an argument in a summary function.

◊ In general, you cannot compare a dynamic parameter with itself. For example, you cannot use two dynamic parameters with the BETWEEN operator.

Many dynamic queries generate result tables containing multiple rows. As an example, consider a query that retrieves a list of the customers of the rare book store who live in a given area.

Dynamic Parameters with Cursors

The user could enter a city, a state/province, a zip/postcode, or any combination of the three.

Step 1: Creating the Statement String

The first step in any dynamic SQL is to place the statement into a host language string variable. Pseudocode to generate the SQL query string for our example can be found in Figure 16-3.

Step 2: Allocating the Descriptor Areas

You allocate a descriptor area with the ALLOCATE DE-SCRIPTOR statement:

```
ALLOCATE DESCRIPTOR descriptor_name
```

For our example, the statements would look something like

```
EXEC SQL ALLOCATE DESCRIPTOR 'input';
EXEC SQL ALLOCATE DESCRIPTOR 'output';
```

The names of the descriptor areas are arbitrary. They can be supplied as literals, as in the above example, or they may be stored in host language string variables.

By default, the scope of a descriptor is local to the program module in which it was created. You can add the keyword GLOBAL after DESCRIPTOR, however, to create a global descriptor area that is available to the entire program.

Unless you specify otherwise, a descriptor area is defined to hold a maximum of 100 values. You can change that value by adding a MAX clause:

```
EXEC SQL ALLOCATE DESCRIPTOR GLOBAL 'input'
    MAX 10;
```

Step 3: Preparing the SQL Statement

Preparing a dynamic SQL statement for execution allows the DBMS to examine the statement for syntax errors and to perform query optimization. Once a query is prepared and stored with a name, it can be reused while the program is still running.

```
String theQuery;
Boolean hasWHERE = false;
String da_street = null, da_city = null, da_state_province = null, da_zip_
postcode = null;

// User enters search values into fields on screen form, which are
// then placed into the appropriate host language variables


theQuery = SELECT first, last, street, city, state_province, FROM customer ";
if (da_street IS NOT NULL)
{
    theQuery = theQuery + "WHERE street = :da_street";
    hasWHERE = true;
}

if (da_city IS NOT NULL)
{
    if (!hasWHERE)
        theQuery = theQuery + "WHERE ";
    else
        theQuery = theQuery + ", ";
     theQuery = theQuery + " city = :da_city";
     hasWHERE = true;
}

if (da_state_province IS NOT NULL)
{
    if (!hasWHERE)
        theQuery = theQuery + "WHERE ";
    else
        theQuery = theQuery + ", ";
     theQuery = theQuery + " state_province = :da_state_province";
     hasWHERE = true;
}

if (da_zip_postcode IS NOT NULL)
{
    if (!hasWHERE)
        theQuery = theQuery + "WHERE ";
    else
        theQuery = theQuery + ", ";
     theQuery = theQuery + " state_postcode = :da_state_postcode";
}
```

Figure 16-3: Setting up a SQL query in a string for use with dynamic parameters

To prepare the statement for execution, use the PREPARE command:

```
PREPARE statement_identifier FROM variable_
holding_command
```

The customer query command would be prepared with

```
EXEC SQL PREPARE sql_statement FROM :theQuery;
```

Steps 4 and 8: Describing Descriptor Areas

The DESCRIBE statement identifies a descriptor area as holding input or output parameters and associates it with a dynamic query. The statement has the following general form:

```
DESCRIBE INPUT/OUTPUT dynamic_statement_name
         USING DESCRIPTOR descriptor_name
```

The two descriptor areas for the customer list program will be written

```
EXEC SQL DESCRIBE INPUT sql_statement USING DE-
SCRIPTOR 'input';
EXEC SQL DESCRIBE OUTPUT sql_statement USING
DESCRIPTOR 'output';
```

Step 5: Setting Input Parameters

Each parameter—input or output—must be associated with an appropriate descriptor area. The SET DESCRIPTOR command needs four pieces of information for each parameter:

◊ A unique sequence number for the parameter. (You can start at 1 and count upwards as you go.)

◊ The data type of the parameter, represented as an integer code. (See Table 16-1 for the codes for commonly used data types.)

◊ The length of the parameter.

◊ A variable to hold the parameter's data.

Table 16-1: Selected SQL data type codes

Data type	Type code
CHAR	1
VARCHAR	12
BLOB	30
BOOLEAN	16
DATE	9
DECIMAL	3
DOUBLE PRECISION	8
FLOAT	6
INT	4
INTERVAL	10
NUMERIC	2
REAL	7
SMALL INT	5

The SET DESCRIPTOR statement has the following general syntax:

```
SET DESCRIPTOR descriptor_area_name
    VALUE sequence_number
    TYPE = type_code LENGTH = parameter_length
    DATA = variable_holding_parameter data
```

The code needed to set the input parameters for the address list query can be found in Figure 16-4.

In addition to what you have just seen, there are two other descriptor characteristics that can be set:

◊ INDICATOR: Identifies the host language variable that will hold an indicator value.

```
INDICATOR =
        :host_langauge_indicator_variable
```

```
Int da_street_type = 12, da_street_length = 30, da_city_type = 12,
    da_city_length = 30, da_state_province_type = 1,
    da_stte_province_length = 2, da_zip_postcode_type = 12,
    da_zip_postcode_length = 12;

Int value_count = 1;

If (da_street IS NOT NULL)
{
    EXEC SQL SET DESCRIPTOR 'input' VALUE :value_count TYPE = :da_street_type
LENGTH = :da_street_length DATA = :da_street;
    value_count ++;
}
if (da_city IS NOT NULL)
{
    EXEC SQL SET DESCRIPTOR 'input' VALUE :value_count TYPE = :da_city_type
LENGTH = :da_city_length DATA = :da_city;
    value_count ++;
}
if (da_state_province IS NOT NULL)
{
    EXEC SQL SET DESCRIPTOR 'input' VALUE :value_count TYPE = :da_state_
province_type LENGTH = :da_state_province_length DATA = :da_state_province;
    value_count ++;
}
if (da_zip_postcod IS NOT NULL)
{
    EXEC SQL SET DESCRIPTOR 'input' VALUE :value_count TYPE = :da_zip_
postcode_type LENGTH = :da_zip_postcode_length DATA = :da_zip_postcode;
}
```

Figure 16-4: Setting input parameters for a dynamic SQL query

◊ TITLE: Identifies the table column name associated with the parameter.

```
TITLE = column_name
```

Steps 6 and 7: Declaring and Opening the Cursor

Declaring a cursor for use with a dynamic SQL statement is exactly the same as declaring a cursor for a static SQL statement. The cursor for the address list program can therefore be declared as

```
EXEC SQL DECLARE CURSOR addresses FOR theQuery;
```

```
int da_first_type = 12, da_first_length = 15, da_last_type = 12,
    da_last_length = 15;
// remaining variables have already been declared

EXEC SQL SET DESCRIPTOR 'output' VALUE 1 TYPE = :da_first_type
    LENGTH = :da_first_type DATA = :da_frist;
EXEC SQL SET DESCRIPTOR 'output' VALUE 2 TYPE = :da_last_type
    LENGTH = :da_last_type DATA = :da_last;
EXEC SQL SET DESCRIPTOR 'output' VALUE 3 TYPE = :da_street_type
    LENGTH = :da_street_type DATA = :da_street;
EXEC SQL SET DESCRIPTOR 'output' VALUE 4 TYPE = :da_city_type
    LENGTH = :da_city_type DATA = :da_city;
EXEC SQL SET DESCRIPTOR 'output' VALUE 5 TYPE = :da_state_province_type
    LENGTH = :da_state_province_type DATA = :da_state_province;
EXEC SQL SET DESCRIPTOR 'output' VALUE 6 TYPE = :da_zip_postcode_type
    LENGTH = :da_zip_postcode_type DATA = :da_zip_postcode;
```

Figure 16-5: Setting output parameters for a dynamic SQL query

Note: You can declare a scrolling cursor for use with dynamic SQL.

The OPEN statement is similar to the static OPEN, but it also needs to know which descriptor area to use:

```
EXEC SQL OPEN addresses USING DESCRIPTOR 'in-
put';
```

Step 9: Setting the Output Parameters

The only difference between the syntax for setting the input and output parameters is that the output parameters are placed in their own descriptor area. The code can be found in Figure 16-5.

Be sure that the output parameters have sequence numbers that place them in the same order as the output columns in the prepared SELECT statement. When you pull data from the result table into the output descriptor area, the SQL command processor will retrieve the data based on those sequence numbers. If they don't match the order of the data, you won't end up with data in the correct host language variables.

Steps 11–13: Fetching Rows and Getting the Data

When you are using dynamic parameters, a FETCH creates a result table in main memory, just as it does with static SQL. Your code must then GET each parameter and pull it into the descriptor area. The end result is that the data from a row in the result table are available in the host language variables identified as holding data, as seen in Figure 16-6.

Steps 14 and 15: Finishing Up

To finish processing the dynamic SQL query, you will close the cursor (if necessary)—

```
EXEC SQL CLOSE addresses;
```

—and deallocate the descriptor areas, freeing up the memory they occupy:

```
EXEC SQL DEALLOCATE DESCRIPTOR 'input';
EXEC SQL DEALLOCATE DESCRIPTOR 'output';
```

Dynamic Parameters without a Cursor

As you saw at the beginning of this section, using dynamic parameters is very similar regardless of whether you are using a cursor. In fact, executing a query that returns a single row is much simpler. You can actually get away without using descriptor areas, although if the descriptor areas have been created, there is no reason you can't use them.

```
EXEC SQL FETCH addresses INTO DESCRIPTOR 'output';
while (strcmp (SQLCODE = '00000')
{
    EXEC SQL GET DESCRIPTOR 'output' VALUE 1 :da_first = DATA;
    EXEC SQL GET DESCRIPTOR 'output' VALUE 2 :da_last = DATA;
    EXEC SQL GET DESCRIPTOR 'output' VALUE 3 :da_street = DATA;
    EXEC SQL GET DESCRIPTOR 'output' VALUE 4 :da_city = DATA;
    EXEC SQL GET DESCRIPTOR 'output' VALUE 5 :da_state_province = DATA;
    EXEC SQL GET DESCRIPTOR 'output' VALUE 6 :da_zip_postcode = DATA;
    // process the data in some way
    EXEC SQL FETCH addresses INTO DESCRIPTOR 'output';
}
```

Figure 16-6: Fetching rows and getting data into host language variables

To execute a prepared statement that does not use either a cursor or a descriptor area, use the EXECUTE command in its simplest form:

Statements without
Cursors or a Descriptor
Area

```
EXECUTE statement_name
USING input_parameter_list
INTO output_parameter_list
```

The USING and INTO clauses are optional. However, you must include a USING clause if your statement has input parameters and an INTO clause if your statement has output parameters. The number and data types of the parameters in each parameter list must be the same as the number and data types of parameters in the query.

For example, assume that you have prepared the following query with the name *book_into*:

```
SELECT author, title
FROM work JOIN book
WHERE isbn = :da_isbn;
```

This query has one input parameter (*da_isbn*) and two output parameters (*da_author*) and (*da_title*). It can be executed with

```
EXEC SQL EXECUTE book_info
USING :da_isbn
INTO :da_author, :da_title;
```

Input parameters can be stored in host languages variables, as in the preceding example, or they can be supplied as literals.

If your parameters have already been placed in a descriptor area, then all you need to do to execute a statement that does not use a cursor is to add the name(s) of the appropriate descriptor area(s) to the EXECUTE statement:

Statements without
Cursors but Using a
Descriptor Area

```
EXEC SQL EXECUTE book_info
USING 'input'
INTO 'output';
```

Part V

Non-Relational

SQL Extensions

17 XML Support

Extensible Markup Language (XML) is a way of representing data and data relationships in text files. Because such UNI-CODE text files have become widespread and are usually platform independent, XML is being used heavily for data transfer, especially between databases and the Web.

As you will see, XML shares some characteristics with HTML. However, the two markup languages have very different goals. HTML is designed to give instructions to a browser about how to display a page. XML, in contrast, is designed to describe the structure of data and to facilitate moving that data from one place to another.

Relational databases can use XML in three ways:

◊ Import XML documents and store the data in one or more relations: At this time, such functionality is not provided within the SQL standard. In practice, it requires program code that is specific to a particular DBMS and therefore is beyond the scope of this book.

◊ Format data stored in relations as XML for output: SQL/XML, which first appeared in the SQL:2003 standard, provides a group of functions for performing this output. The standard also includes detailed instructions for mapping SQL elements to XML.

◊ Store entire XML documents (or portions of documents) in a column of type XML: SQL provides this capability with the XML data type.

This chapter covers the basics of the structure of XML documents. It then looks at the major SQL/XML functions and the XML data type.

XML Basics

XML is a *markup language*. In other words, you place special coding in the text to identify data elements. It shares some contents with HTML, but at the same time is both more and less flexible. (As you will see, this is not a contradiction!)

Note: The following is not intended to be a complete primer on XML. It will, however, give you more than enough background to understand what SQL/XML can and cannot do.

XML Structure

XML data are organized in hierarchies. As an example, consider the hierarchies diagrammed in Figure 17-1, both of which are taken from the rare book store database. Notice that it takes two hierarchies to represent the entire database because a hierarchy does not allow a child element—an element at the "many" end of a 1:M relationship—to have two parent elements (elements at the "one" end of a 1:M relationship). Therefore, we can represent the relationship between a customer, a sale, and a volume *or* the relationship between author, work, book, and volume, but not both within the same hierarchy.

Parent elements may have more than one type of child entity. As an example, consider the hierarchy in Figure 17-2. Each department has many salespeople working for it. A salesperson has many contacts (potential customers) but also makes many sales. Each sale is for one or more customers and contains one or more items. This entire hierarchy can be represented as a whole in an XML document.

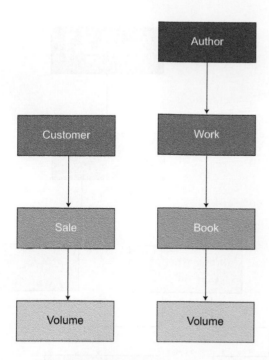

Figure 17-1: Hierarchies for the rare book store database for use in an XML document

Because of their hierarchical structure, XML documents are said to be organized in tree structures. (You will discover later in this chapter that this botanical terminology turns up in other places in XML.)

Each hierarchy has a *root* element, the top element in the hierarchy. In Figure 17-1, there are two root elements—Author and Customer; Figure 17-2 has only one root element, Department.

Attributes

As well as having child elements, an element may have "attributes." An attribute is a single data value that describes an element. For example, in Figure 17-2, a department might have its name and the name of its manager as attributes. In contrast,

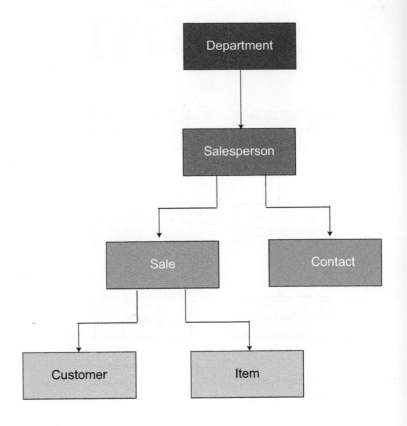

Figure 17-2: A hierarchy that includes parent elements with multiple child element types

salespeople and the data that describe them are represented as child elements.

Attributes do have some limitations. First, they are single-valued; elements can be multi-valued. Because they are a single value attached to an element, attributes can't be related to other attributes or elements. Attributes also make the structure of the XML more difficult to modify should the underlying structure of the data change.

An XML document really has a very simple structure: It is made up of nested pairs of tags. With the exception of the first line in the file, that's all there is to it. (If this were an e-mail rather than a book, a smiley face would go here.)

Elements and their data are identified by *tags* in the text file. These tags are similar to HTML tags but don't come from a fixed set of tags like those available for HTML. Each element begins with an opening tag—

`<element_name>`

—and ends with a closing tab:

`</element_name>`

Unlike HTML, which has some tags that don't come in pairs (for example <LI>), all XML tags must be paired. Between its tags, an element has either a data value or other elements. Nested elements may in turn have data values or other elements.

As mentioned earlier, XML elements may have attributes as well as elements that are nested beneath them. An attribute is a single occurrence of a value that describes an element. Their values are placed within the element's opening tag:

`<element_name attribute_name =`
`    "attribute_value" …>`

Attribute values must be quoted.

If you have a pair of tags that have attributes but no nested elements (an *empty tag*), then you can get away with combining the two tags into one, placing the closing symbol (/) just before the closing symbol (>):

`<element_name element_data/>`

XML Document Structure

Tags

You can find a portion of an XML document that describes some of the data for the hierarchy in Figure 17-2 in Figure 17-3.

Note: The indentation is not required and is included here to make the code easier to read. In fact, the indentation and spacing in some of the longer listings in this chapter have been changed in the interest of space preservation. Nonetheless, the structures of the documents have been maintained through the proper use of nested tags.

Declarations (Prologs)

Each XML document begins with a declaration (or prolog) that identifies the version of XML being used and optionally a character encoding scheme. The particular encoding specified in Figure 17-3 identifies a Western European (and thus also North American) scheme.

The declaration also optionally includes an attribute named STANDALONE. When its value is "yes," the document has no external references needed to understand its content. If the value is "no," then an application processing the XML document will need to consult outside resources to get complete information for understanding the document. Although many of the examples of declarations that you will see include this attribute, in practice it is not widely used.

The declaration is followed by the opening tag for the root element; the last line in the document is the closing tag for the root element. In between the root element tags, the document contains the elements describing the remainder of the data.

Being "Well-Formed"

As you read about XML and XML documents, especially in the context of interactions with databases, you will find references to *well-formed XML documents*. An XML document is well-formed if it meets all the XML syntax rules. Specifically, that means that:

◊ It has one and only one root element.

```
<?xml version "1.0" encoding="ISO-8859-1"?>
<department dept_name = "Hannover" manager_last_name = "Benson"
            manager_first_name = "James">
        <salesperson>
        <first>John</first>
        <last>Doe</last>
        <ext>1234</ext>
            <sale>
                <sale_date>1-12-2012<sale_date>
                <sale_total>152</sale_total>
                <sale_numb>65</sale_numb>
                <customer>
                    <cust_numb>12</cust_numb>
                </customer>
                <item>
                    <item_numb>109</item_numb>
                    <quantity>1</quantity>
                    <sale_numb>65</sale_numb>
                </item>
                <item>
                    <item_numb>85</item_numb>
                    <quantity>1</quantity>
                    <sale_numb>65</sale_numb>
                </item>
            </sale>
            <contact>
                <c_first>Mary</c_last>
                <c_last>Jones</c_last>
                <c_phone>555-525-1111</c_phone>
            </contact>
            <contact>
                <c_first>Sam</c_first>
                <c_last>Smith</c_last>
                <c_phone>555-999-1212</ c_phone >
            </contact>
        </salesperson>
</department>
```

Figure 17-3: A portion of an XML document

◊ Every element has a closing tag or is an empty element.

◊ Tags are case sensitive.

◊ All elements are nested properly.

◊ All attribute values are quoted.

A well-formed XML document is much more likely to be acceptable by many different types of software running on many different platforms.

XML Schemas

To help validate the structure of an XML document, you can create an *XML schema*, a special type of XML document that contains definitions of document structure. An XML schema also defines data types for elements and attributes. It can also contain a number of domain constraints.

Note: XML schemas are a relatively recent addition to XML. The older description of the structure of an XML file is a DTD (Document Type Definition).

Unlike XML documents, XML schemas use predefined element tags and element attributes. An example can be found in Figure 17-4, which contains a schema that describes the structure of the XML in Figure 17-3.

This schema contains the following elements:

◊ *xs:schema*: The root element.

◊ *xs:element*: A declaration of a root element. Each element has a name and a data type. XML includes string, integer, decimal, boolean, date, and time types.

◊ *xs:complexType*: A group of elements that contains multiple data types.

◊ *xs:sequence* (an *indicator*): A group of elements that must appear in the order specified within the pair of sequence tags.

◊ *xs:all* (an indicator): A group of elements that can appear in any order specified within the pair of sequence tags. Each element can appear only once within the group.

At the time this book was written, the SQL standard was not designed to take advantage of SQL schemas for XML

```
<?xml version = "1.0"?>
<xs:schema>
    <xs:complexType name = "department">
        <xs:sequence>
            <xs:element name = "dept_name" type = "xs:string"/>
            <xs:element name = "manager_first_name" type = "xs:string"/>
        </xs:sequence>
        <xs:complexType name = "salesperson">
            <xs:sequence>
                <xs:element name = "first" type = "xs:string"/>
                <xs:element name = "last" type = "xs:string"/>
                <xs:element name = "ext" type = "xs:string"/>
            </xs:sequence>
            <xs:complexType name = "sale" mixed = "true">
                <xs:all>
                    <xs:element name = "sale_date" type = "xs:date"/>
                    <xs:element name = "sale_total" type = "xs:decimal"/>
                    <xs:element name = "sale_numb" type = "xs:string"/>
                </xs:all name = "item" mixed = "true">
                    <xs:sequence>
                        <xs:element name = "item_numb" type = "xs:integer"/>
                        <xs:element name = "quantity" type = "xs:integer"/>
                        <xs:element name = "sale_numb" type = "xs:string"/>
                    </xs:sequence>
                </xs:complexType>
                <xs:complexType name = "customer" mixed = "true">
                    <xs:element name = "cust_numb" type = "xs:integer"/>
                </xs:complexType>
            </xs:complexType>
        <xs:complexType name = "contact">
            <xs:sequence>
                <xs:element name = "c_first" type = "xs:string"/>
                <xs:element name = "c_last" type = "xs:string"/>
                <xs:element name = "c_phone" type = "xs:string"/>
            </xs:sequence>
        </xs:complexType>
    </xs:complexType>
</xs:schema>
```

Figure 17-4: An XML schema that describes the XML document in Figure 17-3

validation. Should you need to determine whether an XML document is well-formed, you will need to examine the document using third-party software.

SQL/XML

SQL/XML, the extensions that provide XML support from within the SQL language, entered the standard in 2003.

Note: XML standards now include a language called XQuery. It is separate from SQL and appeals primarily to XML programmers who need to interact with data stored in a relational database. In contrast, SQL/XML tends to appeal to SQL programmers who need to generate XML documents.

XML Publishing Functions

SQL/XML's publishing functions extract data from tables and produce XML. You can therefore use a series of the functions—most usually within an embedded SQL application—to generate an entire XML document.

XMLCOMMENT

XML documents can include any comments needed. The XMLCOMMENT function has the general syntax:

```
XMLCOMMENT (source_string);
```

The source string can be a literal string or a string stored in a host language variable. The SQL statement

```
SELECT XMLCOMMENT ('High priced volumes');
```

produces the output

```
xmlcomment
----------------------------
<!--High priced volumes-->
```

Notice that the output string is now surrounded by the XML comment indicators.

The XMLPARSE function turns a string of text into XML. It is particularly useful when you need to store a string of text in a column of type XML. The function has the general format:

```
XMLPARSE (type_indicator content_string
whitespace_option)
```

The type indicator takes one of two values: DOCUMENT (for a complete XML document) or CONTENT (for a small chunk of XML that doesn't represent an entire document). Most of the time, the DOCUMENT type is used in an embedded SQL program where an entire XML document can be stored in a host language string variable.

The content string cannot be generated with a SELECT within the XMLPARSE statement. The content string therefore must be either a literal or a host language variable. There is no reason, however, that the host language variable can't be loaded with a long string created by embedded SELECTs and/or other host language string manipulations.

XMLPARSE

The whitespace option tells SQL what to do with any empty space at the end of a string. Its value can be either STRIP WHITESPACE or PRESERVE WHITESPACE.

As a simple example, consider the following:

```
SELECT XMLPARSE (CONTENT 'Converting a literal
to XML' STRIP WHITESPACE);
```

The output looks just like regular text because the interactive SQL command processor strips off the XML tags before displaying the result:

```
        xmlparse
------------------------------
Converting a literal to XML
```

The XMLROOT function is a bit of a misnomer. Its definition says that it modifies an XML root node, but what it really does is create or modify an XML declaration at the very beginning of an XML document. The function has the following general syntax:

XMLROOT

```
XMLROOT (XML_value, VERSION version,
    STANDALONE standalone_property)
```

The first parameter—*xml_value*—is the XML data for which you will be creating or modifying the prolog. You can then set its version (usually supplied as a literal string) and its standalone property.

The standalone property indicates whether all declarations needed for the XML document are contained within the document or whether declarations are contained in an external document. In most cases when you are using XML with a relational database, the standalone property will be set to *yes*.

The following example adds the prolog at the beginning of the XML, sets the version to 1.1 and the standalone property to *yes*—

```
SELECT XMLROOT (XMLPARSE (CONTENT
'<content>something</content>'),
      VERSION '1.1', STANDALONE YES);
```

—and produces the output

```
                               xmlroot
-------------------------------------------------
---------------
<?xml version="1.1"
standalone="yes"?><content>abc</content>
```

XMLELEMENT is one of two ways to generate content for an XML document. It has the following general syntax:

```
XMLELEMENT (NAME name_of_element,
     XMLATTRIBUTES (attribute_value
          AS attribute_name, …), content…)
```

XMLELEMENT

Each element has a name that becomes the element's tag. Attributes are optional. The content may be

◊ A literal value (in quotes)

◊ Data from a database table

◊ Another XML element, typically generated with an embedded call to XMLELEMENT or XMLFOREST

As an example, let's create some XML that contains data about
books (author, title, and ISBN):

```
SELECT XMLELEMENT (NAME "Books",
    XMLELEMENT (NAME "Author",
        author.author_last_first),
    XMLELEMENT (NAME "Title",work.title),
    XMLELEMENT (name "ISBN",book.isbn))
FROM author JOIN book JOIN work;
```

The function call is placed in a SELECT statement as one of
the values that SELECT should return. The FROM clause
identifies the tables from which data will be drawn. This particular example creates an XML element named *Books*. The
contents of the element include three other elements—*Author,
Title, ISBN*—each of which is created with an embedded call to
XMLELEMENT. The SQL statement produces one element
for each row retrieved by the query. In this case, the SELECT
has no WHERE clause and therefore generates an element for
every row in the joined table created by the FROM clause.

The output of this command can be found in Figure 17-5.
Note that the spacing of the output has been adjusted by putting multiple tags on the same line so the output will take up
less space. This isn't a problem because XML is text only; any
spacing between tags is purely cosmetic.

The XMLFOREST function can be used to create elements   **XMLFOREST**
that are part of a higher-level element. Its results are very similar to XMLELEMENT, although its syntax can be simpler
than using multiple embedded XMLELEMENT calls. However, the result of XMLFOREST alone is not a valid XML
document. We therefore often wrap a call to XMLELEMENT
around XMLFOREST.

```
<Books>     <Author>Bronte, Charlotte</Author>
     <Title>Jane Eyre</Title>
     <ISBN>978-1-11111-111-1</ISBN>    </Books>
<Books>     <Author>Bronte, Charlotte</Author>
     <Title>Jane Eyre</Title>
    <ISBN>978-1-11111-112-1</ISBN>    </Books>
<Books>     <Author>Bronte, Charlotte</Author>
     <Title>Villette</Title>
     <ISBN>978-1-11111-113-1</ISBN>    </Books>
<Books>     <Author>Doyle, Sir Arthur Conan</Author>
     <Title>Hound of the Baskervilles</Title>
     <ISBN>978-1-11111-114-1</ISBN>    </Books>
<Books>     <Author>Doyle, Sir Arthur Conan</Author>
     <Title>Hound of the Baskervilles</Title>
     <ISBN>978-1-11111-115-1</ISBN>    </Books>
<Books>     <Author>Doyle, Sir Arthur Conan</Author>
     <Title>Lost World, The</Title>
     <ISBN>978-1-11111-116-1</ISBN>    </Books>
<Books>     <Author>Doyle, Sir Arthur Conan</Author>
     <Title>Complete Sherlock Holmes</Title>
     <ISBN>978-1-11111-117-1</ISBN>    </Books>
<Books>     <Author>Doyle, Sir Arthur Conan</Author>
     <Title>Complete Sherlock Holmes</Title>
     <ISBN>978-1-11111-118-1</ISBN>    </Books>
<Books>     <Author>Twain, Mark</Author>
     <Title>Tom Sawyer</Title>
     <ISBN>978-1-11111-120-1</ISBN>    </Books>
<Books>     <Author>Twain, Mark</Author>
     <Title>Connecticut Yankee in King Arthur's Court, A</Title>
     <ISBN>978-1-11111-119-1</ISBN>    </Books>
<Books>     <Author>Twain, Mark</Author>
     <Title>Tom Sawyer</Title>
     <ISBN>978-1-11111-121-1</ISBN>    </Books>
<Books>     <Author>Twain, Mark</Author>
     <Title>Adventures of Huckleberry Finn, The</Title>
     <ISBN>978-1-11111-122-1</ISBN>    </Books>
<Books>     <Author>Ludlum, Robert</Author>
     <Title>Matarese Circle, The</Title>
     <ISBN>978-1-11111-123-1</ISBN>    </Books>
<Books>     <Author>Ludlum, Robert</Author>
     <Title>Bourne Supremacy, The</Title>
     <ISBN>978-1-11111-124-1</ISBN>    </Books>
<Books>     <Author>Rand, Ayn</Author>
     <Title>Fountainhead, The</Title>
     <ISBN>978-1-11111-125-1</ISBN>    </Books>
```

Figure 17-5: An XML fragment created with calls to XMLELEMENT (*continued on next page*)

```
<Books>      <Author>Rand, Ayn</Author>
     <Title>Fountainhead, The</Title>
     <ISBN>978-1-11111-126-1</ISBN>        </Books>
<Books>      <Author>Rand, Ayn</Author>
     <Title>Atlas Shrugged</Title>
     <ISBN>978-1-11111-127-1</ISBN>        </Books>
<Books>      <Author>Stevenson, Robert Louis</Author>
     <Title>Kidnapped</Title>
     <ISBN>978-1-11111-128-1</ISBN>        </Books>
<Books>      <Author>Stevenson, Robert Louis</Author>
     <Title>Kidnapped</Title>
     <ISBN>978-1-11111-129-1</ISBN>        </Books>
<Books>      <Author>Stevenson, Robert Louis</Author>
     <Title>Treasure Island</Title>
     <ISBN>978-1-11111-130-1</ISBN>        </Books>
<Books>      <Author>Barth, John</Author>
     <Title>Sot Weed Factor, The</Title>
     <ISBN>978-1-11111-131-1</ISBN>        </Books>
<Books>      <Author>Barth, John</Author>
     <Title>Lost in the Funhouse</Title>
     <ISBN>978-1-11111-132-1</ISBN>        </Books>
<Books>      <Author>Barth, John</Author>
     <Title>Giles Goat Boy</Title>
     <ISBN>978-1-11111-133-1</ISBN>        </Books>
<Books>      <Author>Herbert, Frank</Author>
     <Title>Dune</Title>
     <ISBN>978-1-11111-134-1</ISBN>        </Books>
<Books>      <Author>Asimov, Isaac</Author>
     <Title>Foundation</Title>
     <ISBN>978-1-11111-135-1</ISBN>        </Books>
<Books>      <Author>Asimov, Isaac</Author>
     <Title>Foundation</Title>
     <ISBN>978-1-11111-136-1</ISBN>        </Books>
<Books>      <Author>Asimov, Isaac</Author>
     <Title>Last Foundation</Title>
     <ISBN>978-1-11111-137-1</ISBN>        </Books>
<Books>      <Author>Asimov, Isaac</Author>
     <Title>Foundation</Title>
     <ISBN>978-1-11111-138-1</ISBN>        </Books>
<Books>      <Author>Asimov, Isaac</Author>
     <Title>I, Robot</Title>
     <ISBN>978-1-11111-139-1</ISBN>        </Books>
<Books>      <Author>Funke, Cornelia</Author>
<Title>Inkheart</Title>
     <ISBN>978-1-11111-140-1</ISBN>        </Books>
```

Figure 17-5 (continued): An XML fragment created with calls to XMLELEMENT (continued on next page)

```
<Books>      <Author>Funke, Cornelia</Author>
     <Title>Inkdeath</Title>
     <ISBN>978-1-11111-141-1</ISBN>      </Books>
<Books>      <Author>Stephenson, Neal</Author>
     <Title>Anathem</Title>
     <ISBN>978-1-11111-142-1</ISBN>      </Books>
<Books>      <Author>Stephenson, Neal</Author>
     <Title>Snow Crash</Title>
     <ISBN>978-1-11111-143-1</ISBN>      </Books>
<Books>      <Author>Rand, Ayn</Author>
     <Title>Anthem</Title>
     <ISBN>978-1-11111-144-1</ISBN>      </Books>
<Books>      <Author>Rand, Ayn</Author>
     <Title>Anthem</Title>
     <ISBN>978-1-11111-145-1</ISBN>      </Books>
<Books>      <Author>Stephenson, Neal</Author>
     <Title>Cryptonomicon</Title>
     <ISBN>978-1-11111-146-1</ISBN>      </Books>
```

Figure 17-5 (continued): An XML fragment created with calls to XMLELEMENT

By itself, XMLFOREST has the following general syntax:

```
XMLFROEST (content AS element_name, …)
```

As an example, assume that we want to create an XML element for an inventory item, including the ISBN, asking price, and selling price. One way to code the element would be as follows:

```
SELECT XMLELEMENT (NAME "Inventory_item",
     XMLFOREST (volume.isbn, volume.asking_
price, volume.selling_price)) "Volumes"
FROM volume
WHERE selling_price > 75;
```

Notice that the external function call is to XMLELEMENT to create the element named *inventory_item*. The content of the element is produced by a single call to XMLFOREST, which contains the three data values that are part of the inventory item element. Because there is no AS clause, the function uses the column names as the names of the data elements. You can find the output of the sample query in Figure 17-6.

As you will remember from earlier in this chapter, an XML element can have attributes, data values that are part of the element tag. The XMLATTRIBUTES function is used to specify those attributes. Like XMLFOREST, it is most commonly used as part of an XMLELEMENT function call.

XMLATTRIBUTES

The function has the following general syntax:

```
XMLATTRIBUTES (value AS attribute_name)
```

If the attribute's value is a column in a database table, then the AS and the attribute name are optional. SQL will then use the column name as the attribute name.

As an example, let's create an XML element for books with selling prices of more than $75, the results of which appear in Figure 17-7. Notice that text values (e.g., the ISBN) are in quotes.

```
SELECT XMLELEMENT (NAME "High_Priced",
    XMLATTRIBUTES (volume.isbn AS ISBN),
    XMLELEMENT (NAME "Asking_price", volume.
asking_price),
    XMLELEMENT (NAME "Selling_price", volume.
selling_price))
FROM volume
WHERE selling_price > 75;
```

XMLCONCAT

The XML functions we have been discussing generate fragments of XML documents. To paste them together, you use the XMLCONCAT function. It has a relatively simple general syntax:

```
XMLCONCAT (XML_value, XML_value, …)
```

As an example, let's put a comment in front each of the elements that contain data about books with high selling prices:

```
SELECT XMLCONCAT (XMLCOMMENT ('This is a high-
priced book'),
    XMLELEMENT (NAME "High_Priced",
```

```
<Inventory_item>
      <isbn>978-1-11111-111-1</isbn>
      <asking_price>175.00</asking_price>
      <selling_price>175.00</selling_price>          </Inventory_item>
<Inventory_item>
      <isbn>978-1-11111-133-1</isbn>
      <asking_price>300.00</asking_price>
      <selling_price>285.00</selling_price>          </Inventory_item>
<Inventory_item>
      <isbn>978-1-11111-144-1</isbn>
      <asking_price>80.00</asking_price>
      <selling_price>76.10</selling_price>          </Inventory_item>
<Inventory_item>
      <isbn>978-1-11111-121-1</isbn>
      <asking_price>110.00</asking_price>
      <selling_price>110.00</selling_price>          </Inventory_item>
<Inventory_item>
      <isbn>978-1-11111-121-1</isbn>
      <asking_price>110.00</asking_price>
      <selling_price>110.00</selling_price>          </Inventory_item>
<Inventory_item>
      <isbn>978-1-11111-130-1</isbn>
      <asking_price>150.00</asking_price>
      <selling_price>120.00</selling_price>          </Inventory_item>
<Inventory_item>
      <isbn>978-1-11111-126-1</isbn>
      <asking_price>110.00</asking_price>
      <selling_price>110.00</selling_price>          </Inventory_item>
<Inventory_item>
      <isbn>978-1-11111-139-1</isbn>
      <asking_price>200.00</asking_price>
      <selling_price>170.00</selling_price>          </Inventory_item>
<Inventory_item>
      <isbn>978-1-11111-133-1</isbn>
      <asking_price>125.00</asking_price>
      <selling_price>125.00</selling_price>          </Inventory_item>
<Inventory_item>
      <isbn>978-1-11111-130-1</isbn>
      <asking_price>200.00</asking_price>
      <selling_price>150.00</selling_price>          </Inventory_item>
```

Figure 17-6   The results of using XMLFOREST to generate the contents of an XML attribute

```
<High_Priced isbn="978-1-11111-111-1">
     <Asking_price>175.00</Asking_price>
     <Selling_price>175.00</Selling_price>
</High_Priced>
<High_Priced isbn="978-1-11111-133-1">
     <Asking_price>300.00</Asking_price>
     <Selling_price>285.00</Selling_price>
</High_Priced>
<High_Priced isbn="978-1-11111-144-1">
     <Asking_price>80.00</Asking_price>
     <Selling_price>76.10</Selling_price>
</High_Priced>
<High_Priced isbn="978-1-11111-121-1">
     <Asking_price>110.00</Asking_price>
     <Selling_price>110.00</Selling_price>
</High_Priced>
<High_Priced isbn="978-1-11111-121-1">
     <Asking_price>110.00</Asking_price>
     <Selling_price>110.00</Selling_price>
</High_Priced>
<High_Priced isbn="978-1-11111-130-1">
     <Asking_price>150.00</Asking_price>
     <Selling_price>120.00</Selling_price></High_Priced>
<High_Priced isbn="978-1-11111-126-1">
     <Asking_price>110.00</Asking_price>
     <Selling_price>110.00</Selling_price>
</High_Priced>
<High_Priced isbn="978-1-11111-139-1">
     <Asking_price>200.00</Asking_price>
     <Selling_price>170.00</Selling_price>
</High_Priced>
<High_Priced isbn="978-1-11111-133-1">
     <Asking_price>125.00</Asking_price>
     <Selling_price>125.00</Selling_price>
</High_Priced>
<High_Priced isbn="978-1-11111-130-1">
     <Asking_price>200.00</Asking_price>
     <Selling_price>150.00</Selling_price>
</High_Priced>
```

Figure 17-7 The results of using XMLATTRIBUTES to add attributes to an XML element

```
                              XMLATTRIBUTES (volume.isbn AS ISBN),
                              XMLELEMENT (NAME "Asking_price", vol-
ume.asking_price),
                              XMLELEMENT (NAME "Selling_price", vol-
ume.selling_price)))
FROM volume
WHERE selling_price > 75;
```

The results can be found in Figure 17-8. Line breaks have been added to make the result readable. Note, however, that SQL views each occurrence of the comment and the entire element as a single string of text and therefore inserts a line break only at the end of each element.

Note: The x0020 that appears frequently in the output is the ASCII code for a blank.

The XML Data Type

You can declare a column in a table to be of type XML, just as you would with any other data type:

```
CREATE TABLE xmlstuff
    (seq_numb INT,
    xml_text XML,
    PRIMARY KEY (seq_numb));
```

The XML column can then be used to store fragments of XML or entire XML documents. However, doing so has several drawbacks:

```
                                   xmlconcat
-------------------------------------------------------------------------
<!--This is a high-priced book-->
    <High_x0020_Priced isbn="978-1-11111-111-1">
    <Asking_x0020_Price>175.00</Asking_x0020_Price>
    <Selling_x0020_Price>175.00</Selling_x0020_Price>
</High_x0020_Priced>
 <!--This is a high-priced book-->
    <High_x0020_Priced isbn="978-1-11111-133-1">
    <Asking_x0020_Price>300.00</Asking_x0020_Price>
    <Selling_x0020_Price>285.00</Selling_x0020_Price>
```

Figure 17-8: The result of using XMLCONCAT to concatenate XML fragments (continued on next page)

```
</High_x0020_Priced>
 <!--This is a high-priced book-->
     <High_x0020_Priced isbn="978-1-11111-144-1">
     <Asking_x0020_Price>80.00</Asking_x0020_Price>
     <Selling_x0020_Price>76.10</Selling_x0020_Price>
</High_x0020_Priced>
 <!--This is a high-priced book-->
     <High_x0020_Priced isbn="978-1-11111-121-1">
     <Asking_x0020_Price>110.00</Asking_x0020_Price>
     <Selling_x0020_Price>110.00</Selling_x0020_Price>
</High_x0020_Priced>
 <!--This is a high-priced book-->
     <High_x0020_Priced isbn="978-1-11111-121-1">
     <Asking_x0020_Price>110.00</Asking_x0020_Price>
     <Selling_x0020_Price>110.00</Selling_x0020_Price>
</High_x0020_Priced>
 <!--This is a high-priced book-->
     <High_x0020_Priced isbn="978-1-11111-130-1">
     <Asking_x0020_Price>150.00</Asking_x0020_Price>
     <Selling_x0020_Price>120.00</Selling_x0020_Price>
</High_x0020_Priced>
 <!--This is a high-priced book-->
     <High_x0020_Priced isbn="978-1-11111-126-1">
     <Asking_x0020_Price>110.00</Asking_x0020_Price>
     <Selling_x0020_Price>110.00</Selling_x0020_Price>
</High_x0020_Priced>
 <!--This is a high-priced book-->
     <High_x0020_Priced isbn="978-1-11111-139-1">
     <Asking_x0020_Price>200.00</Asking_x0020_Price>
     <Selling_x0020_Price>170.00</Selling_x0020_Price>
</High_x0020_Priced>
 <!--This is a high-priced book-->
     <High_x0020_Priced isbn="978-1-11111-133-1">
     <Asking_x0020_Price>125.00</Asking_x0020_Price>
     <Selling_x0020_Price>125.00</Selling_x0020_Price>
</High_x0020_Priced>
 <!--This is a high-priced book-->
     <High_x0020_Priced isbn="978-1-11111-130-1">
     <Asking_x0020_Price>200.00</Asking_x0020_Price>
     <Selling_x0020_Price>150.00</Selling_x0020_Price>
</High_x0020_Priced>
```

Figure 17-8 (continued): The result of using XMLCONCAT to concatenate XML fragments

◊ The contents of the column are not searchable.[1]

◊ The contents of the column cannot be used in predicates that require comparison operators such as > or =.

◊ The column cannot be indexed.

For that reason, tables that have XML columns need at least a unique sequence number to identify each row. You may also want to include a table that assigns keywords to each document so there is some type of search capability. Such a table might be created with

```
CREATE TABLE keywords
    (seq_numb int,
    keyword char (30),
    PRIMARY KEY (seq_numb, keyword),
    FOREIGN KEY keywords2xmlstuff (seq_numb)
        REFERENCES xmlstuff);
```

As mentioned earlier in the discussion of XMLPARSE, you need to use that function to convert text into XML to store in an XML column. Because you can't generate an input string with a SELECT, the interactive INSERT is limited to XML fragments:

```
INSERT INTO xmlstuff
    VALUES (1, XMLPARSE
            (CONTENT 'This is a test'
            STRIP WHITESPACE);
```

For complete document input, you will generally be working with an embedded SQL application.

If you want to look at the contents of an XML column, you can use an interactive SELECT. SQL strips the XML tags for output. The query

---

1   Some current DBMSs support XQuery, a SQL extension that can be used to search XML data.

```
SELECT * FROM xmlstuff;
```

produces

```
 sequ_numb |    xml_text
-----------+----------------
         1 | this is a test
```

Note: You could store XML in a text column, tags and all. However, when you use an XML column, SQL will check the XML to see that it is well-formed.

The XMLSERIALIZE function is essentially the opposite of XMLPARSE: It takes the contents of an XML column and converts it to a text string:

XMLSERIALIZE

```
XMLSERIALIZE (type_indicator column_name AS
character_type)
```

For example,

```
SELECT XMLSERIALIZE
    (DOCUMENT xmltext AS VARCHAR (256))
    FROM sql_stuff
    WHERE seq_numb = 16;
```

would extract the document from the row with the sequence number of 16, convert it to plain text (removing the tags) and display it on the screen. Because SQL removes the tags from interactive SELECT output, this function is particularly useful in an embedded SQL program.

18

The Object-Relational Data Model

The relational data model has been a mainstay of business data processing for nearly 30 years. Nothing has superseded it in the way the relational data model superseded the simple network data model. However, a newer data model—the object-oriented data model[1]—has come into use as an alternative for some types of navigational data processing.

This chapter presents an overview of some object-oriented concepts for readers who aren't familiar with the object-oriented paradigm. (Chapter 19 looks at the SQL standard's support for object-oriented structures.) If you have object-oriented programming experience, then you can skip over the first parts of this chapter and begin reading with the section *Pure Object-Oriented Databases*.

The object-oriented paradigm was the brainchild of Dr. Kristen Nygaard, a Norwegian who was attempting to write a computer program to model the behavior of ships, tides, and fjords. He found that the interactions were extremely complex and realized that it would be easier to write the program if he

---

1   To be completely accurate, the relational data model is the only data model that has a formal specification. The hierarchical data model and the OO data model do not. The closest thing the simple network data model has is the CODASYL specifications.

separated the three types of program elements and let each one model its own behavior against each of the others.

The object-oriented programming languages in use today (most notably C++, Java, and SmallTalk) are a direct outgrowth of Nygaard's early work. The way in which objects are used in databases today is an extension of object-oriented programming.

Note: This is in direct contrast to the relational data model, which was designed specifically to model data relationships, although much of its theoretical foundations are found in mathematical set theory.

Getting Started: Object-Orientation without Computing

To understand the role of objects in relational databases, you must first understand the object-oriented paradigm as it is used in object-oriented programming and pure object-oriented databases. The easiest way to do so is to begin with an example that has absolutely nothing to do with programming at all.

Assume that you have a teenage daughter (or sister, whichever is more appropriate) named Jane and that your family is going to take a long car trip. Like many teens, Jane is less than thrilled about a trip with the family and in particular with spending so much time with her 12-year-old brother. In self-defense, Jane needs something to keep her brother busy so he won't bother her as she reads while her parents are driving. She therefore decides to write up some instructions for playing solitaire games for him.

The first set of instruction is for the most common solitaire game, Klondike. As you can see in Figure 18-1, the deal involves seven piles of cards of increasing depth, with the top card turned over. The rest of the deck remains in the draw pile. Jane decides to break the written instructions into two main parts: information about the game and questions her brother might ask. She therefore produces instructions that look something like Figure 18-2. She also attached the illustration of the game's deal.

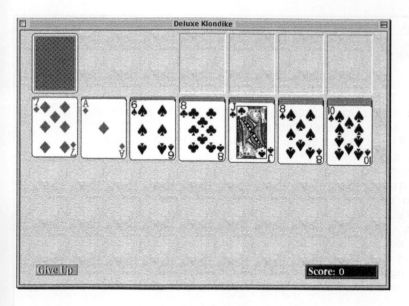

Figure 18-1: The starting layout for Klondike

The next game she tackles is Canfield. Like Klondike, it is played with one deck, but the deal and play are slightly different (see Figure 18-3). Jane uses the same pattern for the instructions as she did for Klondike because it cuts down the amount of writing she has to do (see Figure 18-4).

And finally, just to make sure her brother doesn't get too bored, Jane prepares instructions for Forty Thieves (see Figure 18-5). This game uses decks of cards and plays in a very different way from the other two games (see Figure 18-6). Nonetheless, preparing the instructions for the third game is fairly easy because she has the template for the instructions down pat.

After completing three sets of instructions, it becomes clear to Jane that having the template for the instructions makes the process extremely easy. Jane can use the template to organize any number of sets of instructions for playing solitaire. All she has to do is make a copy of the template and fill in the values for the information about the game.

```
Information about the book
      Name: Klondike
      Illustration: See next page
      Decks: One
      Dealing: Deal from left to right
            First pass: First card face up six cards down.
            Second pass: First card face up on top of pile #2, five
                  cards down on remaining piles.
            Third pass: First card face up on top of pile #3; four
                  cards down on remaining piles.
            ...repeat pattern for total of seven passes.
            Place remaining cards in draw pile, face down.
      Playing: One or two cards can be turned from the draw pile
            at a time. As encountered, put aces above layout. Build up
            from aces in suits. Build down on the deal, opposite suit
            colors. Can move from the middle of a stack moving card
            and all cards built below it.
            Move only kings into empty spots on the layout.
            If turning one card, make only one pass through the draw
                  Pile.
            If turning three cards, make as many passes as you like
                  through the draw pile.
      Winning: All cards built on top of their aces.
Questions to Ask
      What is the name of the game?
            Read Name section.
      How many decks do I need?
            Read Decks section.
      What does the layout look like.
            Read Illustration section.
      How do I deal the game?
            Read Dealing section.
      How do I play the game?
            Read Playing section.
      How do I know when I've won?
            Read Winning section.
```

Figure 18-2: Instructions for playing Klondike

Basic OO Concepts

The object-oriented paradigm shares some characteristics with the Entity-Relationship model used for database design. However, OO extends the idea of relationships between entities by adding actions that the entities can perform.

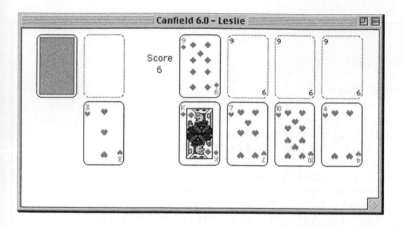

Figure 18-3: The starting deal for Canfield

Objects

If someone were writing an object-oriented computer program to manage the instructions for playing solitaire, each game would be known as an *object*. It is a self-contained element used by the program. It has things that it knows about itself: its name, an illustration of the layout, the number of decks needed to play, how to deal, how to play, and how to determine when the game is won. In object-oriented terms, the values that an object stores about itself are known as *attributes* or *variables* or, occasionally, *properties*.

Each solitaire game object also has some things it knows how to do: explain how to deal, explain how to play, explain how to identify a win, and so on. In object-oriented programming terminology, actions that objects know how to perform are called *methods, services, functions, procedures*, or *operations*.

Note: It is unfortunate, but there is no single accepted terminology for the object-oriented paradigm. Each programming language or DBMS chooses which terms it will use. You therefore need to recognize all of the terms that might be used to describe the same thing.

An object is very security-minded. It typically keeps the things it knows about itself private and releases that information only

```
Information about the book
      Name: Canfield
      Illustration: See next page
      Decks: One
      Dealing: Deal four cards face up.
              Place one additional card above the first four as the
                  starting card for building suits.
              The remaining cards stay in the draw pile.
      Playing: Turn one card at a time, going through the deck as many
                  times as desired.
              Build down from deal, opposite suit colors.
              Can move cards from the middle of stack, moving card and
                  all cards built below it.
              Place cards of the same value as the initial foundation
                  card above the deal as encountered.
              Build up in suits from the foundation cards.
              Any card can be placed in any empty space in the deal.
      Winning: All cards built on top of the foundation cards.
Questions to Ask
      What is the name of the game?
              Read Name section.
      How many decks do I need?
              Read Decks section.
      What does the layout look like.
              Read Illustration section.
      How do I deal the game?
              Read Dealing section.
      How do I play the game?
              Read Playing section.
      How do I know when I've won?
              Read Winning section.
```

Figure 18-4: Instructions for playing Canfield

through a method whose purpose is to share data values (an *accessor method*). For example, a user or program using one of the game objects cannot access the contents of the Dealing variable directly. Instead, the user or program must execute the How Do I Deal the Game? method to see that data.

Objects also keep private the details of the procedures for the things they know how to do, but they make it easy for someone to ask them to perform those actions. Users or programs

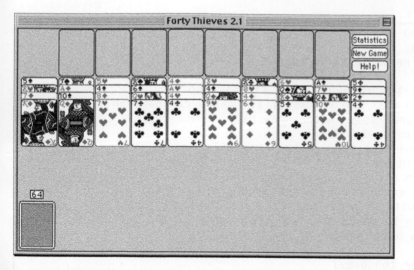

Figure 18-5: The starting layout for Forty Thieves

cannot see what is inside the methods. They see only the result of the method. This characteristic of objects is known as *information hiding* or *encapsulation*.

An object presents a public interface to other objects that might use it. This provides other objects with a way to ask for data values or for actions to be performed. In the example of the solitaire games, the questions that Jane's little brother can ask are a game's public interface. The instructions below each question represent the procedure to be used to answer the question. A major benefit of data encapsulation is that as long as the object's public interface remains the same, you can change the details of the object's methods without needing to inform any other objects that might be using those methods. For example, the card game objects currently tell the user to "read" the contents of an attribute. However, there is no reason that the methods couldn't be changed to tell the user to "print" the contents of an attribute. The user would still access the method in the same way, but the way in which the method operates would be slightly different.

```
Information about the book
      Name: Forty Thieves
      Illustration: See next page
      Decks: Two
      Dealing: Make 10 piles of four cards, all face up.
             Jog cards so that the values of all cards can be seen.
             Remaining cards stay in the draw pile.
      Playing: Turn one card at a time.
             Make only one pass through the draw pile.
             Build down in suits.
             Only the top card of a stack can be moved.
             As aces are encountered, place at top of deal and build up
                  in suits from the aces.
             Any card can be moved into any open space in the layout.
      Winning: All cards built on top of their aces.
Questions to Ask
      What is the name of the game?
             Read Name section.
      How many decks do I need?
             Read Decks section.
      What does the layout look like.
             Read Illustration section.
      How do I deal the game?
             Read Dealing section.
      How do I play the game?
             Read Playing section.
      How do I know when I've won?
             Read Winning section.
```

Figure 18-6: Instructions for playing Forty Thieves

An object requests data or an action by sending a *message* to another object. For example, if you were writing a computer program to manage the instructions for solitaire games, the program (an object in its own right) could send a message to the game object asking the game object to display the instructions for dealing the game. Because the actual procedures of the method are hidden, your program would ask for the instruction display and then you would see the instructions on the screen. However you would not need to worry about the details of how the screen display was produced. That is the job

```
Information about the book
        Name:
        Illustration:
        Decks:
        Dealing:
        Playing:
        Winning:
Questions to Ask
        What is the name of the game?
                Read Name section.
        How many decks do I need?
                Read Decks section.
        What does the layout look like.
                Read Illustration section.
        How do I deal the game?
                Read Dealing section.
        How do I play the game?
                Read Playing section.
        How do I know when I've won?
                Read Winning section.
```

Figure 18-7: The solitaire game instruction template

of the game object rather than the object that is asking the game to do something.

An object-oriented program is made up of a collection of objects, each of which has attributes and methods. The objects interact by sending messages to one another. The trick, of course, is figuring out which objects a program needs and the attributes and methods those objects should have.

The template on which the solitaire game instructions are based is the same for each game. Without data it might be represented as in Figure 18-7. The nice thing about this template is that it provides a consistent way of organizing all the characteristics of a game. When you want to create the instructions for another game, you make a copy of the template and "fill in the blanks." You write the data values for the attributes. The procedures that make up the answers to the questions someone might ask about the game have already been completed.

Classes

In object-oriented terminology, the template on which similar objects like the solitaire game objects are based is known as a *class*. When a program creates an object from a class, it provides data for the object's variables. The object can then use the methods that have been written for its class. All of the objects created from the same class share the same procedures for their methods. They also have the same types of data, but the values for the data may differ, for example, just as the names of the solitaire games are different.

A class is also a data type. In fact, a class is an implementation of what is known as an *abstract data type*, which is just another term for a user-defined data type. The implication of a class being a data type is that you can use a class as the data type of an attribute in a relation.

Suppose, for example, you were developing a class to handle data about the employees in your organization. The attributes of the class might include the employee ID, the first name, the last name, and the address. The address itself is made up of a street, city, state, and zip. Therefore, you would probably create an address class with those attributes and then, rather than duplicating those attributes in the employee class, simply indicate that an object of the employee class will include an object created from the address class to contain the employee's address.

Types of Classes

There are three major types of classes used in an object-oriented program:

◊ *Control classes*: Control classes neither manage data nor have visible output. Instead, they control the operational flow of a program. For example, *application classes* represent the programs themselves. In most cases, each program creates only one object from an application class. The application class's job includes starting the execution of the program, detecting menu selections (or other user interface events), and executing the correct program code to satisfy the user's requests.

◊ *Entity classes:* Entity classes are used to create objects that manage data. The solitaire game class, for example, is an entity class. Classes for people, tangible objects, and events (for example, business meetings) are entity classes. Most object-oriented programs have at least one entity class from which many objects are created. In fact, in its simplest sense, the object-oriented data model is built from the representation of relationships among objects created from entity classes.

◊ *Interface classes:* Interface classes handle the input and output of information. For example, if you are working with a graphic user interface, then each window and menu used by the program is an object created from an interface class.

In an object-oriented program, entity classes do not do their own input and output (I/O). Keyboard input is handled by interface objects that collect data and send it to entity objects for storage and processing. Screen and printed output is formatted by interface objects that get data for display from entity objects. When entity object become part of a database, the DBMS takes care of the file I/O; the rest of the I/O is handled by application programs or DBMS utilities.

Why is it so important to keep data manipulation separate from I/O? Wouldn't it be simpler to let the entity object manage its own I/O? It might be simpler in the short run, but if you decided to change a screen layout, you would need to modify the entity class. If you keep them separate, then data manipulation procedures are independent of data display. You can change one without affecting the other. In a large program, this not only can save you a lot of time, but also can help you avoid programming errors. In a database environment, the separation of I/O and data storage becomes especially critical because you do not want to modify data storage each time you decide to modify the look and feel of a program.

Many object-oriented programs also use a fourth type of class: a *container* class. Container classes exist to "contain," or manage, multiple objects created from the same class. Because they gather objects together, they are also known as *aggregations*. For example, if you had a program that handled the instructions for playing solitaire, then that program would probably have a container class that organized all the individual card game objects. The container class would keep the objects in some order, list them for you, and probably search through them as well. Many pure object-oriented DBMSs require container classes, known as *extents*, to provide access to all objects created from the same class. However, as you will see, container classes are not used when objects are integrated into a relational database.

Types of Methods

Several types of methods are common to most classes, including the following:

◊ *Constructors*: A constructor is a method that has the same name as the class. It is executed whenever an object is created from the class. A constructor therefore usually contains instructions to initialize an object's variables in some way.

◊ *Destructors*: A destructor is a method that is executed when an object is destroyed. Not all object-oriented programming languages support destructors, which are usually used to release system resources (for example, main memory allocated by the object). Java in particular does not use destructors.

◊ *Accessors*: An accessor, also known as a *get method*, returns the value of a private attribute to another object. This is the typical way in which external objects gain access to encapsulated data.

◊ *Mutators*: A mutator, or *set method*, stores a new value in an attribute. This is the typical way in which external objects can modify encapsulated data.

The remaining methods defined for a class depend on the specific type of class and the specific behaviors it needs to perform.

One of the characteristics of a class is its ability to contain *overloaded* methods, methods that have the same name but require different data to operate. Because the data are different, the public interfaces of the methods are distinct.

Method Overloading

As an example, assume that a human relations program has a container class named AllEmployees that aggregates all objects created from the Employee class. Programs that use the AllEmployees class create one object from the class and then relate all employee objects to the container using some form of program data structure.

To make the container class useful, there must be some way to locate specific employee objects. You might want to search by the employee ID number, by first and last name, or by telephone number. The AllEmployees class therefore contains three methods named "find." One of the three requires an integer (the employee number) as input, the second requires two strings (the first and last name), and the third requires a single string (the phone number). Although the methods have the same name, their public interfaces are different because the combination of the name and the required input data is distinct.

Many classes have overloaded constructors. One might accept interactive input, another might read input from a file, and a third might get its data by copying data from another object (a *copy constructor*). For example, most object-oriented environments have a Date class that supports initializing a date object with three integers (day, month, year), the current system date, another Date object, and so on.

The benefit of method overloading is that the methods present a consistent interface to the programmer. In the case of our example of the AllEmployees container class, whenever a programmer wants to locate an employee, he or she knows to use a method named "find." Then the programmer just uses whichever of the three types of data he or she happens to have. The object-oriented program locates the correct method by using the entire public interface (its *signature*), made up of the name and the required input data.

Class Relationships

The classes in an object-oriented environment aren't always independent. The basic object-oriented paradigm has two major ways to relate objects, distinct from any logical data relationships that might be included in a pure object-oriented database: inheritance and composition.

Inheritance

As a developer or database designer is working on an object-oriented project, he or she may run into situations where there is a need for similar—but not identical—classes. If these classes are related in a general to specific manner, then the developer can take advantage of one of the major features of the object-oriented paradigm, known as *inheritance*.

Inheriting Attributes

To see how inheritance works, assume that you are writing a program (or developing a database) to manage a pet shop. One of the entity classes you will use is Animal, which will describe the living creatures sold by the shop. The data that describe objects created from the Animal class include the English and Latin names of the animal, the animal's age, and the animal's gender. However, the rest of the data depend on what type of animal is being represented. For example, for reptiles, you want to know the length of the animal, but for mammals, you want to know the weight. And for fish, you don't care about the weight or length, but you do want to know the color. All the animals sold by the pet shop share some data, yet have pieces of data that are specific to certain subgroups.

You could diagram the relationship as in Figure 18-8. The Animal class provides the data common to all types of animals. The subgroups—Mammals, Reptiles, and Fish—*add* the data specific to themselves. They don't need to repeat the common data because they *inherit* them from animals. In other words, Mammals, Reptiles, and Fish all include the four pieces of data that are part of Animal.

If you look closely at Figure 18-8, you'll notice that the lines on the arrows go from the subgroups to Animal. This is actually contrary to what is happening: The data from Animal are flowing down the lines into the subgroups. Unfortunately, the direction of the arrows is dictated by convention, even though it may seem counterintuitive.

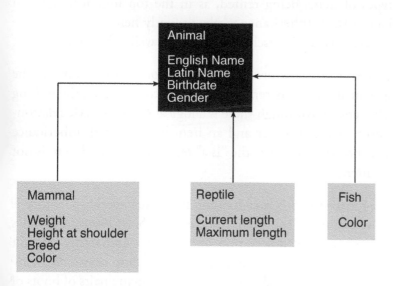

Figure 18-8: The relationship of classes for an object-oriented environment for a pet shop

In object-oriented terminology, the subgroups are known as *subclasses* or *derived classes*. The Animal class is a *superclass* or *base class*.

The trick to understanding inheritance is to remember that subclasses represent a more specific occurrence of their superclass. The relationships between a base class and its derived classes therefore can be expressed using the phrase "is a":

◊ A mammal is an animal.

◊ A reptile is an animal.

◊ A fish is an animal.

If the "is a" phrasing does not make sense in a given situation, then you are not looking at inheritance. As an example, assume that you are designing an object-oriented environment for the rental of equipment at a ski rental shop. You create a class for a generic merchandise item and then subclasses for the specific types of items being rented, as in the top four rectangles in Figure 18-9. Inheritance works properly here because skis are a specific type of merchandise item, as well as boots and poles.

However, you run into trouble when you begin to consider the specific items being rented and the customer doing the renting (the renter). Although there is a logical database-style relationship between a renter and an item being rented, inheritance does not work because the "is a" test fails. A rented item is not a renter!

The situation with merchandise items and rental inventory is more complex. The Merchandise Item, Skis, Boots, and Poles classes represent description of types of merchandise but not physical inventory. For example, the ski shop may have many pairs of one type of ski in inventory and many pairs of boots of the same type, size, and width. Therefore, what is being rented is individual inventory items, represented by the Item Rented

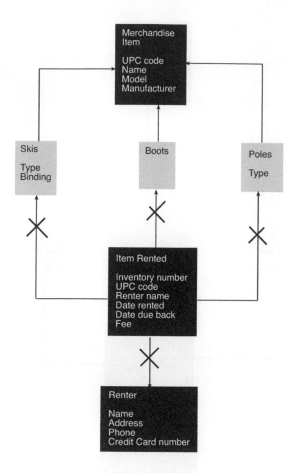

Figure 18-9: Inheritance and no inheritance in an object-oriented environment for a ski equipment rental

class. A given inventory item is either skis, boots, or poles. It can only be *one*, not all three as shown in Figure 18-9. Therefore, an item rented is not a pair of skis, a pair of boots, or a set of poles. (You also have the problem of having no class that can store the size or length of an item.)

The solution to the problem is to create a separate rented item class for each type of merchandise, as in Figure 18-10. When you are looking at this diagram, be sure to pay attention to

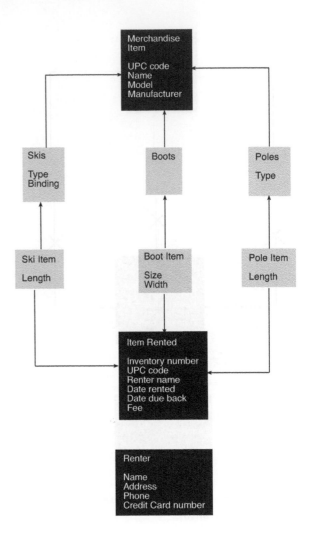

Figure 18-10: Multiple inheritance in the data environment for a ski shop

the direction of the arrows. The physical layout of the diagram does not correspond to the direction of the inheritance. Remember that, by convention, the arrows point from the derived class to the base class.

The Ski Item class inherits information about the type of item it is from the Skis class. It also inherits information about an item being rented from the Item Rented class. A ski item "is a" pair of skis; a ski item "is a" rented item as well. Now the design of the classes passes the "is a" test for appropriate inheritance. (Note that it also gives you a class that can contain information such as the length and size of a specific inventory item.) The Renter class does not participate in the inheritance hierarchy at all.

Multiple Inheritance

When a class inherits from more than one base class, you have *multiple inheritance*. The extent to which multiple inheritance is supported in programming languages and DBMSs varies considerably from one product to another.

Abstract Classes

Not every class in an inheritance hierarchy is necessarily used to create objects. For example, in Figure 18-10 it is unlikely that any objects are ever created from the Merchandise Item or Item Rented classes. These classes are present simply to provide the common attributes and methods that their derived classes share.

Such classes are known as *abstract*, or *virtual*, classes. In contrast, classes from which objects are created are known as *concrete* classes.

Note: Many computer scientists use the verb "instantiate" to mean "creating an object from a class." For example, you could say that abstract classes are never instantiated. However, I find that term rather contrived (although not quite as bad as saying "we will now motivate the code" to mean "we will now explain the code") and prefer to use the more direct "create an object from a class."

Inheriting Methods: Polymorphism

In general, methods are inherited by subclasses from their superclass. A subclass can use its base class's methods as its own. However, in some cases it may not be possible to write a generic method that can be used by all subclasses. For example, assume that the ski rental shop's Merchandise Item class has a method named printCatalogEntry, the intent of which is to print a properly formatted entry for each distinct type of merchandise item. The subclasses of Merchandise Item, however, have attributes not shared by all subclasses and the printCatalogEntry method therefore must work somewhat differently for each subclass.

To solve the problem, the ski rental shop can take advantage of *polymorphism*, the ability to write different bodies for methods of the same name that belong to classes in the same inheritance hierarchy. The Merchandise Item class includes a *prototype* for the printCatalogEntry method, indicating just the method's public interface. There is no body for the method, no specifications of how the method is to perform its work (a *virtual method*). Each subclass then redefines the method, adding the program instructions necessary to execute the method.

The beauty of polymorphism is that a programmer can expect methods of the same name and same type of output for all the subclasses of the same base class. However, each subclass can perform the method according to its own needs. Encapsulation hides the details from all objects outside the class hierarchy.

Note: It is very easy to confuse polymorphism and overloading. Just keep in mind that overloading applies to methods of the same class that have the same name but different signatures, whereas polymorphism applies to several subclasses of the same base class that have methods with the same signature but different implementations.

Composition

Inheritance can be described as a general–specific relationship. In contrast, *composition* is a whole–part relationship. It specifies that one class is a component of another and is often read as "has a."

To help you understand how composition can be used, let's assume that the ski rental shop wants to offer packages of items for rent (skis, boots, and poles). The packages will come in three qualities—good, better, and best—based on the retail value of the items in the package.

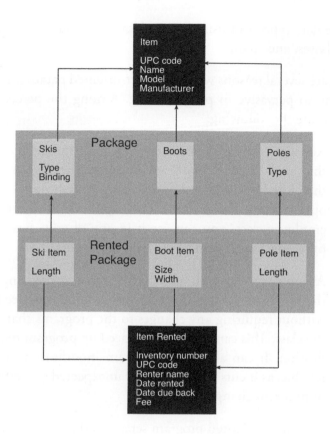

Figure 18-11: Composition

As you can see in Figure 18-11, each package contains three types of merchandise items, so the package class "has a" boot, "has a" pole, and "has a" ski. An object created from this class would be used to indicate which types of items could be rented as a bundle. In contrast, the rented package class contains actual rental items and therefore indicates which specific inventory items have been rented together.

Some pure object-oriented DBMSs take composition to the extreme. They provide simple data types such as integers, real numbers, characters, and Booleans. Everything else in the database—even strings—is built by creating classes from these simple data types and using those classes to build more complex classes, and so on.

Benefits of Object-Orientation

There are several reasons why the object-oriented paradigm has become so pervasive in programming. Among the perceived benefits are the following:

◊ An object-oriented program consists of modular units that are independent of one another. These units can therefore be reused in multiple programs, saving development time. For example, if you have a well-debugged employee class, you can use it in any of your business programs that require data about employees.

◊ As long as a class's public interface remains unchanged, the internals of the class can be modified as needed without requiring any changes to the programs that use the class. This can significantly speed up program modification. It can also make program modification more reliable, as it cuts down on many unexpected side effects of program changes.

◊ An object-oriented program separates the user interface from data handling, making it possible to modify one independent of the other.

◊ Inheritance adds logical structure to a program by relating classes in a general to specific manner, making the program easier to understand and therefore easier to maintain.

Where Objects Work Better Than Relations

There are some database environments—especially those involving a great deal of inheritance—in which object-orientation is easier to implement than a relational design. To see why this is so, let's look at a hobby environment that just happens to be one of the best examples of the situation in question that I've ever encountered.

The database catalogs Yu-Gi-Oh cards (one of those animé related trading card games). The collector for whom this database and its application were developed has thousands of cards, some of which are duplicates. They are stored in three binders. Within each binder there may be several sections; the pages are numbered within each section.

There are three major types of cards: monsters, spells, and traps. The monster card in Figure 18-12 is fairly typical. Notice that it has a title, an "attribute" at the top right, a "level" (count the circles below the name), an "edition" (first, limited, or other), a set designation, a type (and optionally two subtypes), a description, attack points, and defense points. At the bottom left, there may be a code number, which is missing from some of the early cards.

A card with the same name may appear in many sets and the same set may have more than one card of the same name. What distinguishes them is their "rarity," determined by how the title is printed (black or white for common cards and silver or gold for rare cards) and how the image is printed (standard color printing or holofoil printing). There are a variety of combinations of printing to generate common, rare, super rare, ultra rare, and ultimate rare cards.

Note: If you want an interesting challenge before you see the relational design for this database, try to figure out the primary key for a card!

Most cards can be used for game play, but some have been banned from specific types of games. Others have caveats ("rulings") attached to them by the game's governing board that affect how the card can be used in a game.

Spell cards, which as you might expect can be used in the game to cast spells, share a number of attributes with the monster card, but don't have things such as type and subtypes. The third type of card, a trap, also shares some attributes with monsters,

Figure 18-12: A typical Yu-Gi-Oh monster card

but is missing others and has a property that is unique to this type of card. Spells also have properties, but the list of possible properties differs between spells and traps.

You can find an entity-relationship diagram for the card database in Figure 18-13. As you might have guessed, there is an entity for the card, which has three subclasses, one for each specific type of card. There are also many holdings for each card.

To design the relational database, we create one relation for each entity, including the superclass (in this example, Card) and its subclasses (Monster card, Trap card, and Spell card). With an object-oriented DBMS, we would create objects only from the subclasses; no object would ever be created from the

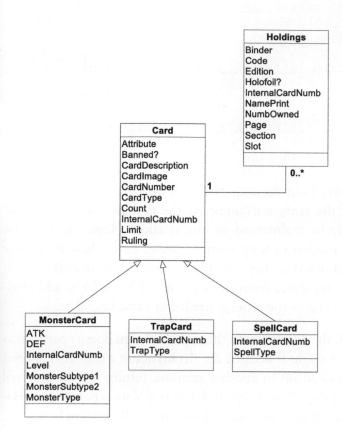

Figure 18-13: The ER diagram for the card database

superclass. The subclasses "inherit" the attributes of their parent. For the relational database, we have to do that manually, using some type of primary key–foreign key relationship to connect the subclass tables to the parent table. Differences in where cards of a given name appear and how they are printed are handled by Holdings. Therefore, the design of the card database looks like this:

```
Card (InternalCardNUMB, Attribute, Banned?,
    CardDescription?, CardImage, CardName,
    CardNumber, CardType, Count, Limit,
    Ruling)
```

```
Monster card (InternalCardNumb, ATK, DEF,
     Level, MonsterSubtype1, MonsterSubtype2,
     MonsterType)

Trap card (InternalCardNumb, TrapType)

Spell card (InternalCardNumb, SpellType)

Holdings (InternalCardNumb, Code, Edition,
     Holofoil?, NamePrint, NumberOwned, Binder,
     Page, Section, Slot)
```

Why have both the trap and spell card relations if they have exactly the same attributes? At the current time they could certainly be maintained in one relation. However, there are several reasons to keep them separate. First, there is no way to guarantee that they will always have the same attributes. If they are separated from the start, it will be easier to add attributes to one or the other if needed at some later date.

Second, the major reason this type of design doesn't perform as well as it might is because the details about a card always need to be looked up in another relation, joining on the internal card number. If we keep spell and trap data separate, the relations will remain smaller and the joins will perform better.

Note: Here's the answer to the primary key challenge: A Holding actually represents one or more physical cards in the inventory. It has a name (represented by the internal card number) and a set designation. When cards of the same name are printed in different ways in the same set, they have different set designations. Therefore, the concatenation of the internal card number and the set designation uniquely identifies a card (although not a physical card in the inventory, given that there may be duplicate cards in the inventory). The only other alternative is to assign unique inventory numbers to each physical card and to use them. For some collectors, this may make sense, given that they would want to track the condition of each and every card.

There is an alternative design for this type of database: Rather than use one relation for each entity, create only a single relation in which many attributes may be null, depending on the type of card. Such a relation might look like this:

```
Card (InternalCardNumb, Attribute, Banned?,
     CardDescription, CardImage, CardName,
     CardNumber, CardType, Count, Limit,
     Ruling, ATK, DEF, Level, MonsterSubtype1,
     MonsterSubtype2, MonsterType, TrapType,
     spellType)
```

The CardType attribute indicates which of the type-specific attributes should have data. For example, if CardType contained "M" for Monster, you would expect to find data in the ATK, DEF, and level attributes but not the spell type or trap type. The supposed benefit of this design is that you avoid the joins to combine the separate relations of the earlier design. However, when a DBMS retrieves a row from this relation, it pulls in the entire row, empty fields and all. Practically, in a performance sense, you haven't gained much and you're stuck with a design that can waste disk space.

Note: Personally, I prefer the multiple relation design because it's cleaner, wastes less space, and is much more flexible as the design of the relations needs to change over time.

A pure object-oriented design for the same database would include the five entity classes, although the Card class would be an abstract class. It would also include a class to aggregate all objects created from subclasses of the Card class, letting users handle all cards, regardless of type, as a single type of object. The nature of these data—the major need for inheritance—suggests that an object-oriented database may well perform better than a relational database.

Pure Object-Oriented Databases

Representing Data Relationships

A pure object-oriented database management system (OOD-BMS) defines all of its data using object-oriented data structures. There are no tables, but only objects and groups of objects. There are no required primary keys nor any foreign keys.

An object-oriented database indicates relationships by requiring each object to contain identifiers for the objects to which it is related. To make this work, when an object is created it is given a unique internal identifier. The user (a programmer or someone working interactively) never sees this identifier. In fact, it may be created from the information needed to locate the object's data in a physical database file.

Exactly which containers an object will have depends on the types of relationships in which it is participating:

◊ 1:1: Each object will have an attribute that stores the identifier for the object to which it is related.

◊ 1:M: The object at the "one" end of the relationship will have a container for the identifiers of the objects to which it is related. If the relationship is to support inverse access ("many-to-one"), each object at the "many" end of the relationship will have an attribute to hold the identifier of its parent object.

◊ M:M: A pure object-oriented database can represent a M:M relationship directly, without the use of a relationship object (a composite entity), something a relational database cannot do. (An OO design may still need the equivalent of a composite entity if it needs to store relationship data.) Each object will have a container for the identifiers for objects at the other end of the relationship.

The objects in an OO database are not required to have unique keys (the equivalent of a primary key). However, most classes are designed with a variable to hold a unique identifier to ensure retrieval of each specific object.

Object-oriented databases are what we call *navigational*. This means that access to related objects must follow the predefined linkages created by the containers for related objects. For example, to find all the purchases made by a customer, a program in an object-oriented database environment would do the following:

Navigating the Relationships

1. Find the customer object, perhaps using an aggregate object that collects all the customer objects.

2. Retrieve the first related-object identifier from the customer object.

3. Use the purchase object's identifier to locate the purchase object and process it as needed.

4. Retrieve the next related-object identifier from the customer object.

5. Repeat steps 3 and 4 until all purchase objects have been processed.

Relationships in a relational database are all two-way (inverse). In other words it is possible to go from the entity at the "one" end of a relationship to entities at the "many" end. It is also possible to take a single entity at the "many" end of a relationship and find its parent entity. However, not all OODBMSs require inverse relationships. When the database developer creates the schema, he or she must indicate which relationships will be inverse and which will be one-way. One-way relationships therefore mean that a relationship can be navigated in only one direction.

The Object-Relational Data Model

The *object-relational* (OR) data model—which is sometimes known as *post-relational*—is a combination of the relational data model that we discussed in Chapter 1 and some of the object-oriented concepts that—in the opinion of some database theorists and users—make up for shortcomings in the relational data model. The purpose of this discussion is to help you understand how OR designs differ from both pure OO designs and pure relational designs. With that in hand, you will be able to understand the strengths and weaknesses of SQL's support for object-related structures that are discussed in Chapter 19.

ER Diagrams for Object-Relational Designs

The style of ER diagramming that you saw in Chapter 1 (the *Information Engineering*, or IE, approach) does not lend itself to the inclusion of objects because it has no way to represent a class. Therefore, when we add objects to a relational database, we have to use another ERD style.

Although there are many techniques or object-oriented ERDs, one of the most commonly used is the *Unified Modeling Language* (UML). When used to depict a post-relational database design, UML looks a great deal like the IE style, but indicates relationships in a different way.

An example of an ER diagram using UML can be found in Figure 18-14. This design is of a purely object-oriented database and includes some elements that therefore won't appear in a hybrid design. It has been included here to give you an overview of UML so that you can better understand the portions of the modeling tool that we will be using in Chapter 19.

The basic features of UML include the following:

◊ A regular class is represented by a rectangle, divided into three parts (name, attributes, procedures).

◊ An aggregate class (a *metaclass* in the diagram)—a class that collects all objects of a given class—is represented

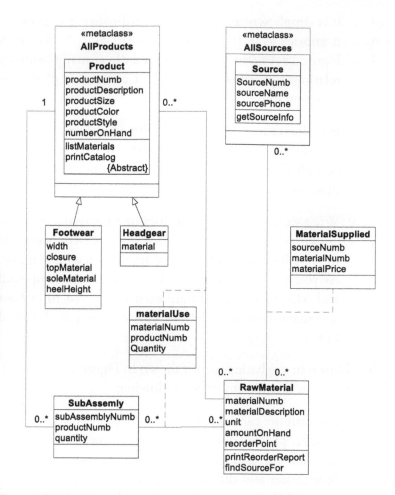

Figure 18-14: An object-oriented database design using UML

by a rectangle containing its name and the rectangles of the classes whose objects it aggregates. For example, in Figure 18-14, the Product and Source classes are within their aggregate classes, AllProducts and AllSources, respectively.

◊ Relationships between entities are shown with lines with plain ends. The cardinality of a relationship is represented as n, n..n, or n..*. For example, if the cardinality is 1, it is simply written as 1. If the cardinality is 0 or more, it appears as 0..*; 1 or more appears as 1..*. Notice in Figure 18-14 that there are several direct many-to-many relationships, shown with 0..* at either end of the association line.

◊ Inheritance is shown by a line with an open arrow pointing toward the base class. In Figure 18-14, the Footwear and Headgear classes have such arrows pointing toward Product.

◊ What we call composite entities in a relational database are known as *association classes*. They are connected to the relationship to which they apply with a dashed line. As you can see in Figure 18-14, the MaterialSupplied and MaterialUse classes are each connected to at least one many-to-many relationship by the required dashed line.

In addition to the basic features shown in Figure 18-14, UML diagrams can include any of the following:

◊ An attribute can include information about its visibility (public, protected, or private), data type, default value, and domain. In Figure 18-15, for example, you can see four classes and the data types of their attributes. Keep in mind that in an object-oriented environment, data types can be other classes. Therefore, the Source class uses an object of the TelephoneNumber class for its phoneNumber attribute and an object of the Address class for its sourceAddress attribute. In turn, source, Address, and TelphoneNumber all contain attributes that are objects of the String class.

◊ Procedures (officially called *operations* by UML) can include their complete program signature and return data type. If you look at Figure 18-15, for example, you can see each operation's name followed by the type of data

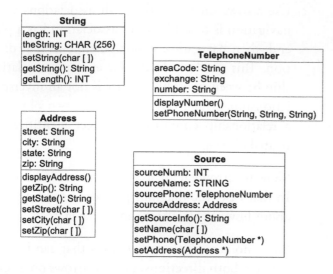

Figure 18-15: UML classes showing attribute data types

it requires to perform its job (*parameters*). Together, the procedure's name and parameters make up the procedure's signature. If data are returned by the operation, then the operation's signature is followed by a colon and the data type of the return value, which may be an object of another class or a simple data type such as an integer.

◊ Solid arrows can be used at the end of associations to indicate the direction in a relationship can be navigated.

Note: As mentioned earlier in this chapter, pure object-oriented databases are navigational, meaning that traversal through the database is limited to following predefined relationships. Because of this characteristic, some theorists feel that the object-oriented data model is a step backwards rather than forward and that the relational data model continues to have significant advantages over any navigational data model.

There are three possible ways to use the arrows:

o Use arrows on the ends of all associations where navigation is possible. If an association has a plain end, then navigation is not possible in that direction. This would indicate, for example, a relationship between two objects that is not an inverse relationship, where only one of the two objects in a relationship contains the object identifier of a related object.

o Show no arrows at all, as was done in Figure 18-15. In that case, the diagram provides no information about how the database can be navigated.

o Show no arrows on associations that can be navigated in both directions, but use arrows on associations that can be navigated in only one direction. The drawback to this approach is that you cannot differentiate associations that can be navigated in both directions from associations that cannot be navigated at all.

◊ An association that ends in a filled diamond indicates a whole–part relationship. For example, if you were representing a spreadsheet in a database, the relationship between the spreadsheet and its cells could be diagrammed as in Figure 18-16. The filled diamond can also be used to show aggregation instead of placing one object within another as was done in Figure 18-14.

◊ When an association is between more than two objects, UML uses a diamond to represent the relationship. If an association is present, it will be connected to the diamond, as in Figure 18-17. The four classes in the illustration represent entities from a poetry reading society's database. A "reading" occurs when a single person reads a single poem that was written by one or more poets.

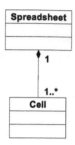

Figure 18-16: A UML representation of a whole–part relationship

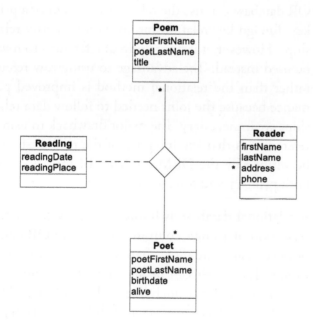

Figure 18-17: The UML representation of a relationship between more than two classes

Features of the OR Data Model

The association entity indicates when and where the reading took place.

There is no accepted standard for the object-relational data model. However, a commonly used model is based on the elements supported by recent SQL standards. As you will see, these features violate many of the rules applied to relational databases:

◊ A relational database should have no data structures other than tables. An OR database, however, allows an attribute to support a reference to a row in another table. These references are the internal object identifiers used by OO databases described earlier in this chapter. An OR database can use the relational concept of a primary key–foreign key relationship to indicate entity relationships. However, it is not required; references to rows can be used instead. The advantage to using row references rather than the relational method is improved performance because the joins needed to follow data relationships are unnecessary. The major drawback to using row references is that the integrity of the relationships can't be verified by the DBMS; referential integrity requires both primary and foreign key values.

◊ A relational database is limited to one value at the intersection of a single column and row. An OR database, however, can store more than one value in the same location. The values can be an array of the same type of data, a row of data (much like a table within a table), an unordered collection of data of different data types, or an entire object.

◊ Classes are implemented as *user-defined data types* (UDTs). A new UDT may inherit from an existing UDT, although multiple inheritance is not allowed. A UDT will have default accessor and mutator methods as well as a default constructor, each of which can be overridden by a database programmer. There is nothing in the relational data model that prohibits UDTs. However, to be used in a relational database, a custom data type must hold only a single value.

◊ UDTs may have methods defined with them. Methods may be overloaded. Polymorphism is supported. Relational databases have no concept of storing procedures with data.

Object-Relational Support

The SQL:2003 standard introduced a variety of object-relational features. Although not all relational DBMSs support this part of the standard, you will find at least some OR features in most of today's major DBMSs.

Note: There are some people who cling to the pure relational data model like a lifeline. However, in practice there is nothing that requires you to avoid SQL's OR features. If those features can help model your database environment, then those designing your database shouldn't be afraid to use them. Just be aware of the referential integrity issues that can arise when you store more than one piece of data in a single column in a single row.

SQL provides four column data types for OR storage as well as support for user-defined data types (UDTs). The SQL programming constructs discussed in Chapter 14—along with extensions for accessing OO structures—are used to write methods for UDTs when they are needed.

Note: Some of the OR features covered in this chapter require programming. As when we discussed triggers, stored procedures, and embedded SQL, in those instances this chapter assumes that you have programming experience.

An Additional Sample Database

For some of the examples in this chapter we will be working with a classic home computer application: recipes. You can find the ERD in Figure 19-1. (It has been designed to illustrate OR concepts and therefore is probably missing elements that would be part of a commercial application.)

The *recipe* class is an abstract class that stores data common to all types of recipes. The six subclasses represents categories of recipes, each of which has at least one unique attribute.

The *ingredient*, *instruction*, and *ingredient_amount* classes are more traditional entities. A recipe has many instructions. Each instruction uses zero, one, or more ingredients. The *ingredient_amount* class therefore stores relationship data: the amount of a given ingredient used in a given instruction.

SQL Data Types for Object-Relational

SQL's OR features include three column data types for storing multiple values: ROW, ARRAY, and MULTISET. You can use these data types without using any of the other OR features (in particular, typed tables to store objects). Because they do not act as objects, these columns cannot have methods.

Row Type

A column declared as a *row* type holds an entire row of data (multiple pieces of data). This gives you the equivalent of a table within a table. The contents of the row—called *fields*—can be declared as built-in data types or UDTs.

As an example, we'll create a table for customers of the rare book store that stores the customer's address in a single column using the ROW data type:

```
CREATE TABLE customer
    (first_name CHAR (20),
     last_name CHAR (20),
     address ROW (street CHAR (50),
                  city CHAR (30),
                  state CHAR (2),
                  zip CHAR (10),
                  phone CHAR (12)));
```

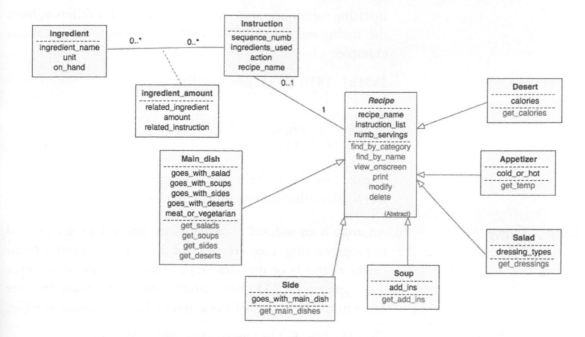

Figure 19-1: An object-relational ERD

Notice that the ROW column is given a name, just as a single-valued column. The data type is followed by the contents of the row in parentheses. The row's fields are declared in the same way as any other SQL column (name followed by data type).

We use "dot" notation to access the individual fields in a column of type ROW. For example, to reference the *street* field in the *address* column without qualifying the table name you would use

```
address.street
```

When the SQL statement requires a table name (for example, for use in a join or for display by a query in which the field appears in multiple tables), you preference the field reference with the table name, as in

```
customer.address.street
```

Inserting values into a row column is only a bit different from the traditional INSERT statement. Consider the following example:

```
INSERT INTO customer VALUES
     ('John','Doe',
       ROW ('123 Main
Street,'Anytown','ST','11224'),
      '555-111-2233');
```

The data for the *address* column are preceded by the keyword ROW. The values follow in parentheses.

Array Type

An *array* is an ordered *collection* of elements. Like arrays used in programming, they are declared to have a maximum number of elements of the same type. That type can be a simple data type or a UDT. For example, we might want to store order numbers as part of a customer's data in a *customer* table:

```
CREATE TABLE customer
     (first CHAR (20),
      last CHAR (20),
      orders INT ARRAY[100],
      numb_orders INT,
      phone CHAR (12));
```

The array column is given a name and a data type, which are followed by the keyword ARRAY and the maximum number of elements the array should hold (the array's *cardinality*), in brackets. The array's data type can be one of SQL's built-in data types or a UDT.

Access to values in an array is by the array's *index* (its position in the array order). Although you specify the maximum number of elements in an array counting from 1, array indexes begin at 0. An array of 100 elements therefore has indexes from 0 to 99. The sample *customer* table above includes a column (*numb_orders*) that stores the total number of elements in the array. The last used index will be *numb_orders – 1*.

You can input multiple values into an array at one time when you first insert a row:

```
INSERT INTO customer VALUES
    ('John','Doe',
      ARRAY (25,109,227,502,610),
      5,'555-111-2233');
```

The keyword ARRAY precedes the values in parentheses.

You can also insert or modify a specific array element directly:

```
INSERT INTO customer (first, last, orders[0],
    numb_orders,phone)
      VALUES ('John','Doe',25,1,'555-111-2233');
```

When you query a table and ask for display of an array column by name, without an index, SQL displays the entire contents of the array, as in:

```
SELECT orders
FROM customer
WHERE first = 'John' AND last = 'Doe';
```

Use an array index when you want to retrieve a single array element. The query

```
SELECT orders [numb_orders - 1]
FROM customer
WHERE first = 'John' AND last = 'Doe';
```

displays the last order stored in the array.

Processing each element in an array requires programming (a trigger, stored procedure, or embedded SQL). Declare a variable to hold the array index, initialize it to 0, and increment it by 1 each time an appropriate loop iterates—the same way you would process all elements in an array using any high-level programming language.

Note: Although many current DBMSs support arrays in columns, not all automatically perform array bounds checking. In other words, they do not necessarily validate that an array index is within the maximum number specified when the table was created. Check your software's documentation to determine whether array bounds constraints must be handled by an application program or can be left up to the DBMS.

Manipulating Arrays

Restrictions of content and access notwithstanding, there are two operations that you can perform on arrays:

◊ Comparisons: Two arrays can be compared (for example, in a WHERE clause) if the two arrays are created from data types that can be compared. When making the comparison, SQL compares the elements in order. Two arrays A and B therefore are equivalent if A[0] = B[0], A[1] = B[1], and so on; all comparisons between all the pairs of values in the array must be true. By the same token, A > B if A[0] > B[0], throughout the arrays.

◊ Concatenation: Two arrays with compatible data types (data types that can be converted into a single data type) can be concatenated with the concatenation operator (||). The result is another array, as in Figure 19-2. Notice that the data from array A have been converted to real numbers because SQL will always convert to the format that has the highest precision.

Multiset Type

A *multiset* is an unordered collection of elements of the same type. The following table contains a multiset to hold multiple phone numbers:

```
CREATE TABLE customer
    (first CHAR (20),
     last CHAR (20),
     orders INT ARRAY[100],
     phones CHAR (20) MULTISET);
```

You specify the contents of a multiset when you insert a row into a table much like you do for an array. The only differ-

(A)	(B)	(C)
16	96.05	16.00
52	295.82	52.00
109	303.00	109.00
85	105.88	85.00
33	22.16	33.00
203	111.23	203.00
384	88.22	384.00
23	45.99	23.00
	18.62	96.05
	35.88	295.82
		303.00
		105.88
		22.16
		111.23
		88.22
		45.99
		18.62
		35.88

(Column A) || (Column B) = (Column C)

Figure 19-2: Concatenating arrays

ence is the use of the keyword MULTISET to indicate that the values in parentheses are intended as a single group:

```
INSERT INTO customer (first, last,
orders[0],numb_orders,phones)
     VALUES ('John','Doe',25,1, MULTISET ('555-
111-2233','555-222-1122'));
```

Because a multiset is unordered, you cannot access individual elements by position as you do with array elements. You can, however, display the entire contents of the multiset by using its name in a query:

```
SELECT phones
FROM customer
WHERE first = 'John' AND last = 'Doe';
```

Updating a multiset is an all or nothing proposition. In other words, you can't pull one value out or put in a single value. An UPDATE statement such as

```
UPDATE customer
    SET phones =
    MULTISET ('555-111-2233','555-333-1122');
```

replaces the entire contents of the *phones* column.

Manipulating Multisets

As with arrays, there are a few operations that can be performed on multisets with compatible data types:

◊ Multisets can be compared, just as arrays. Multisets A and B will be true if they contain exactly the same elements.

◊ Union: The MULTISET UNION operator returns a multiset that contains all elements in the participating multisets. For example,

```
UPDATE some_table
    SET big_multiset = small_multiset1
MULTISET UNION small_multiset2
```

puts the two small multisets into the big multiset.

◊ Intersect: The MULTISET INTERSECT operator returns all elements that two multisets have in common. For example,

```
SELECT table1.multiset MULTISET INTER-
SECT table2.multiset
FROM table1 JOIN table2;
```

works on each row in the joined tables, returning the elements that the multisets in each row have in common.

◊ Difference: The MULTISET EXCEPT operation returns the difference between two multisets (all elements they *don't* have in common). The query

```
SELECT table1.multiset MULTISET EXCEPT
table2.multiset
FROM table1 JOIN table2;
```

functions exactly like the previous example but returns elements from each row that the multisets don't share.

The union, intersect, and difference operators have two options. If you include ALL after the operator, SQL includes duplicate elements in the result. To exclude duplicates, use DISTINCT.

The more classic SQL object-oriented features are built from UDTs and typed tables. The UDT defines a class and the typed table defines a place to store objects from that class. Even if you choose not to use OR elements in a database, you may want to use a UDT as a domain.

A user-defined data type is a structured, named group of attributes of existing data types (either built-in types or other UDTs). In its simplest form, the UDT has the following general syntax:

```
CREATE TYPE type_name AS (column_definitions);
```

We could create a very simple type to hold a date, for example:

```
CREATE TYPE date_type AS
    (month int,
     day int,
     year int);
```

We could then specify *date_type* as the data type for a column in a table:

```
CREATE TABLE people
    (first CHAR (20),
     last CHAR (20),
     birthdate date_type);
```

User-Defined Data Types and Typed Tables

UDTs as Domains

UDTs as Classes

More commonly, we use a UDT to define a class. For example, we could create a type for the *Ingredient* class with

```
CREATE TYPE ingredient_type AS OBJECT
    (ingredient_name CHAR (256),
     unit char (20),
     on_hand int);
```

Notice the AS OBJECT clause that has been inserted after the UDT's name. This indicates that rather than being used as the domain for a value in a table, this class will be used as the structure of a typed table.

Note: UDTs can have methods, just like a class created in an object-oriented programming language. We'll look at them at the end of this chapter.

Creating Typed Tables Using UDTs

Once you have created a class as a UDT, you then use that UDT to create a *typed table*:

```
CREATE TABLE table_name OF UDT_name
    REF IS reference_column_name (method_to_
generate_row_ID)
```

SQL creates a table with one column for each column in the UDT on which the table is based along with a column for the self-referencing object ID. There are three options for creating the object ID of a row:

◊ The user generates the object ID (REF USING *existing_data_type*)

◊ The DBMS generates the object ID (REF IS *identifier_name* SYSTEM GENERATED)

◊ The object ID comes from the values in a list of attributes (REF FROM *attribute_list*)

You may want to use a primary key as a source for an object ID. Although this makes sense logically, it also provides the slowest retrieval performance.

By default, the object ID value is generated by the SQL command processor whenever a row is inserted into the typed table, using the method that was specified when the table was created. However, an insert operation can override the default object ID, placing a user-specified value into the ID column. Once created, the object ID cannot be modified.

To create the *ingredient* table, we could use

```
CREATE TABLE ingredient OF ingredient_type
    (REF IS ingredient_ID SYSTEM GENERATED);
```

Note: Only base tables or views can be typed tables. Temporary tables cannot be created from UDTs.

One of the most important OO features added to the SQL:2003 standard was support for inheritance. To create a *subtype* (a *subclass* or *derived class*, if you will), you create a UDT that is derived from another and then create a typed table of that subtype.

Inheritance

As a start, let's create the *Recipe* type that will be used as the superclass for types of recipes:

```
CREATE TYPE recipe_type AS OBJECT
    (recipe_name CHAR (256),
     instruction_list instruction ARRAY[20],
     numb_servings INT)
    NOT INSTANTIABLE,
    NOT FINAL;
```

The two last lines in the preceding example convey important information about this class. *Recipe* is an abstract class: Objects will never be created from it directly. We add NOT INSTANTIABLE to indicate this property.

By default, a UDT has a *finality* of FINAL. It cannot be used as the parent of a subtype. (In other words, nothing can inherit from it.) Because we want to use this class as a superclass, we must indicate that it is NOT FINAL.

To create the subtypes, we indicate the parent type preceded by the keyword UNDER. The subtype declaration also includes any attributes (and methods) that are not in the parent type that need to be added to the subtype. For example, we could create the *Desert* type with:

```
CREATE TYPE desert_type
     UNDER recipe_type (calories INT);
```

Because this type will be used to create objects and because no other types will be derived from it, we can accept the defaults of INSTIABLE and FINAL.

Note: As you have just seen, inheritance can operate on UDTs. It can also be used with typed tables, where a typed table is created UNDER another.

Reference (REF) Type

Once you have a typed table, you can store references to the objects (in other words, the rows) in that table in a column of type REF that is part of another type. For example, there is one REF column in the recipe database: the attribute in the *ingredient_amount* table (*related_ingredient*) that points to which ingredient is related to each occurrence of *ingredient_amount*.

To set up the table that will store that reference, use the data type REF for the appropriate column. For example,

```
CREATE TABLE ingredient_amount
     (related_ingredient REF ingredient_type
SCOPE IS ingredient,
     amount decimal (5,2));
```

creates a table with a column that stores a reference to an ingredient. The SCOPE clause specifies the table or view that is the source of the reference.

To insert a row into a table with a REF column, you must include a SELECT in the INSERT statement that locates the row whose reference is to be stored. As you would expect, the object being referenced must exist in its own table before a reference to it can be generated. We must therefore first insert an ingredient into the *ingredient* table:

```
INSERT INTO ingredient VALUES
    ('Unbleached flour,' 'cups',25);
```

Then we can insert a referencing row into *ingredient_amount*:

```
INSERT INTO ingredient_amount
    (SELECT REF (i) FROM ingredient i
    WHERE i.ingredient_name =
        'Unbleached flour')
    VALUES (2.5);
```

Dereferencing for Data Access

An application program that is using the recipe database as its data store will need to use the reference stored in the *ingredient_amount* table to locate the name of the ingredient. The DEREF function follows a reference back to the table being referenced and returns data from the appropriate row. A query to retrieve the name and amount of an ingredient used in a recipe instruction could therefore be written:

```
SELECT
    DEREF(related_ingredient).ingredient_name,
    amount
FROM ingredient_amount
WHERE DEREF(related_instruction).recipe_name =
    'French toast';
```

Note that the DEREF function accesses an entire row in the referenced table. If you don't specify otherwise, you will retrieve the values from every column in the referenced row. To retrieve just the value of a single column, we use "dot" notation. The first portion—

```
DEREF(related_ingredient)
```

—actually performs the dereference. The portion to the right of the dot specifies the column in the referenced row.

Some DBMSs provide a dereference operator (->) that can be used in place of the DEREF function. The preceding query might be written:

```
SELECT
    related_ingredient->ingredient_name, amount
FROM ingredient_amount;
```

Methods

The UDTs that we have seen to this point have attributes, but not methods. It is certainly possible, however, to declare methods as part of a UDT and then to use SQL programming to define the body of the methods. Like classes used by OO programming languages such C++, SQL the body a method is defined separately from the declaration of the UDT.

You declare a method after declaring the structure of a UDT. For example, we could add a method to display the instructions of a recipe with

```
CREATE TYPE recipe_type AS OBJECT
    (recipe_name CHAR (256),
     instruction_list instruction ARRAY[20],
     numb_servings INT)
     NOT INSTANTIABLE,
     NOT FINAL
     METHOD show_instructions ();
```

This particular method does not return a value and the declaration therefore does not include the optional RETURNS clause. However, a method to compute the cost of a recipe (if we were to include ingredient costs in the database) could be declared as

```
CREATE TYPE recipe_type AS OBJECT
     (recipe_name CHAR (256),
      instruction_list instruction ARRAY[20],
      numb_servings INT)
     NOT INSTANTIABLE,
     NOT FINAL
     METHOD show_instructions ()
     METHOD compute_cost ()
          RETURNS DECIMAL (5,2));
```

Methods can accept input parameters within the parentheses following the method name. A method declared as

```
METHOD scale_recipe (IN numb_servings INT):
```

accepts an integer value as an input value. The parameter list can also contain output parameters (OUT) and parameters used for both input and output (INOUT).

As mentioned earlier, although methods are declared when UDTs tables are declared, the bodies of methods are written separately. To define a method, use the CREATE METHOD statement:

Defining Methods

```
CREATE METHOD method_name FOR UDT_name
BEGIN
     // body of method
END
```

A SQL-only method is written using the language constructs discussed in Chapter 14.

Random programming note: Like the C++ and Java "this," SQL methods use SELF to refer to the object to which the method belongs.

Executing a method uses the "dot" notation used in C++:

Executing Methods

```
typed_table_name.method_name (parameter_list);
```

Such an expression can be, for example, included in an IN-SERT statement to insert the method's return value into a column. It can also be included in another SQL method, trigger, or stored procedure. Its return value can then be captured across an assignment operator. Output parameters return their values to the calling routine, where they can be used as needed.

Part VI
Appendices

Appendix A

Common Acronyms and Abbreviations

Abbreviation/ Acronym	Definition
1:1	One-to-one
1:M	One-to-many
ANSI	American National Standards Institute
API	Application Program (or Programmer) Interface
ASCII	American Standard Code for Information Interchange
CHAR	Character
CLI	Command-line interface
CTE	Common table expression
DBA	Database administrator or Database administration
DBMS	Database management system
DTD	Document type definition
ER	Entity relationship
ERD	Entity relationship diagram
FK or fk	Foreign key
GUI	Graphic user interface
HTML	Hypertext markup language
IE	Information Engineering
INT	Integer

ISO	International Standards Organization
JDBC	Java Database Connectivity
M:M	Many-to-many
M:N	Many-to-many
NIST	National Institute for Standards and Technology
OO	Object-oriented
OODBMS	Object-oriented database management system
OOP	Object-oriented programming
OR	Object-relational
PK or pk	Primary key
PSM	Persistent stored modules
RDMBS	Relational database management system
SQL	Structured query language
UDF	User-defined function
UDT	User-defined type; user-defined data type
URI	Uniform resource identifier
URL	Uniform resource locator
UML	Unified modeling language
VARCHAR	Character varying
XML	Extended (Extensible) Markup Language

Appendix B

SQLSTATE Return Codes

This appendix contains a numeric listing of the SQLSTATE return codes specified in the SQL standard (Table B-1). SQLSTATE is a five-character string. The leftmost two characters represent the error class; the rightmost three characters represent the subclass. Because SQLSTATE is a string, an embedded SQL program will need to use a substring function if it needs to separate the two parts of the code.

Table B-1: SQLSTATE return codes

Class	Class definition	Subclass	Subclass definition
00	Successful completion	000	*None*
01	Warning	000	*None*
		001	Cursor operation conflict
		002	Disconnect error
		003	Null value eliminated in set function
		004	String data, right truncation
		005	Insufficient item descriptor area
		006	Privilege not revoked
		007	Privilege not granted
		008	Implicit zero-bit padding
		009	Search expression too long for information schema
		00A	Query expression too long for information schema
		00B	Default value too long for information schema
		00C	Result sets returned
		00D	Additional result sets returned
		00E	Attempt to return too many result sets
		00F	Statement too long for information schema
		010	Column cannot be mapped (XML)
		011	SQL-Java path too long for information schema
		02F	Array data, right truncation
02	No data	000	*None*
		001	No additional result sets returned
07	Dynamic SQL error	000	*None*
		001	Using clause does not match dynamic parameter
		002	Using clause does not match target specifications

		003	Cursor specification cannot be executed
		004	Using clause required for dynamic parameters
		005	Prepared statement not a cursor specification
		006	Restricted data type attribute violation
		007	Using clause required for result fields
		008	Invalid descriptor count
		009	Invalid descriptor index
		00B	Data type transform function violation
		00C	Undefined DATA value
		00D	Invalid DATA target
		00E	invalid LEVEL value
		00F	Invalid DATETIME_INVERTVAL_CODE
08	Connection exception	000	*None*
		001	SQL client unable to establish SQL connection
		002	Connection name in use
		003	Connection does not exist
		004	SQL server rejected establishment of SQL connection
		006	Connection failure
		007	Transaction resolution unknown
09	Triggered action exception	000	*None*
0A	Feature not supported	000	*None*
		001	Multiple server transactions
0D	Invalid target type specification	000	*None*
0E	Invalid schema name list specification	000	*None*
0F	Locator exception	000	*None*
		001	Invalid specification
0K	Resignal when handler not active	000	*None*
0L	Invalid grantor	000	*None*

0M	Invalid SQL-invoked procedure reference	000	*None*
0N	SQL/XML mapping error	000	*None*
		001	Unmappable XML name
		002	Invalid XML character
0P	Invalid role specification	000	*None*
0S	Invalid transform group name specification	000	*None*
0T	Target table disagrees with cursor specification	000	*None*
0U	Attempt to assign to non-updatable column	000	*None*
0V	Attempt to assign to ordering column	000	*None*
0W	Prohibited statement encountered during trigger execution	000	*None*
0X	Invalid foreign server specification	000	*None*
0Y	Pass-through specific condition	000	*None*
		001	Invalid cursor option
		002	Invalid cursor allocation
0Z	Diagnostics exception	001	Maximum number of stacked diagnostics area exceeded
		002	Stacked diagnostics accessed without active hander
10	XQuery error	000	*None*
20	Case not found for CASE statement	000	*None*
21	Cardinality violation	000	*None*
22	Data exception	000	*None*
		001	String data, right truncation
		002	Null value, no indicator
		003	Numeric value out of range
		004	Null value not allowed
		005	Error in assignment
		006	Invalid interval fomat
		007	Invalid datetime format

008	Datetime field overflow
009	Invalid time zone displacement value
00B	Escape character conflict
00C	Invalid use of escape character
00D	Invalid escape octet
00E	Null value in array target
00F	Zero-length character string
00G	Most specific type mismatch
00H	Sequence generator limit exceeded
00J	Nonidentical notations with the same name (XML)
00K	Nonidentical unparsed entities with the same name (XML)
00L	Not an XML document
00M	Invalid XML document
00N	Invalid XML content
00P	Interval value out of range
00Q	Multiset value overflow
00R	XML value overflow
00S	Invalid XML comment
00T	Invalid XML processing instruction
00U	Not an XQuery document node
00V	Invalid XQuery context item
00W	XQuery serialization error
010	Invalid indicator parameter value
011	Substring error
012	Division by zero
015	Interval field overflow
017	Invalid data specified for datalink
018	Invalid character value for cast
019	Invalid escape character

01A	Null argument passed to datalink constructor
01B	Invalid regular expression
01C	Null row not permitted in table
01D	Datalink value exceeds maximum length
01E	Invalid argument for natural logarithm
01F	Invalid argument for power function
01G	Invalid argument for width bucket function
01J	XQuery sequence cannot be validated
01K	XQuery document node cannot be validated
01L	No XML schema found
01M	Element namespace not declared
01N	Global element not declared
01P	No XML element with the specified QName
01Q	No XML element with the specified namespace
01R	Validation failure
01S	invalid XQuery regular expression
01T	Invalid XQuery option flag
01U	Attempt to replace a zero-length string
01V	Invalid XQuery replacement string
021	Character not in repertoire
022	Indicator overflow
023	Invalid parameter value
024	Unterminated C string
025	Invalid escape sequence
026	String data, length mismatch
027	Trim error
029	Noncharacter in UCS string
02A	Null value in field reference

		02D	Null value substituted for mutator subject parameter
		02E	Array element error
		02F	Array data, right truncation
		02H	Invalid sample size
23	Integrity constraints violation	000	*None*
		001	Restrict violation
24	Invalid cursor state	000	*None*
25	Invalid transaction state	000	*None*
		001	Active SQL transaction
		002	Branch transaction already active
		003	Inappropriate access mode for branch transaction
		004	Inappropriate isolation level for branch transaction
		005	No active SQL transaction for branch transaction
		006	Read-only SQL transaction
		007	Schema and data statement mixing not supported
		008	Held cursor requires same isolation level
26	Invalid SQL statement name	000	*None*
27	Triggered data change violation	000	*None*
28	Invalid authorization specification	000	*None*
2A	Syntax error or access rule violation in direct SQL statement	000	*None*
2B	Dependent privilege descriptors still exist	000	*None*
2C	Invalid character set name	000	*None*
2D	Invalid transaction termination	000	*None*
2E	Invalid connection name	000	*None*
2F	SQL routine exception	000	*None*
		002	Modifying SQL data not permitted
		003	Prohibited SQL statement attempted

		004	Reading SQL data not permitted
		005	Function executed but no return statement
2H	Invalid collation name	000	*None*
30	Invalid SQL statement identifier	000	*None*
33	Invalid SQL descriptor name	000	*None*
34	Invalid cursor name	000	*None*
35	Invalid condition number	000	*None*
36	Cursor sensitivity exception	000	*None*
		001	Request rejected
		002	Request failed
37	Syntax error or access rule violation in dynamic SQL statement	000	*None*
38	External routine exception	000	*None*
		001	Containing SQL not permitted
		002	Modifying SQL not permitted
		003	Prohibited SQL statement attempted
		004	Reading SQL data not permitted
39	External routine invocationexception	000	*None*
		004	Null value not allowed
3B	Savepoint exception	000	*None*
		001	Invalid specification
		002	Too many
3C	Ambiguous cursor name	000	*None*
3D	Invalid catalog name	000	*None*
3F	Invalid schema name	000	*None*
40	Transaction rollback	000	*None*
		001	Serialization failure
		002	Integrity constraint violation
		003	Statement completion unknown
42	Syntax error or access rule violation	000	*None*
44	With check option violation	000	*None*
45	Unhandled user defined exception	000	*None*
46	Java DDL	000	*None*

		001	Invalid URL
		002	Invalid JAR name
		003	Invalid class deletion
		005	Invalid replacement
		00A	Attempt to replace uninstalled JAR
		00B	Attempt to remove uninstalled JAR
		00C	Invalid JAR removal
		00D	Invalid path
		00E	Self-referencing path
46	Java execution	000	*None*
		102	Invalid JAR name in path
		103	Unresolved class name
		110	Unsupported feature
		120	Invalid class declaration
		121	Invalid column name
		122	Invalid number of columns
		130	Invalid profile state
HV	FDW-specific condition	000	*None*
		001	Memory allocation error
		002	Dynamic parameter value needed
		004	Invalid data type
		005	Column name not found
		006	Invalid data type descriptors
		007	Invalid column name
		008	Invalid column number
		009	Invalid use of null pointer
		00A	Invalid string format
		00B	Invalid handle
		00C	Invalid option index
		00D	Invalid option name
		00J	Option name not found

		00K	Reply handle
		00L	Unable to create execution
		00M	Unable to create reply
		00N	Unable to establish connection
		00P	No schemas
		00Q	Schema not found
		00R	Table not found
		010	Function sequence error
		014	Limit on number of handles exceeded
		021	Inconsistent descriptor information
		024	Invalid attribute value
		090	Invalid string length or buffer length
		091	Invalid descriptor field identifier
HW	Datalink exception	000	*None*
		001	External file not linked
		002	External file already linked
		003	Referenced file does not exist
		004	Invalid write token
		005	Invalid datalink construction
		006	Invalid write permission for update
		007	Referenced file not valid
HY	CLI-specific condition	000	*None*
		001	Memory allocation error
		003	Invalid data type in application descriptor
		004	Invalid data type
		007	Associated statement is not prepared.
		008	Operation canceled
		009	Invalid use of null pointer
		010	Function sequence error
		011	Attribute cannot be set now

012	Invalid transaction operation code
013	Memory management error
014	Limit on number of handles exceeded
017	Invalid use of automatically-allocated descriptor handle
018	Server declined the cancelation request
019	Non-string data cannot be sent in pieces
020	Attempt to concatenate a null value
021	Inconsistent descriptor information
024	Invalid attribute value
055	Non-string data cannot be used with string routine
090	Invalid string length or buffer length
091	Invalid descriptor field identifier
092	Invalid attribute identifier
093	Invalid datalink value
095	Invalid FunctionID specified
096	Invalid information type
097	Column type out of range
098	Scope out of range
099	Nullable type out of rage
103	Invalid retrieval code
104	Invalid LengthPrecision value
105	Invalid parameter mode
106	Invalid fetch orientation
107	Row value of range
109	Invalid cursor position
C00	Optional feature not implemented

Appendix C

SQL Syntax Summary

This appendix contains a summary of SQL syntax used throughout this book. The first table (Table C.1) describes SQL statements, arranged alphabetically command. The notation is as follows:

◊ Keywords that must be typed exactly as they appear are in uppercase characters, such as REFERENCES.

◊ Parts of commands that are determined by the user appear in italics and name the item that must be supplied, such as *table_name.*

◊ Optional portions of a command are surrounded by brackets ([and]).

◊ Portions of commands that form a single clause are grouped within braces ({ and }).

◊ Sets of options from which you choose one or more are separated by vertical lines (|).

◊ Portions of commands that may be repeated as needed are followed by an ellipsis (…)

The second table (Table C.2) describes SQL built-in functions discussed in this book, including input data types. In Table C.3 you will find SQL operators covered in the text.

Table C.1: SQL statements

Allocate space for a descriptor area for a dynamic SQL statement

```
ALLOCATE DESCRIPTOR descriptor_name
     [ WITH MAX number_of_parameters ]
```

Change the specifications of a domain

```
ALTER DOMAIN domain_name
     { SET DEFAULT default_value }
     | { DROP DEFAULT }
     | { ADD constraint_definition_clause }
     | { DROP CONSTRAINT constraint_name }
```

Change the specifications of a table

```
ALTER TABLE table_name
     { ADD [COLUMN] column_defintion }
     | { ALTER [COLUMN]
         {SET DEFAULT default_value }
         | { DROP DEFAULT }
         | { DROP [COLUMN] column_name RESTRICT | CASCADE }}
     | { ADD table_constraint_definition_clause }
     | { DROP CONSTRAINT constraint_name RESTRICT | CASCADE }
```

Declare host language variables for use in an embedded SQL statement

```
BEGIN DECLARE SECTION
     Declarations
END DECLARE SECTION
```

Close an embedded SQL cursor

```
CLOSE cursor_name
```

Commit a transaction, making its changes permanent

```
COMMIT [ WORK ]
```

Connect to a database, specify its cluster, catalog, and schema if necessary

```
CONNECT TO {cluster.catalog.schema.database_name
     { [ AS connection_name ] }
     { [ USER user_name
       | DEFAULT ] }}
```

Create an assertion, a constraint that is not attached to a specific table

```
CREATE ASSERTION assertion_name
    CHECK ( check_predicate )
        [ { INITIALLY DEFERRED } | { INITIALLY IMMEDIATE } ]
        [ DEFERRABLE | { NOT DEFERRABLE } ]
```

Create a domain

```
CREATE DOMAIN domain_name
    [ AS ] data_type
        [ DEFAULT default_value ]
        CHECK ( check_clause )
        { [ INITIALLY DEFERRED ] | [ INITIALLY IMMEDIATE ] }
        [ DEFERRABLE | { NOT DEFERRABLE } ]
```

Define a method for a UDT

```
CREATE METHOD method_name FOR UDT_name
BEGIN
    // body of method
END
```

Create an index

```
CREATE INDEX index_name ON table_name (index_key_column_list)
```

Note: Indexes are no longer part of the SQL standard, but are still supported by most relational DBMSs.

Create a schema

```
CREATE SCHEMA { schema_name
    | AUTHORIZATION authorization_ID
    | schema_name AUTHORIZATION authorization_ID }
```

Create a table

```
CREATE [ [ GLOBAL | LOCAL ] TEMPORARY ] table_name
    ( { column_name { data_type | domain_name }} [ column_size ]
    [ column_constraint … ] , …
    [ DEFAULT default_value ]
    [ table_constraint ], …
    [ ON COMMIT DELETE | PRESERVE ROWS ] )
```

Create a user-defined data type (UDT)

```
CREATE TYPE type_name AS [ OBJECT ](column_definitions)
    [ INSTANTIABLE | { NOT INSTANTIABLE } ]
    [ FINAL | { NOT FINAL } ]
    [ { METHOD method_name (parameter_list) }, … ]
```

Create a typed table

```
CREATE TABLE table_name OF UDT_name
    [ UNDER supertype_name (added_column_list) ]
    [ REF IS reference_column_name
            ( { REF USING existing_data_type }
            | { REF IS identifier_name SYSTEM GENERATED }
            | { REF FROM attribute_list } ) ]
```

Create a database user account and password

```
CREATE USER | LOGIN implementation_specific_syntax
```

Note: Creating user accounts is not part of the SQL standard and much of the syntax is implementation dependent.

Create a view

```
CREATE VIEW view_name [ (column_list ) ]
    AS (complete_SELECT_statement
    [ WITH [ CASCADED | LOCAL ] CHECK OPTION ])
```

Remove a dynamic SQL descriptor area from main memory

```
DEALLOCATE DESCRIPTOR descriptor_name
```

Declare a cursor for processing an embedded SQL SELECT that returns multiple rows

```
DECLARE CURSOR cursor_name [ INSENSITIVE ] [ SCROLL ] CURSOR FOR
    (complete_SELECT_statement)
        [ FOR ( { READ ONLY } | UPDATE [ OF column_name, … ] ) ]
    | prepared_dynamic_SQL_statement_name
```

Delete rows from a table

```
DELETE FROM table_name
    [ { WHERE row_selection_predicate }
    | { WHERE CURRENT OF cursor_name } ]
```

Describe the dynamic parameters in a prepared dynamic SQL statement for a descriptor area

```
DESCRIBE [ INPUT | OUTPUT ]
     Prepared_dyamic_SQL_statement_name
     USING SQL DESCRIPTOR descriptor_name
```

Disconnect from a database

```
DISCONNECT connection_identifier
```

Remove an assertion from a schema

```
DROP ASSERTION assertion_name
```

Remove a domain from a schema

```
DROP DOMAIN domain_name CASCADE | RESTRICT
```

Remove an index from a schema

```
DROP INDEX index_name
```

Remove a schema from a catalog

```
DROP SCHEMA schema_name CASCADE | RESTRICT
```

Remove a table from a schema

```
DROP TABLE table_name CASCADE | RESTRICT
```

Remove a view from a schema

```
DROP VIEW view_name CASCADE | RESTRICT
```

Execute an embedded SQL statement

```
EXEC SQL complete_SQL_statement
```

Execute a prepared dynamic SQL statement

```
EXECUTE [ GLOBAL | LOCAL ] prepared_dynamic_SQL_statement
     [ INTO { parameter, … }
     | { SQL DESCRIPTOR [ GLOBAL | LOCAL ] descriptor_name } ]
     [ USING { parameter, … }
     | { SQL DESCRIPTOR [ GLOBAL | LOCAL ] descriptor_name } ]
```

Execute a dynamic SQL statement immediately, without a separate preparation step

```
EXECUTE IMMEDIATE SQL_statement_text_literal_or_variable
```

Retrieve a row from an open cursor's result table

```
FETCH [ NEXT | PRIOR | FIRST | LAST | ABSOLUTE
        | { RELATIVE row_number } ]
    FROM cursor_name
    INTO host_language_variable, …
```

Retrieve information from a dynamic SQL descriptor area

```
GET DESCRIPTOR descriptor_name
     { host_language_variable = COUNT | KEY_TYPE | DYNAMIC_FUNCTION |
DYNAMIC_FUNCTION_CODE | TOP_LEVEL_COUNT }
     |   VALUE descriptor_number { host_language_variable =
             descriptor_ field }, …
```

Note: Descriptor field most common used are TYPE (data type of parameter), DATA (actual value of parameter), and INDICATOR (value of indicator variable associated with parameter).

Grant access rights to other users

```
GRANT { ALL PRIVILEGES }
        | SELECT
        | DELETE
        | INSERT [ (column_name, …) ]
        | UPDATE [ (column_name, …) ]
        | REFERENCES { (column_name, …) }
        | USAGE
   ON { [ TABLE ] table_name }
        | { DOMAIN domain_name }
   TO { user_id, … } | PUBLIC
   [ WITH GRANT OPTION ]
```

Insert new rows into a table

```
INSERT INTO table_name
    [ (column_name, …) ]
    { VALUES (value1, value2, …) }
    | complete_SELECT_statement
    | DEFAULT VALUES
```

Conditionally update, delete, or insert data from one table into another

```
MERGE INTO target_table_name USING source_table_name ON merge_condition
WHEN MATCHED THEN
      Update/delete specifications
WHEN NOT MATCHED THEN
      insert specification
```

Open a cursor, executing the SELECT and positioning the cursor at the first row

```
OPEN cursor_name
     [ { USING host_language_variable_or_literal, … }
     | { SQL DESCRIPTOR descriptor_name } ]
```

Prepare a dynamic SQL statement for execution

```
PREPARE [ GLOBAL | LOCAL ]
     prepared_dynamic_SQL_statement_name
     FROM SQL_statement_text_literal_or_variable
```

Remove access rights from a user

```
REMOVE [GRANT OPTION FOR ]
            { ALL PRIVILEGES }
            | SELECT
            | DELETE
            | UPDATE
            | REFERENCES
            | USAGE
     ON [ TABLE ] table_name
            | DOMAIN domain_name
     FROM PUBLIC | { user_id, … }
     CASCADE | RESTRICT
```

Roll back a transaction

```
ROLLBACK [ WORK ]
```

Retrieve rows from a table

```
SELECT [DISTINCT]
          { { summary_function, … }
          | { data_manipulation_expression, … }
          | { column_name, … } }
    FROM { { table_name [ AS ] [ correlation_name ] }
          | joined_tables
          | complete_SELECT_statement }
    [ WHERE row_selection_predicate ]
    [ GROUP BY column_name, … ]
         [ HAVING group_selection_predicate ]
    [ UNION | INTERSECT | EXCEPT [CORRESPONDING BY (column_name, …) ]
         complete_SELECT_statement ]
    [ ORDER BY (column_name [ ASC | DESC ], …) ]
```

Retrieve rows from a common table expression (CTE)

```
WITH [ RECURSIVE ] CTE_name (column_list) AS
    ( SELECT_statement_defining_table )
complete_SELECT_using_result_of_CTE_query
```

Choose the current catalog

```
SET CATALOG catalog_name
```

Choose an active connection

```
SET CONNECTION connection_name | DEFAULT
```

Choose when constraints are checked

```
SET CONSTRAINTS MODE { constraint_name, … | ALL }
    DEFERRED | IMMEDIATE
```

Store values in a SQL descriptor area

```
SET DESCRIPTOR [ GLOBAL | LOCAL ]
          descriptor_name { COUNT = integer_value }
    | {VALUE descriptor_number { descriptor_field = value, …}, …}
```

Choose the current schema

```
SET SCHEMA schema_name
```

Choose the characteristics of the next transaction

```
SET TRANSACTION
    { ISOLATION LEVEL
        { READ UNCOMMITED }
      | { READ COMMITTED }
      | { REPEATABLE READ }
      | { SERIALIZABLE } }
  | { READ ONLY } | { READ WRITE }
```

Begin a transaction

```
START TRANSACTION transaction_mode
```

Remove all rows from a table leaving the table structure intact

```
TRUNCATE TABLE table_name
```

Change the data in a table

```
UPDATE table_name
    SET { column_name = { value
                        | NULL
                        | DEFAULT }, … }
        [ { WHERE row_selection_predicate }
        | { WHERE CURRENT OF cursor_name } ]
```

Table C.2: SQL functions

Function	Returns	Input Data
AVG ( )	Average of values	Numeric values
COUNT (*)	Number of rows in a result set	none
LOWER ( )	Convert to lowercase	Character value
MAX ( )	Maximum value	Number, character, or datetime values
MIN ( )	Minimum value	Number, character, or datetime values
SUBSTRING ( )	Portion of a character string	Character value
SUM ( )	Sum of values	Numeric values

TRIM ( )	Remove trailing blanks	Character value
UPPER ( )	Convert to uppercase	Character value
	Create XML element attributes	Attribute value, attribute name
XML COMMENT ( )	Append comment to XML document string	Character value
XMLCONCAT ( )	Concatenate XML fragments	Character values containing XML text
XMLELEMENT ( )	Create an XML element	Element name, optional attributes, content of element
XMLFOREST ( )	Create nested XML element	Element content, element name
XMLPARSE ( )	Convert text to XML	Element type, content of element
XMLROOT ( )	Modify XML Prolog	XML character string, XML version, standalone property
XMLSERIALIZE ( )	Covert an XML string to text	Character string formatted as XML

Table C.3: SQL operators

Operator	Use	Operates on:
Arithmetic	Compute arithmetic quantities	
+	Preserve the sign of a value	Numeric value
-	Change the sign of a value	Numeric value
*	Multiply two values	Numeric values
/	Divide one value by another	Numeric values
+	Add two values	Numeric values
-	Subtract one value from another	Numeric values
Comparison	Compare two values	
=	Equality	Any compatible data types
>	Greater than	Any compatible data types

>=	Greater than or equal to	Any compatible data types
<	Less than	Any compatible data types
<=	Less than or equal to	Any compatible data types
!= *or* <>	Note equal to	Any compatible data types
Logical		
AND	Determine if two expressions are true	Expressions returning a Boolean value
OR	Determine if at least one of two expressions is true	Expressions returning a Boolean value
NOT	Change the truth value	Expression returning a Boolean value
= *or* :=	Assignment	Any compatible data types
||	Concatenate two strings	Character strings
Specialty operators		
BETWEEN	Determine if a value falls inside an interval	Numeric, characters, or datetime values
DISTINCT	Remove duplicate rows	Table
EXCEPT	Find the difference between two tables	Tables
EXISTS	Determine if a subquery result table contains at least one row	Table
EXTRACT	Pull out portion of a datetime	Datetime
IN	Determine if a value is in a set	Any set of values of the same datatype
INTERSECT	Find rows in common of two tables	Tables
IS NULL	Determine if a value is null	Any data type
IS NOT NULL	Determine if a value is not null	Any data type
JOIN	Combine two tables horizontally	Tables
LIKE	Perform string pattern matching	Character value
MULTISET EXCEPT	Find elements unique to each of two multisets	Multisets

MULTISET INTERSECT	Find elements common to two multisets	Multisets
MULTISET UNION	Combine two multisets vertically	Multisets
NOT IN	Determine if a value is not in a set of vaues	Any sets of values of the same data type
OVERLAPS	Determine if two datetime intervals overlap	Datetimes
UNION	Combine to tables vertically	Tables

Glossary

Abstract class: A class from which no objects are created.

Abstract data type: In an object-oriented environment, a user-defined data type; a class.

Accessor method: A function that returns the values of private data stored about an object.

Aggregate function: A SQL function—for example, AVG and SUM—that computes a variety of measures based on values in one or more numeric columns.

Aggregation: In an object-oriented environment, a class that manages objects created from another class.

Array: In a SQL database, an ordered collection of elements of the same data type stored in a single column and row of a table.

Assertion: A constraint that is not attached to a table but is instead a distinct database object. It can therefore be used to enforce rules that apply to multiple tables or to verify that tables are not empty.

Attribute (relational database): A column in a relation.

Attribute (XML element): A data value that describes an XML element and is part of the element's tag rather than appearing in a separate element nested under the parent element.

Base class: A class at the "general" end of an inheritance relationship; a parent class.

Base table: A relation whose contents are physically and permanently stored in a database.

Before-image file: A file that contains images of every action taken by a transaction and is used to undo actions when a transaction is rolled back.

Case sensitive: Aware of the difference between upper- and lower-case letters.

Catalog: A group of schemas, usually composed of all schemas handled by a single DBMS.

Class: A declaration of data and methods that describe a single entity and that will be used as a template to create objects.

Cluster: A group of catalogs. Cluster definition is specific to a given DBMS.

Commit (a transaction): End a transaction, making any changes that it made permanent. A committed transaction is never rolled back.

Common table expression (CTE): A virtual table created by a SQL query that is used as the data source for another query. Unlike a view, the definition of a CTE is not stored in the database and must be used immediately after it is created.

Composition: A relationship between two classes where objects created from one class are part of objects created from the other.

Concrete class: A class from which objects are created.

Concatenated foreign key: A foreign key made up of two or more columns that references a concatenated primary key.

Concatenated primary key: A primary key made up of the combination of two or more columns.

Concatenation: Combining two strings by placing one at the end of the other.

Concurrent execution: The simultaneous handling of multiple transactions by a single database.

Connect (to a database): Establish a user session with a database.

Constraint (on a relation): A rule to which data stored in a relation must adhere.

Container class: In an object-oriented environment, a class that manages groups of objects created from another class.

Control class: A class that controls the operational flow of an object-oriented program.

Correlated subquery: A subquery that a DBMS cannot process completely before turning to the outer query. The DBMS must execute the subquery repeatedly for every row in the outer query.

Correlation name: An alias for a table used in a SQL query.

Cursor: A pointer to a row in the result table generated when an embedded SQL SELECT returns multiple rows.

Constructor: In an object-oriented environment, a method that is executed automatically every time an object is created from a class.

Data dictionary: In the broadest sense, documentation of a logical structure of a database. In relational database terms, a collection of tables that store data about the database.

Data dictionary driven: A property of a relational database where all access to data begins with a check of the data dictionary to determine whether the requested database elements are present in the database and whether the user has the necessary access rights to perform the requested action.

Database: A place to store data long with information about the relationships between the data.

Database management system (DBMS): Software that manipulates a database, isolating the user from the physical file storage structures.

Declaration (in an XML document): A statement at the beginning of an XML document that identifies the version XML being use and optionally a character encoding scheme.

Derived class: A class at the "specific" end of an inheritance relationship; a child class.

Destructor: In an object-oriented environment, a method that is run each time an object is destroyed (removed from main memory).

Difference: A relational algebra operation that returns the rows found in one table but not in another.

Dirty read: The problem that arises when a transaction reads the same data more than once, including data modified by concurrent transactions that are later rolled back.

Disconnect (from a database): Terminate a user session with a database.

Divide: A relational algebra operation that searches for multiple rows in a table.

Domain: An expression of the set of values from which the values stored in a column of a relation are taken.

Drop: Delete an element of database structure from a database.

Dynamic embedded SQL: Embedded SQL in which the entire SQL statement cannot be assembled prior to running the program. The SQL statement is therefore completed and processed during the program run.

Dynamic parameter: A value given to an embedded SQL statement at runtime rather than when the program in which the statement is contained is compiled.

Embedded SQL: SQL statements placed within a host language, allowing SQL to be executed by application programs.

Entity: Something about which we store data in a database environment, such as customer, an inventory item, or a sale.

Entity class: In an object-oriented environment, a class that is used to create objects that manipulate data.

Entity-relationship diagram (ERD): A graphic method for depicting the relationships in a database environment.

Equi-join: A join that combines two tables based on matching (equivalent) data in rows in the two tables.

Escape character: A character, usually \, that removes the special meaning of whatever follows in a literal string.

Exclusive lock: A lock on a database element that prevents other transactions from updating or viewing the database element while the lock is held.

Extensible markup language (XML): A way of representing data and data relationships in text files, typically for data exchange between software of different types.

Field: A piece of data contained within a column of the ROW data type.

Foreign key: A column or combination of columns that is the same as the primary key of some table in the database.

Frame (in a windowing query): A portion of a windowing query's window that "slides" to present to the DBMS the rows that share the same value of the partitioning criteria.

Function: A small program that performs one task and returns a single value. It may be built into the SQL language or written by a user, database administrator, or application programmer.

Get method: A function that returns the values of private data stored about an object.

Grant: Give access rights to database elements to users. The user that creates a database element has all rights to that element. Other users have no access unless they are specifically granted access rights.

Granularity (of a lock): The size of the database element on which a lock is placed (usually a table or a row within a table).

Grouping query: A query that groups rows of data based on common values in one or more columns and that optionally computes summary values from each group.

Hierarchy: A structure for data relationships where all relationships are one-to-many and no child entity may have more than one parent entity.

Host language: A programming language in which SQL statements are embedded.

Identifier chain: The fully qualified name of an element in a SQL database, including the catalog, schema, table, and column of the element.

Indeterminate cursor: A cursor in which the effects of updates by the same transaction on the result table are left up to each DBMS.

Index: A data structure that provides a fast-access path to one or more columns in a relation.

Indicator variable: A variable that accompanies an embedded SQL dynamic parameter to indicate the presence of nulls in the parameter.

Inheritance: A general to specific relationship between classes in an object-oriented environment.

Inner join: A join that excludes rows for which there is no match between the tables being joined.

Input parameter: A value sent by an embedded SQL statement to the DBMS.

Insensitive cursor: A cursor for which the contents of the result table to which it points are fixed.

Instance (of a relation): A relation containing one or more rows of data.

Interactive SQL: Individual SQL statements entered from the keyboard and processed immediately.

Interface class: In an object-oriented environment, a class that handles input and output operations.

Interleaved execution: A sequence of executing concurrent transactions in which the actions of two or more transactions alternate.

Intersect: A relational algebra operation that returns all rows common to two tables.

Isolation level: The degree to which a transaction can view data modified by other transactions running concurrently.

Join: A relational algebra operation that combines two tables making new rows that are a combination of one row from each of the two source tables.

Locking: The processing of giving a transaction exclusive rights to view and/or update a database element to prevent problems that arise with interleaved transaction execution.

Lost update: An error condition that occurs when the interleaved execution of a transaction wipes out an update of another transaction.

Markup language: A set of special codes placed inside a text document to identify the elements of the document and optionally to give instructions to software using the document.

Message: Requests for data manipulation sent from one object to another.

Method (class): A program module that acts on objects created from a class in an object-oriented program.

Method (SQL): A program module that is part of a user-defined data type that is used to create objects.

Module: A group of SQL routines.

Multiset: In a SQL database, an unordered collection of elements of the same data type that is stored in a single column and row.

Mutator method: A function that modifies the values of private data stored about an object.

Natural equi-join: An equi-join.

Nonprocedural: A process that specifies "what" but not "how," leaving the manner in which the result is obtained up to the DBMS.

Nonrepeatable read: The difference in result tables that occurs when a nonserialized transaction reads the same data twice and retrieves different values but the same rows as the result of the actions of other interleaved transactions.

Null: A value, distinct from 0 or a blank, that means "unknown."

Object: An instance of a self-contained element used by an object-oriented program, containing data that describe the specific element and links to program modules that operate on the element.

Object-oriented: A programming and database environment in which elements in the environment are conceptualized as entities and data and programs are stored together.

Outer join: A join that preserves all rows from both source tables. Where a new row cannot be formed by combining rows, the outer join places nulls in empty columns.

Output parameter: A value returned by an embedded SQL statement to the host language program.

Overloading: In an object-oriented environment, two methods of the same class that have the same name but different signatures (input parameters and data types).

Partition (in a windowing query): A set of rows for which an aggregate function will compute a summary value.

Persistent stored module (PSM): A SQL program written using the SQL programming language.

Phantom read: The difference in result tables that occurs when a nonserialized transaction reads the same data twice and different rows are retrieved as a result of the actions of other interleaves transactions.

Polymorphism: The redefinition of the body of a superclass method inherited by a subclass. The polymorphic method retains the same signature.

Precedence: The order in which a DBMS evaluates operators in a predicate when multiple operators are present.

Precision: In a floating-point number, the number of digits to the right of the decimal point.

Precompiler: A program processor that examines a source code file for SQL statements and translates them into calls to routines in external program libraries. The result is another source code file that can be compiled by a normal programming language compiler.

Predicate: A logical expression used to qualify the rows that are affected by a data manipulation request.

Primary key: One or more columns whose values uniquely identify every row in a relation.

Procedural: A process that is expressed in a step-by-step manner. It specifies "how" as well as "what."

Procedure: A SQL routine that is stored in a database and executed with the SQL CALL statement. It does not return a value.

Product: A relational algebra operation that forms all possible combinations of rows from two source tables.

Project: A relational algebra operation that takes a vertical subset of a table. In other words, it extracts complete columns.

Prolog (of an XML document): A statement at the beginning of an XML document that identifies the version of XML being used and optionally a character encoding scheme.

Query optimizer: A part of a DBMS that examines a nonprocedural data manipulation request and makes a determination of the most efficient way to process that request.

Read lock: A lock on a database element that prevents other transactions from updating the database element while the lock is held.

Recursive query: A query that queries itself.

Referential integrity: A constraint on a relation that states that every nonnull foreign key value must reference an existing primary key value.

Relation: The defintion of the structure of a two-dimensional table with columns and rows.

Relational algebra: A set of procedural operations used to manipulate relations.

Relational calculus: A set of nonprocedural operations used to manipulate relations.

Restrict: A relational algebra operation that takes a horizontal subset of the rows in a table, usually choosing the rows that meet the logical criteria specified in a predicate.

Revoke: Remove previously granted access rights from a user.

Roll back (a transaction): End a transaction, undoing any changes made by the transaction and restoring the database to the state it was in before the transaction began.

Root (of an XML hierarchy): The top node in a hierarchy, providing a single point of access to the hierarchy.

Routine: The smallest unit of a SQL PSM. Typically it performs a single action, such as updating a total or inserting a row in a table.

Schema (relational database): In database design theory, the overall logical design of a database. In a SQL DBMS, a group of tables and supporting elements such as views and indexes.

Schema (XML): A special type of XML document that contains definitions of document structure used to validate XML documents that contain data.

Signature (of a function): The name and parameters of a function.

Scope (of a temporary table): The visibility of a temporary table. Local temporary tables can be seen only by the program module that created them. Global temporary tables can be seen by the entire database session.

Scrollable cursor: A cursor that can move to the first, last, or prior row in a table rather than just to the next row.

Serial execution: A sequence of executing concurrent transactions in which one transaction runs from start to finish before a second transaction begins.

Serializable: A property of interleaved transaction execution such that the result of the interleaved execution is the same as the result of serial execution.

Session: A block of time during which a user interacts with a database.

Set function: A SQL function—for example, AVG and SUM—that computes a variety of measures based on values in one or more numeric columns.

Set method: A function that modifies the values of private data stored about an object.

Shared lock: A lock on a database element that prevents other transactions from updating the database element while the lock is held.

Static embedded SQL: Embedded SQL in which the entire SQL statement can be specified when the program is written, allowing the statement to be precompiled before the program is executed.

Stored procedure: A SQL program module that is invoked by an application program using the SQL CALL command. Stored procedures are stored in the database they manipulate.

Subclass: A class at the "specific" end of an inheritance relationship; a child class.

Subquery: A complete SELECT statement that is part of another SELECT.

Substring: A portion of a string.

Superclass: A class at the "general" end of an inheritance relationship; a parent class.

Tag: The markup device in an XML file. XML tags exist in pairs, with an opening tag before the element being identified and a closing tag after it.

Temporary table: A relation whose contents are not stored in the database but that exists only during the database session in which it was created.

Θ-join (theta-join): A join that combines two tables on some condition, which may be equality or something else such as greater than or less than.

Three-valued logic: A system of logic in which logical expressions can be evaluated to true, false, or maybe. It is the result of the presence of nulls in relations.

Transaction: A unit of work presented to a database. The transaction may be committed, in which case any changes it made to the database are permanent or it may be rolled back, in which case any changes it made to the database are rolled back.

Tree structure: A structure for data relationships where all relationships are one-to-many and no child entity may have more than one parent entity.

Trigger: A SQL program module that is executed when a specific data modification activity occurs. Triggers are stored in the database they manipulate.

Truncate (a table): Remove all rows from a table, leaving the structure of the table in the database's data dictionary.

Tuple: A row in a relation.

Two-phase locking: A locking scheme in which a transaction is given a shared lock on a database element when it retrieves a value. The shared lock is upgraded to an exclusive lock when the transaction attempts to modify the value.

Typecast: Change the data type of a value for output or use in a SQL program.

Typed table: A table created as a class using a user-defined data type to define the structure of the objects to be stored in the table. Each row contains one object.

Uncorrelated subquery: A subquery that a DBMS can process completely before processing the query in which the subquery is contained.

Union: A relational algebra operation that combines two tables by merging their rows into the same structure.

Union compatible: A property of two tables where all columns in both tables are drawn from the same logical domains.

Updatability: A property of a view that indicates whether it can be used to perform updates that can then be propagated to the base table from which it was derived.

User-defined data type (UDT): In a SQL database, a declaration of a structured data type that can be used as the domain of a column or as an object.

View: A stored SQL query from which a virtual table is created for use each time the name of the view is used.

Virtual class: A class from which no objects are created.

Virtual table: A table that exists only in main memory. It may be created by the end user as a temporary table or it may be created by a DBMS to hold the results of a query.

Wait state: A hold placed by a DBMS on the execution of a transaction because the transaction is unable to obtain a needed lock on a database element, usually because the element is locked by another transaction. The transaction must wait until the lock can be placed.

Well-formed XML document: An XML document that meets all the XML syntax rules including having only one root element, paired tags, case sensitive tags, proper tag nesting, and quoted attribute values.

Window: A set of rows for which an aggregate function will compute a summary value.

Windowing: A SQL technique for computing aggregate measures for groups of rows that also displays the individual rows in each group.

Windowing function: A function that computes an aggregate measure about a partition in a windowing query.

Write lock: A lock on a database element that prevents other transactions from updating or viewing the database element while the lock is held.

XML: A way of representing data and data relationships in text files, typically for data exchange between software of different types.

XML schema: A special type of XML document that contains definitions of document structure used to validate XML documents that contain data.

Index

Printed and bound by CPI Group (UK) Ltd, Croydon, CR0 4YY

03/10/2024

01040310-0007